A View from the Castle

Published by New Generation Publishing in 2018

Copyright © David L Smallman 2018

First Edition

Digitally typeset in Bookman Old Style 11 pt.

Cover photo by David L Smallman

A CIP catalogue for this book is available from the British Library

www.newgeneration-publishing.com

New Generation Publishing

Also by David L Smallman

Quincentenary: A Story of St Helena 1502 – 2002

One of The Queen's Men

A View from the Castle
- four years at St Helena

An autobiographical narrative of the times, trials and successes of
His Excellency David L Smallman, Esq, LVO
Twenty-ninth Governor under the Crown and Commander-in-Chief of the British Overseas Territory of St Helena and the associated Dependencies of Ascension and Tristan da Cunha in the South Atlantic Ocean

Acknowledgements

The quotations from letters, reports, books and print are acknowledged in the text. Every effort has been made to obtain the necessary permissions with reference to copyright material. I apologise for any omissions in this respect.

I single out the liberty I have taken in quoting from the poem 'New Year Honours' by the late U Myint Thein, Uncle Monty to all of us who came in close contact with him in Burma, published in his book of verse "When at Nights I Strive to Sleep" (1971). He would have truly appreciated the humour in this context.

Dedication

This book is dedicated to my dear wife, Sandi, my First Lady, who gave so much with so little in return, and whose love and support was freely given to enable the story herein to be told. I owe her a significant debt of gratitude for foregoing any possibility of a career of her own during my service as a Diplomat and particularly for her contribution to whatever success I might have had.

'Tis sad to be slighted.
I have not been knighted,
Blighted in my aim in life
To make a lady of my wife.

Maung Myint Thein, 1900-1994

CONTENTS

Foreword

The reader might well ask why now? The bulk of the events covered in the pages of the volume that follows happened some 20 years ago. Why then do I feel the need to write about them in 2018?

Well, jocular references from friends, being fed scraps of press cuttings and having my leg pulled about *"your airport"* in the several years leading up to 2017; together with critical press comment about the saga, some would say fiasco, surrounding the provision, or not, of an airport on the tiny South Atlantic Island of St Helena; explaining that it was not my airport, prompted me to revisit the time that Sandi and I spent on the Island when I was appointed to act as its Governor.

Further, the news that the *Royal Mail Ship St Helena* was to finally be paid off and sold after its very last journey from Jamestown to Cape Town is a seminal moment in the Island's history as well as our own lives: we travelled 54,500 miles embarked on the *RMS* during my gubernatorial term.

Having lived for four years on what writer Richard Madden described in a *Daily Telegraph* travel feature as *"A green and pleasant Alcatraz"*; and having published a brief history of the first five hundred years of the Island's history I felt, at least, quite well qualified to write about the Island and our time there! I had seen and experienced what made the Island, its politicians and masters in London tick. I had been a part of it. I spent four years involved with colleagues in the attempt to bring St Helena into the last years of the 20th Century when it had been running on a sort of 1950s-benevolence model, or at least that is the framework that politicians had sought to maintain.

After nearly a quarter of a century it is hopefully no longer quite as I have described its politicians and the political process, but I believe the story needs telling for posterity anyway. There had been no place in *Quincentenary*, an historical record of the first five hundred years since the discovery of St Helena, to record the more contemporary history that was personal to my own gubernatorial term. So, in writing here of my own years on the personal note missing from *A Story of St Helena 1502 – 2002*, I now have the opportunity to comment upon those events of four years of the 1990s; and to put much else that has been viewed from a much wider perspective into closer Island focus. It is warts and all!

As an aid to understanding the abbreviations and acronyms in use in the context of this book I append a list below.

APM	Aid Planning Mission
BAM	Budgetary Aid Mission
CPA	Commonwealth Parliamentary Association
DfID	Department for International Development
DSRs	Diplomatic Service Regulations
DWS	Diplomatic Wireless Service
ExCo	Executive Council
FCO	Foreign & Commonwealth Office
HOMS	Heads of Mission Section
LegCo	Legislative Council
MLC	Member of Legislative Council
ODA	Overseas Development Administration
RIB	Rigid Inflatable Boat
RNLI	Royal National Lifeboat Institution
SAAD	South Atlantic & Antarctic Department
SHPF	St Helena Police Force

INTRODUCTION

An Introduction to the Island of St Helena

Running before the warm South-east Trade Wind in the vast and trackless wastes of the South Atlantic Ocean on his homeward journey from Goa some five hundred years ago a Portuguese 'admiral', João da Nova, made an exciting discovery. Some 15° south of the equator he had made an unexpected landfall - an uncharted island with a sheltered anchorage. The surprise sighting of this previously unknown island in 1502 opened a new chapter in the unfolding history of European discovery and trade with the Indies.

Da Nova, the *Capitão Môr* (literally, chief captain) of the third *Carriera da India* that had set sail from Lisbon on 25th March 1501, was from Galicia. Following the custom of Portuguese discovery, it has long been believed that he named the island after the Saint upon whose day it had first been sighted - Saint Helena. However, it is now a matter of conjecture whether da Nova sighted the island on 21st May 1502, as has long been the English belief or on another day in another month altogether. An academic paper by Ian Bruce, "*St Helena Day*", draws attention, to the discrepancy between the 21st May and the feast day of St Helena in the Roman Catholic Church, which actually celebrates the Saint's day on 18th August. The Eastern Orthodox Church celebrates a Saint's Day for St Helena Day on 21st May, as does the Protestant Church. However, da Nova was a Catholic and there is no credible explanation why he might have used the Orthodox Church calendar on this occasion: in 1502, of course, the Protestant Church had yet to be formed.

Bruce has conducted a pretty forensic examination of the record and points to the most likely explanation being that the island of St Helena was quite probably first sighted on 3rd May 1502 – the Roman Catholic day devoted to the Feast of the True Cross, consecrated to the memory of the Empress Helena who, as Sir Thomas Herbert writing about the discovery of St Helena after visiting for six days in 1629, noted was *"She that first found the Crosse"*. Furthermore, Bruce suggests that firstly Jan Hügen van Linschoten, a Dutchman, writing of his travels in 1596 (erroneously) used the Dutch Reformed Church liturgical calendar, in which St Helena day is marked as 21st May, to pin point the date of discovery; and that the English author Thomas Brooke simply compounded the error, without further research, when writing the first complete history of St Helena in 1808.

It was, perhaps, coincidence or even fate that this Helena, the mother of the Emperor Constantine, was born in England - in the Roman garrison town of Colchester. Whichever it was, the island was destined to play its part in the growth of what much later became the British Empire. The fact that since 1945, when 21st May was designated as 'St Helena Day', Saints have been celebrating their National Day on the Protestant Saint's day dedicated to Helena rather than the actual date of the island's discovery is perhaps apt: nothing is ever what it seems on St Helena!

*   *   *

St Helena is associated with the Mid-Atlantic Ridge and is of volcanic origin. It is in fact the deeply eroded summit of an enormous volcano with a base of over 80 miles in diameter, reaching up from the seabed more than 13,000 feet below the waves to nearly 2,700 feet above sea level. The island was formed by volcanic activity on the Atlantic sea floor around fifty million years ago, and continued to form on this magma growth for the following thirty-seven to forty million years as the volcano moved away from the Mid-Atlantic Ridge. Geologists estimate that the growing volcano rose out of the sea about fourteen million years ago and that the last major volcanic event probably happened about seven million years ago. However, volcanic activity on St Helena has been extinct for so long that the course of erosion has had millennia to shape the island's topography and for its flora and fauna to evolve.

Although the active era of volcanic eruptions spanned a period seven to fourteen million years ago, it is evident that the activity was far from continuous even then. Indeed, there were several periods, lasting for centuries, when there was no activity at all. Then, winds and sea currents would have

4

brought plant life, birds and sea creatures to the newly forming island's shores. During the most recent active period, some eight million years ago, the peak of the volcano was probably over 4,500 feet above sea level, and the island perhaps as much as 100 sq miles in size – more than twice its area today. But even when volcanic activity was spewing forth lava and ash in one part of the island, plant and mammal colonies would, nevertheless, have been able to begin establishing themselves elsewhere. From time to time it is very likely that an established colony, perhaps centuries old, would be wiped out by further eruptions and lava flows.

The action of the sea on the volcano's slopes has led to the formation of a narrow shelf around the island, just below sea level, and has had a major impact in the formation of the high cliffs that surround St Helena. The effects of marine erosion are still continuing, as the South-east Trade Winds drive the wave formations to eat away at the coast in their path, while the seasonal Atlantic rollers pound the cliffs on the north and west of the island. Over a period of some fourteen million years rain and wind acted together to form the inland topography of St Helena. Streams and torrents have cut deep runnels into the original volcano, leaving deep valleys, and exposed pinnacles and ridges of harder rock which now give the island its most distinctive sky-line and scenery, of which Lot and Lots Wife, the Barn and the Heart-shape Waterfall are all classic examples.

Fish and marine mammals, and seabirds would have been very early visitors, arriving in the vicinity as soon as the volcanic cone was within a short distance of the sea's surface. A similar process is happening over the two volcanoes yet to emerge from the Atlantic within the vicinity of St Helena, the Napoleon and Grattan Seamounts, the highest points of which are currently between 200 – 350 feet below the present sea level. Shallow water species of fish would have attracted both larger fish, and mammals such as seals, that could prey upon them. Seals and turtles were probably the first of the marine mammals to colonise the island, while some of the oceanic seabirds would have followed quite soon afterwards. The latter would also have helped to establish insect populations by carrying parasites with them: other insects would have arrived borne on the winds.

Plant-life would have found a ready home in the ashy soils of the developing volcano, but it is far from clear how the many endemic and indigenous species of flora actually became established on St Helena. The island lies far from any landmass, and dispersal of seeds purely on the wind over such distances is difficult, although it is not entirely impossible for spores to be carried far over the ocean. Some species will undoubtedly have been wind-borne, while others (such as the three original endemics - ebony, dwarf ebony and redwood) probably arrived on the tide or were inadvertently carried by transiting birds.

Man has introduced a number of land-birds to St Helena. Some, such as pheasant, partridge and pigeon were introduced for feeding the crews of ships using the island as a re-victualing stop, while other colourful species, such as the cardinal, canary, and waxbill, came as more exotic and decorative immigrants and evoke the island's links with its maritime past: Madagascar, the Canary Islands, and the East Indies. The common mynah has a more utilitarian background, having been introduced from India in 1829 in the hope that it would make an impact on the parasitical insects infesting cattle. Instead it has flourished on domestic fruits and become a pest. Due to its extreme isolation the island's native bird population consists of only eight species of locally breeding seabird, including the fairy tern which nests in the forests and hovers above the walker like a guardian angel (perhaps appropriate in an island of Saints); an indigenous moorhen; and St Helena's wirebird, the sole endemic species – a flightless variety of small plover.

There are more than thirty endemic species of plants, most of which are types of tree or shrub growing on the highlands of the central mountain chain of the island. These include cabbage trees (both He Cabbage and She Cabbage) distantly related to groundsel; gumwoods, a distant relation to some herbaceous species; ebonies and redwood; whitewood and boxwood; the St Helena ebony; and some flowering shrub and herb-like varieties, which include such island oddities as babies toes, hair grass, goosefoot and salad plants.

St Helena is roughly the size of Jersey in the Channel Islands and has eroded over the millennia into a lozenge shape, lying on a south-west/north-east axis. A mountainous ridge dominates this major axis and the island comprises an almost continuous line of high, sheer cliffs cut only by a few narrow and steep-sided valleys around the coastline. It is criss-crossed by valleys up to 1,000 feet deep, and slopes steeply from the central ridges to the sea. There is little flat land and while bush and semi-tropical growth is found on the high central peaks, and grassland a little lower, the 1,200 feet contour generally marks the lower limit of cultivation. Most of the land below this is semi-barren or barren. In da Nova's day it is recorded that the island was wooded to the ocean's edge, but goats and man have subsequently had a devastating impact.

The island, at most some ten miles long and six miles wide, occupies just forty-seven square miles in the South Atlantic some 1,700 miles northwest of Cape Town. It is hardly surprising that it remained undiscovered and unknown for so long and remained remote by modern day standards. The nearest land is at Ascension Island, itself a mere speck on the ocean's surface some 700 miles to the north. The major link with the outside world at the time of our arrival was Cape Town, five days away by sea.

Like da Nova and hundreds since, the ships of today's travellers find anchorage in James Bay. There is no port or harbour. On shore, in the lee of the South-east Trade Winds in a narrow defile on the Northwest coast, a rocky valley gives shelter to the island's capital, Jamestown. Crumbling fortifications stand guard on the bare cliffs overlooking the bay and, as in the days those defensive works were built, all visiting vessels have to lie at anchor while passengers and cargo leave over the ship's side to be ferried ashore by lighter to the quay.

Today, however, apart from the occasional cruise ships in the southern summer season, St Helena now sees few ships. A contrast to the days of sail, when the island was first settled. During those earlier times, and particularly before the Suez Canal was built, there were many hundreds of ships calling annually to take on water and other fresh supplies. In the days of the English East India Company, the Company's ships returning from the East Indies would gather at St Helena to be protected from pirates and other predatory shipping by the Royal Navy during their onward journey through the North Atlantic. The withdrawal of the Union Castle Line mail service from Southampton to the

Cape prompted the first of many agonising discussions on access to this remote island and introduced the concept of a vessel dedicated to serving the island and its needs. This ship, the *Royal Mail Ship St Helena*, then played an important part in the lives of the South Atlantic islands of St Helena, Ascension and Tristan da Cunha, all of which were then linked with Cape Town. The dedicated passenger and cargo service fulfilled by the *RMS St Helena* drew to a close in early 2018 as hopes for a new era of air travel were spurred on by the arrival of the first commercial air service to St Helena on 14th October 2017.

First impressions, however, can be deceptive. St Helena is not a few acres of Britain in a sub tropical environment. Its remote location and history have conspired to produce a breed of people without equal who, given their lack of natural resources and the relationship with those responsible over the centuries for their governance, have developed a unique personality of their own. A view that Saints, as they are familiarly called, are heavily suntanned Englishmen, and wholly British down to Scouts, Guides, brass bands and church-every-Sunday is sadly wide of the mark, illustrating the visitor's capacity for self-deception.

St Helena was uninhabited before the English East India Company's formal settlement of the island in 1659. Subsequently people of many races gradually settled it. Some came voluntarily but many arrived involuntarily as slaves or slaves freed from slave ships arrested by the Royal Navy. They have since both intermarried and associated outside marriage widely. The result is a very mixed population of all shades and colours. But no one really belongs and, as a result there is no deep-rooted culture, nor traditions unassociated with colonialism. This background produces a strange and unusual people: individualists with a basic feeling of insecurity. They have none of the accepted emotions of tradition, or tribe, or caste, which could give them a foundation upon which they can rely.

Saints have a Britishness in the same way that other colonial and former colonial peoples do. But, theirs is a distinctive brand of Saint Helenian Britishness, including their English language and vocabulary. By the same token, they share with all isolated and consanguineous communities a parochial turn of mind, an obsessive concern with the activities of their fellow islanders, and what they may in turn think of them, which extinguishes any real possibility of their exercising impartial administration of rules or regulations, which exist for others - not themselves. Their inclination to small-mindedness, what might be termed their infinite capacity for thinking small, is not untypical of other small, remote island communities. In St Helena's case there are historical reasons for this that become evident in due course. However, they can, by and large, be summed up as the result of almost total dependence on 'Britain' for nearly three hundred and fifty years. There is a tendency to argue that certain courses to break free of this dependency are unacceptable, and a will not to admit of the need to see the other point of view.

That this dependence is not a modern phenomenon, springing from the twentieth century British welfare state, it is necessary only to turn to the work entitled *St Helena* by J C Melliss and published in 1875. John Charles Melliss, being born on the island, was well placed to understand; but, more than that, he was an acute observer of things Saint Helenian. He wrote of the island's people that:-

> "*The habits of dependence and indolence, as well as ignorance, which so long a period of slavery had engrafted, remain to this day evident, not only in individuals, but pervading the whole character of the place.*"

The following chapters examine the issues current in 1995-1999 that tend to establish this and illustrate why Melliss' observation might be as true on the day that we arrived, as it was apposite over one hundred and twenty-five years earlier.

St Helena's geographic position has, nonetheless, managed to preserve a veneer of Englishness where, superficially at least, family values were strong, and a sense of community important, which in turn created a society in which there was no overt racism, there were no muggings, or murders, no hard drugs or organised crime and where it was still the rule rather than the exception to leave one's house and car unlocked. Nonetheless, drink related crimes, battered wives and domestic violence, and even incest, were not uncommon; and the local jail customarily had a majority of its inmates (an average of between 4 – 6 convicted prisoners) serving sentences for sex offences: yet, AIDS was still non-existent. Familial relationships twist and turn throughout the community – recognised here, but not there – usually without malice or seriously detrimental effects.

The Island, and particularly the capital Jamestown, came to life when the ship was in port or on its short journey to and from Ascension Island, presenting an appearance of a bustling, lively, colonial enclave. The visitor benefits from the casual greeting, as between islanders – the wave from car to passing car – and a feeling that there is warmth and friendship, and that nothing is too much trouble for the stranger in the island community.

It was not surprising that visitors, especially those who were officials and advisers from London (categorised by the islanders as 'two-day' or 'seven-day visitors'), failed to obtain any real concept of what life was like for Saint Helenians when their life-line to the outside world sailed away for two weeks to the Cape, or five to six weeks at a time when the RMS sailed north to Britain. Life can be harsh; unemployment a very real problem; and alcohol the island's solace and salve since the early settlement of St Helena,

If, as it seemed to the outsider, St Helena and its people displayed many of the values of the 1950s, nostalgically evoked by those critical of society in the developed world, it was hard to understand how many of those same people, when representing British officialdom, could be so impatient at the way in which St Helena was struggling to adapt to the pragmatic financial imperatives of the late twentieth century. St Helena is different; and it is its location and history that made it so.

The original party of settlers, augmented by those families offered passage and land after the fire of London in 1666, and again in 1673, together with other Britons in the service of the English East India Company formed the early nucleus of the population of this formerly uninhabited island. Few of the more senior of the Company's servants settled permanently. This early population grew with the arrival of soldiers and sailors - some of whom settled - and the adoption of the social model found in colonial garrison towns all around the world where couples would form relationships that neither partner expected to be permanent. The population was also increased by the many hundreds of slaves trafficked by the East India Company before emancipation and by freed slaves thereafter. Africans and Asians out-numbered the population of European origin throughout the period of slavery which, taken with the continuing extraordinary level of promiscuity, has resulted in a genuinely 'rainbow' population today.

There has, however, been no new immigration to parallel that of the settlement of other British territories. Land and mineral resources, which fuelled those population movements in the nineteenth century, are conspicuously absent on St Helena. In the twentieth century the population began to decline and immigration, increasingly unpopular with local politicians as the century drew to a close, was generally limited to a minimal number of spouses of Saint Helenians married abroad returning with them, often in retirement. Indeed, migration has largely tended to be in the opposite direction, with large exoduses following the period of Napoleon's imprisonment and the two World Wars. Since the Falklands conflict, when Saint Helenian labour was sought after to cater to the rapidly expanded Armed Forces' presence on nearby Ascension Island, there has been an outward flow of contract workers, firstly to Ascension; and subsequently to the Falkland Islands. This has had far reaching affects on the island's economy, the capacity for development on St Helena and for social cohesion.

In 1995 it was by far the poorest of Britain's remaining colonies, known since 1999 as Overseas, rather than Dependent, Territories instead of Colonies. It was the only British dependency still in receipt of long-term grant-in-aid-of-expenses-of-administration to balance the Budget. Although the volcanic eruption in Montserrat and the hurricane of 2016 in the Virgin Islands brought about the short-term need for grant-in-aid for those Territories, St Helena has a structural dependence on such funding from Britain due to its lack of natural resources; negligible capital base and consequent lack of assets; a very small internal market; poor access; isolation from potential export markets; and small population. In short, it has insufficient economic resources for sustainable development.

St Helena is linked to two further Dependencies, Ascension and Tristan da Cunha, as St Helena & Its

Dependencies. The latter two territories are not, however, dependent upon the St Helena Government, but are separate United Kingdom Overseas Territories, forming part of a single territorial grouping under the sovereignty of the British Crown. They have been linked, for administrative convenience, under the one Governor, who exercises the Crown's executive authority in their respect.

The Governor of St Helena is both The Queen's representative, and represents The Queen, in the Territory. This is more than just a matter of semantics. A Governor, within his colony, is not a civil servant, nor even a 'senior official'. The powers and duties of colonial Governors vary from one dependency to another according to the constitutional provisions of the Territory. The common factor being, in the lapidary words of William Strang, former Head of the Foreign Office and one-time political adviser to Field Marshall Montgomery, that *"...he stands at the nodal point in the traffic of business, the point at which instructions from above meet recommendations from below"*.

It is also, in part, the Governor's responsibility in St Helena (as it is the rôle of Governors and other senior officials appointed by the British Government in all Overseas Territories) to project Britain in the Territory. The Governor has to ensure that St Helena's legitimate interests are represented to the United Kingdom while at the same time he must reflect the UK point of view as far as he can without losing his credibility with the island's population as their chief representative. The Governor should thus, consequently be conscious of his responsibility to both Governments in all that he does, and the Foreign & Commonwealth Office has to rely to a very considerable extent on the Governor to judge where the balance is best struck. If the British case is under-represented in public in the Territory, then this has to be accepted in London as the necessary consequence of supporting the Governor whom the FCO have appointed. Whether a Governor does retain that support is, of course, a moot point!

The Territory of St Helena can be said to have come of age in 1985 with the grant of Armorial Bearings by Royal Warrant. As one of Her Britannic Majesty's overseas possessions the national flag of St Helena is the Union Flag of the United Kingdom of Great Britain and Northern Ireland:

the 'Union Jack'. But there is a defaced blue ensign, which is flown to identify Saint Helena as a Territory. The ensign had a flag badge, depicting an East Indiaman and the rocky coast of St Helena, which was replaced in 1985 to include the St Helena Coat of Arms. The Arms include the heraldic items of the flag badge with the addition of a wirebird set in the upper part. This flag flies above the Supreme Court building in Jamestown, and on other Government buildings on Island occasions, such as St Helena Day.

Despite its remoteness, St Helena made the headlines in Britain, and elsewhere in the English-speaking world, in its campaign for British citizenship in the 1990s; and more recently over the fiasco of providing air access. But, for many it is still an unknown, vaguely associated in the mind with Napoleon, situated in the Mediterranean, or perhaps Caribbean? Even though it has been somewhat neglected by the mandarins of Whitehall, as (arguably) the second oldest remaining British dependency, it was a fascinating example of British colonial rule in the twentieth century.

It was immediately obvious to me that I was no longer a diplomat, but a politician. From a career of offering, hopefully sensible and sound advice, to senior officials and politicians, I was now to be the recipient of such advice and ultimately responsible for possibly life-changing decisions affecting a community that had had no choice whatsoever in putting me in that position. I recalled my often vigorous philosophical political discussions with the Trinidadian politician Basdeo Panday: by contrast his opposite number Michael Manning didn't 'do' philosophical and had seemed to live in a 'policy free zone' when Leader of the Opposition himself. I could see that it was going to be important to explain to an unsophisticated Saint Helenian public, used to Government occupying the commanding heights of the economy, what our ultimate aim was and how we expected to achieve it. Despite the constitutional responsibility of the elected representatives to make the political decisions and enact the legislation, I realised that it would be my determination and personal engagement that would have the most influence on the Government's economic programme and its success. A big ask, and a situation with which a British diplomat was rarely faced. I hoped that I was up to the challenge.

To support me in meeting this challenge I fortunately had a first rate team of officials, senior among whom was the Chief Secretary, John Perrott. The Office of the Chief Secretary was headed by the St Helena Government Deputy Secretary, Ethel Yon, who ran this secretariat, the function of which was to directly support the office of Governor and co-ordinate Government policy across the board. Ethel Yon was the most senior Saint Helenian civil servant and an experienced and skilled bureaucrat occupying a position somewhat similar to the Cabinet Secretary in the British Government machine. She attended, but did not take part in the meetings of the Executive Council (c.f. Cabinet). Then there was our local 'Chancellor of the Exchequer', the Financial Secretary, Bob Perrott (no relation to John); and the Attorney General, David Jeremiah. In addition to these officials I could call upon the Government Economist, Tom Pengelly, and the Head of the Audit Department who was an accountant formerly with Price Waterhouse and who had both economics and management skills – Ken Jones. These six individuals, and in time their successors, came to form an informal advisory group that would be joined by other heads of department when discussion required.

My career had been fashioned by my belief in the adage that the essence of good management is to make the right decisions, not those which might be most popular. It might not always have stood me in good stead and I soon realised that his might be especially true in a political context!

CHAPTER ONE

In the Beginning

I had no burning childhood ambition, nor even a dream, to be a Colonial Governor even though during my childhood Great Britain sat at the centre of an Empire upon which the sun never set. The Sovereign was described on the nation's coinage from the farthing to the half-crown as *Georgivs VI, G: REX ET IND: IMP,* that is George VI *Dei gratia Rex et Ind. Imp.* The mystique of Empire was captured for me on 2nd June 1953 after watching the Coronation procession of Queen Elizabeth II on the Mall with my parents. With martial music still ringing in my young ears and the uniforms of so many marching men still colouring my mind's eye, we walked up the steps from St James' Park to King Charles Street. There I caught sight of the statue of Robert Clive staring calmly back over the park towards Buckingham Palace. The plinth is simply annotated with the name 'Clive' and the dates 1725 – 1774, expecting all who read it to know just who Clive was. It was many years later, and from the vantage point of the Foreign & Commonwealth Office, that I realised that he stood sentinel over Clive Steps outside what had once been the India Office.

*   *   *

As a child I had had the ambition to join the Navy. During my teens that developed into a desire to combine a life at sea with flying by joining the Royal Navy's Fleet Air Arm. It was possible to join on a direct entry scheme (by-passing Dartmouth) at the age of 17. In the event I was persuaded to stay on at school to sit 'A Levels'; and went on to University to study geography. As a member of the University Air Squadron I learnt to fly, but after opting to join the RAF as a pilot decided that perhaps my potential for command lay outside the confines of a light blue uniform. However, I had no career Plan B in place and it was not until catching sight of a Civil Service circular calling for volunteers for the

Diplomatic Service some years later that my future began to be mapped. The call was part of the process of creating the new Diplomatic Service, to replace members of the Colonial and Commonwealth Relations Offices who wished to remain members of the home civil service rather than become members of the Diplomatic Service, with its obligation, like those in the Foreign Office, for overseas service. Circumstances change, but I still had no notion of becoming a Colonial Governor.

Her Majesty's Diplomatic Service was established as a uniformed Service of State by an Order-in-Council on 1st January 1965. Distinct and separate from the Civil Service, its officers held a commission from The Queen similar to a military commission. Even in the 1990s the Service numbered less in total than the staff of Harrods department store in London. There had, of course, been diplomats and a foreign service before 1965, but the mid sixties was another of those eras of periodic assault by Government on the structure of the public services, which went under the guise of "modernisation".

Broadly speaking, the Diplomatic Service was established to staff all of Britain's overseas representative missions – embassies, delegations to international organisations, high commissions, consulates - and to provide the core staff in the London offices then dealing with them - the Foreign, Colonial, and Commonwealth Relations Offices.

A 'foreign office' had existed as part of the machinery of government in London since 1640 taking on something of its modern shape in 1782, when it became a separate Department of State with Charles James Fox as His Majesty's Principal Secretary of State for Foreign Affairs.

An office dealing with the colonies can be traced back to the Council of Foreign Plantations set up in 1660 to deal with the affairs of the settlements in North America and the West Indies. For some years during the nineteenth century the colonies were the responsibility of the Secretary of State for War, but a separate Colonial Office was established in 1854.

The India Office was constituted to take political responsibility for the governance of India from the English East India Company in 1857, following the 'Indian mutiny'. Much later, in 1925, a Dominions Office was set up to deal with the significant developments in the Empire; and to handle relations with Canada, Australia, New Zealand, South Africa, Newfoundland, and the Irish Free State. Then, following the transfer of power to the independent Governments of India and Pakistan in 1947, the India and Dominions Offices were translated into the Commonwealth Relations Office. We had affairs with foreigners, but relations with members of the British Commonwealth – as it was then, before the 'winds of change' in Africa.

During the early 1960s, first Harold Macmillan's Government and then Harold Wilson's examined our post-colonial relationship with the rest of the world. Both concluded that one Service and one Department of State dealing with 'abroad' better suited Britain's reduced power and place in the post-war world.

After HM Diplomatic Service was established in 1965, a Diplomatic Service Administration Office was set up to manage the merger and to administer the cadres of the former Foreign Office and Commonwealth Relations Office. The Colonial Office and the Commonwealth Relations Office merged to become the Commonwealth Office in 1967. The Commonwealth Office was, in its turn, merged with (some would say taken over, lock stock and barrel, by) the Foreign Office in October 1968 and renamed the Foreign & Commonwealth Office - the FCO or (as the diehards would have it) Foreign Office for short. Indeed, the latter form is now more commonly used by the Service itself, the media and the public.

I finally started my diplomatic career as an Assistant Telegraph Officer in 1966 – on loan to the Colonial Office, during its final months of existence. In that capacity I met Sir Cosmo Haskard, Governor of the Falkland Islands, while his wife in Port Stanley was struggling with encyphering telegraphic messages to the Colonial Office reporting on the (unsuccessful) invasion attempt by a handful of Argentinian terrorists, known as Condors, who had crash-landed their DC4 aircraft on the Island's Race Course. They had taken several islanders hostage for a short time before the Royal Marine detachment dealt with them. While stirring the imagination it didn't prompt a career ambition! Nevertheless, in the early 1990s David Gilmore, then Head of the Diplomatic Service and with whom I had served closely in the

FCO's Defence Department in the late 1970s, sought to establish a cadre of officers willing to serve in the remaining colonies. In the light of my earliest experiences in the Service I did put my name forward, but I have no way of knowing how or whether that might have led to my posting to St Helena in 1995.

A career in Her Majesty's Diplomatic Service, that started in the Colonial Office, was then to take me all over the territories acquired by Clive's Honourable East India Company - from Aden to Singapore; to the Indian sub-continent and Burma; and, via Trinidad, finally to that minute speck in the South Atlantic Ocean, best more widely known for its infamous prisoner, Napoleon Buonaparte.

*   *   *

Between 1990 and 1994 I had been posted at Port of Spain in the Caribbean isle of Trinidad, where for a year I had acted as the British High Commissioner, and *inter alia* been much involved with Trinidad's politicians, cricket and the building of new High Commission offices. No ministerial visit could be offered for an official opening, but as luck would have it we received news that The Duke of Edinburgh would be visiting Trinidad in April 1994 in a capacity that would usually mean he would conduct no official engagements for HMG. I was able, however, through contacts that I had established as the head of the Royal Matters secretariat at the FCO in the period before my posting to Port of Spain, to reach agreement that His Royal Highness would, in addition to the obligatory courtesy call on the President, make an exception to the 'no engagements' stricture and formally open the new High Commission building. During the post-official opening drinks, His Royal Highness asked, in the knowledge that I had been *en poste* for some four years, whether I knew where I would next be posted. I replied that I knew not, to which he responded, "*Typical bloody Foreign Office*" turned on his heel and strode away! At least, I thought, he had sent me a personal congratulatory telegram on my appointment as a Lieutenant of the Royal Victorian Order in 1990 after working as the Royal Family's man at the FCO.

Thus, Sandi and I returned to spend the summer of 1994 in England. I made my rounds of colleagues in the FCO in

London and Departments in Whitehall de-briefing on Trinidad and Tobago. Naturally I called on 'personnel', but had no hints about my future and learnt that the Board making appointments in the next round would not now sit until the end of September. The three appointments to be decided and for which I was qualified were the posts of British High Commissioner at Belmopan, Belize, and that at Georgetown, Guyana, and as Governor of St Helena and Its Dependencies.

There was a strong politico/military element in the job at Belmopan (Belize). Guatemala was still making threats to the country's borders, established in colonial days, and the RAF had a detachment of Harrier jets stationed there together with a battalion size army deployment to deter potential cross-border aggression. I had picked up quite a lot about Belize in Trinidad, as the current High Commissioner at Belmopan had been a nephew of the lawyer Gerald Furness-Smith's wife. She frequently passed on to us the latest developments and news. Belize was small, jungle clad and quite claustrophobic she reported. Whereas Guyana was important neither commercially nor politically to the UK. A posting to Georgetown would, I saw, allow lots of intra-Caribbean travel for business and pleasure; and together with its proximity to Trinidad, it was my reason entirely for having it as a Post preference. I discussed the opportunities available in the bidding round with a colleague similarly placed, but he kept his cards very close to his chest, but I thought he might be a well placed candidate for St Helena.

I still have no idea what he might have preferred personally, but the telephone call informing me of the decision to appoint me to St Helena was a complete shock. But not nearly so much as a shock as it was to Sandi! A posting to the place she least wanted had become a nightmare reality! I hurried to London and discussions with 'personnel'. Refusing this posting could, I learnt, have had the result of triggering a move for my early retirement: an unwelcome choice. Tucked away in DSRs was a paragraph that could be interpreted as meaning a posting was an order rather than a request. So, St Helena it was. We couldn't refer to the appointment until it had been submitted to the Prime Minster and agreed by The Queen; and then announced in the Court Circular. My predecessor, however, asked that any announcement should be delayed until a date several months hence, to prevent him from feeling a lame duck Governor.

We read that St Helena had been established, almost as an afterthought of history, as a victualing station in the South Atlantic Ocean, by the English East India Company for its fleets to gather safely on their route from the Indies to England. It was, we further read, the deeply eroded summit of an enormous volcano that had formed from volcanic activity associated with the Mid-Atlantic Ridge about fifty million years ago. Geoffrey Martin, our Chief Justice, who became a good friend, described St Helena succinctly in his memoirs thus-

"Centuries of seamen have anchored there and attempted to describe it. None has fully succeeded; words cannot capture the wild forbidding beauty of the place. For that, one must see it. Jamestown Bay is hardly a bay, more a slight indentation where a bleak steep sided valley meets the sea. From the anchorage, some half mile from shore, we could see the sea wall, and just behind it a long rampart joining the two walls of the valley. Beyond it appears a thin ribbon of buildings, at first two streets wide but rapidly narrowing to one squeezed between bare rock walls. There are a few trees in the town, a couple of jacarandas shining blue amongst the pink and brown roofs. A square church tower peeps over the rampart, comfortingly English. Half way up each valley wall old fortifications cling to the rock. Slightly inland on a high knoll sits a walled fortress. Up on a cliff top to the right is a cluster of houses, some elderly naval guns and a flagstaff. To right and left stretch bare cliffs, rising steeply out of the sea like castle walls. Not one beach or pebbly bay can be seen. From the sea, the island is a fortress crudely chopped from the towering rock. There is no hint of the lovely landscape within, reminiscent of the West Country in England."

St Helena is roughly the size of Jersey in the Channel Islands, but surrounded by high cliffs and dominated by a mountainous ridge criss-crossed with valleys up to 1,000 feet deep. There was but one town, more a village really, the capital Jamestown; and a population of less than 6,000. And, finally - there was no airport. After our four years in Trinidad this, to echo Napoleon, sounded more like a penal colony!

The formalities took some time to work their way through the system following the Foreign and Commonwealth Secretary's submission of 15th November that,

> "Mr Douglas Hurd, with his humble duty to Your Majesty, has the honour respectfully to submit for Your Majesty's approval that Mr D L Smallman, LVO be appointed Governor of St Helena, in succession to Mr A N Hoole..."

It was not until the end of November, when I received a letter from the FCO's Personnel Management Department, that I had official confirmation –

> "...that Her Majesty the Queen has been pleased to approve your appointment as Governor of St Helena." And that "The announcement of your appointment will not be made until April/May 1995."

I had a lot to learn despite my early experience in the Colonial Office of the 1960s. Colonial administration was obviously quite different to representing the British Government overseas and the rôle of a British colonial Governor was markedly different to one of Her Britannic Majesty's Ambassadors. Although both are The Queen's representatives in the country in which they reside; and both are responsible to the Secretary of State for Foreign and Commonwealth Affairs in London, in the Ambassador's case the buck truly rests with the Secretary of State, while for the Governor, in practice, the buck invariably stops on his desk. The fundamental difference in their respective rôles being that the Governor also represents the executive authority of The Queen in her rôle as Head of State. Although those Ambassadors to other Royal Courts then only wore

Diplomatic Service uniform, e.g. in Oslo and Bangkok, Governors still wore uniform in their Territories. Glamorous as such a rôle may appear to the casual observer, it is not one for which applications were over-subscribed as the job did not lead automatically to the topmost appointments in the FCO or HM Diplomatic Service.

It was not until 5th April in 1995, that the Announcements section of the Court Circular carried the bald statement "*Mr David Leslie Smallman to be Governor and Commander-in-Chief of St Helena*" squeezed between the appointment of Mr Peter Ord as Resident Factor for the Royal Estate at Balmoral and that of Mr James Daly as British High Commissioner to the Government of Vanuatu *The Daily Telegraph's* 'Peterborough' column carried the following tongue-in-cheek piece:-

"*IT IS announced that David Smallman will in August become Governor of St Helena. In the diplomatic world this is considered to be a little like opening the winning envelope on Blind Date* [a popular TV programme at the time, the prizes in which could include glamorous overseas destinations], *only to pull out a weekend in Swanage.*

What can Smallman and his wife Sandi expect? St Helena is 48 sq miles, with a population of 5,500. You reach it by boat, which calls every three to five weeks. The Governor's residence was built by the East India Company 200 years ago and is atop a hill in woods with a tennis court (one of only four on the island). The Governor also has a 1989 Jaguar XJ6, plus driver.

Television was introduced last week. The outgoing Governor, Alan Hoole, is just finishing his second stint there. 'The first thing most people notice is the very British way of life. The most popular pursuits are skittles, camping and euchre drives {euchre being a cross between whist and rummy}.' Gossiping is also something of a national pastime, its subject most often being...the Governor."

We never found out who had contributed the information for this article: but it was clearly someone who had both the knowledge that the preferred form of Sandi's name was Sandi (not the more common form - Sandy) and not her given name, Sandra; and that he or she possessed some correct detail about life on St Helena. I mused that it appeared that the most obvious requirement for the job seemed to be a sense of humour.

Since the demise of the Colonial Service, Governor's had generally been appointed from the ranks of HM Diplomatic Service, which had, in effect, replaced it. In the larger colonies officers had progressed up the promotion ladder from District Officer, to perhaps Chief Secretary, and eventually to Governor, and then perhaps from one colony to a bigger one as Governor. The last Colonial Service Governor of St Helena was Geoffrey Guy who had been a District Commissioner in Sierra Leone; Commissioner and Administrator of the Turks and Caicos Islands; Administrator and then Governor of Dominica, and Administrator of Ascension Island before taking up his appointment as Governor at St Helena in 1976. Unusually, he stayed on in St Helena for some years and in retirement became the Speaker of the St Helena Legislative Council.

There are no set qualifications for a British Colonial Governor. There was no high level administrative examination. Each brought his own unique, and usually diplomatic, experience to the rôle. Alan Hoole was the first contracted official to be appointed as the Governor of St Helena, but the practice is becoming more common both in the South Atlantic as well as elsewhere. Alan Hoole, who was Governor from 1991 – 1995, was an English lawyer who had been recruited as Attorney General on the Island from 1978 – 1981; and had then served as Deputy Governor of Anguilla for two years before his appointment to St Helena.

John Perrott, a Diplomatic Service First Secretary then acting as the St Helena Government Chief Secretary (the most senior public servant in the colony) and who was to be my deputy in St Helena, was fortuitously on leave in London. The Foreign Office desk officer in the FCO's South Atlantic and Antarctic Department (SAAD) arranged a meeting for us on the day my appointment became official. We got on well and to better know them, Sandi and I met John and Wendy, his wife, for lunch in Westminster a fortnight later.

A few days later, on 22nd April and following an arrangement made by my SAAD desk officer contact, I drove down to Fordingbridge in Hampshire to attend the annual meeting of the Tristan da Cunha Society. Tristan da Cunha, along with Ascension Island, is a separate colony described as a Dependency of St Helena: both islands share the same Governor (of St Helena). I met the handful of Tristanians then resident in Britain. Also there were the small (and declining) group of expatriates who had served on Tristan da Cunha over the years, together with a number of others who had visited the islands or were simply just interested in that distant archipelago in the South Atlantic. I was vaguely aware of the dramatic story of the evacuation of the population from Tristan da Cunha following the volcanic eruption there in the 1960s, but the meeting stirred my imagination and gave me the first feeling that I really wanted to go and explore my new domain.

On the day before my birthday I picked up the small bright red Rover Metro car that we had ordered from the Rover export department, bearing its export registration M65 DXP that we were to take to St Helena. A short while later I returned to the Savile Row establishment of Alan Bennett, the tailors producing my official uniform, for a final fitting. On 16th May it was ready for collection.

My diary for the weeks between May and August were mapped out in consultation with SAAD and my contact in the Heads of Mission Section. I was to embark on the comprehensive series of meetings that went with an appointment as Governor of St Helena and Its Dependencies, the most important of which was the Audience with The Queen. This, coincidentally, marked the beginning of my formal programme of briefing calls prior to our departure for St Helena.

I spent many hours at the feet of the FCO's resident colonial guru, and days with my head inside files, before it was possible to venture outside the FCO in public as Governor-designate. It had, however, become crystal clear that some form of economic re-generation was going to be needed to fill the vacuum left by the loss of the Island's flax industry in the late 1960s. St Helena seemed to lack any credible (or legal) means with which to earn a living. The economy had been shrinking by between 2 and 3% per annum for the previous three years. The solution appeared to require the development of an enterprise culture; to encourage moves from the unacceptably high reliance on public sector employment into the private sector without pushing unemployment to unacceptable levels; and to improve the economy of an island with a limited domestic economic base and few natural or local resources. St Helena, then alone of the UK Dependent Territories, relied on a grant-in-aid of the expense of administration of the Colony from HMG to balance expenditure and those revenues that the Government of St Helena was able to generate. This latter funding now came from the budget of the Aid Wing of the FCO, the Overseas Development Administration (ODA). Wow! What had I taken on?

The ODA could recruit and fund economists and advisers for the Government in St Helena, but I needed to understand the problem and potential solutions. So, as a first step, I sought and received independent advice from the Adam Smith Institute, one of the world's leading think tanks promoting free markets and limited government. As the Institute's web site says today *"It engineers policies to increase Britain's economic competitiveness, inject choice into public services, and create a freer, more prosperous society."* From the discussions and help that I received in those early days before arriving in St Helena I felt prepared to enter into a useful and hopefully productive dialogue with those upon whom I would have to rely on the Island to put any programme of restructuring into effect.

With this done I could then embark on the series of meetings that go with an appointment as Governor of St Helena. The most important of which was the Audience with The Queen. The tradition that Her Britannic Majesty's Ambassadors and Her Governors in the Dependent Territories overseas were summoned to the Royal presence to receive their instructions is maintained. The ceremony was earlier known as the 'kissing of hands'. Now it was simply an Audience – but a formal occasion for all that. The news was conveyed in a letter from Heads of Mission Section instructing that *"...dress for you is morning coat with black waistcoat (a hat and gloves are not essential as you would hand them to a page on arrival in any case). The Palace have advised that there are no restrictions as to your choice of tie. For your wife, a day dress or dressy suit would be acceptable, with hat and gloves. Unrelieved black should be avoided."* Further instructions ended with the information that an official car had been booked to pick us up from the FCO Park Door (Ambassador's Entrance) at 11:40 a.m. to take us to Buckingham Palace for our noon engagement.

On Wednesday 17th May we drove down to London picking up a hired morning suit from Moss Bros in Regent Street en route to the FCO. There, in the ample accommodation of the Heads of Mission we changed. Sandi looked stunning in a gold silk skirt and jacket and navy-blue hat that she had chosen specially for the occasion. We walked out through the Ambassador's Entrance overlooking St James' Park to the waiting car.

We were met on the steps of the Grand Entrance in the inner courtyard of Buckingham Palace by one of my former interlocutors at the Palace, (Sir) Robert Fellowes, The Queen's Private Secretary, and escorted to the Ante-room to the Audience Chamber. He briefed us on the etiquette of the Audience and were told that Her Majesty would indicate when our fifteen minutes were up, so that we could leave.

I had seen The Queen before, of course, but never really close up. I first saw her properly on the occasion that she did a 'drive about' in the days immediately after the Coronation in 1953 when, together with the other pupils at St Clement Danes Grammar School, I had lined nearby Wood Lane to wave to her as she had driven by. We had been in her company before, at the Garden Parties and Receptions at Buckingham Palace; and at my investiture as a Lieutenant of the Royal Victorian Order in 1990 she had been standing on the raised part of the Throne Room and had seemed, if anything, taller than I. As we were ushered into The Queen's presence her diminutive stature was most remarkable: one sees pictures and TV coverage when it is obvious that she is quite small, but to see her closely across the room underlines it: that and her intensively blue eyes. She bade us sit and her easy manner dispelled any nervousness that we might have felt.

We must have spoken about a lot of things; but my clearest recollection of our conversation was of The Queen saying that her most distinct memory of St Helena (which she had visited in 1947 with her father King George VI and Queen Elizabeth on the way back to Britain from a tour of South Africa) was seeing arum lilies growing in the wild for the first time. She also remembered seeing Jonathan an aged tortoise, 'who couldn't possibly be still alive'. I was able to assure her that to the best of my knowledge he was alive and well, and promised to send photographic evidence after we reached the Island. The Queen must be very practiced in keeping her Audiences to the conditioned fifteen minutes. However and for whatever reason, we finally received the sign and made our exit after a full thirty minutes, keeping Admiral Sir Michael Layard, Commander-in-Chief Naval Home Command, waiting in the Ante-room for his audience before taking up his appointment.

However, it was not until August that I received the Commission that The Queen had been "...*graciously pleased to grant to you under the Royal Sign Manual and Signet, constituting and appointing you Her Majesty's Governor and Commander-in-Chief in St Helena and Its Dependencies.*" There had been, as is often the case in politics, a cabinet reshuffle in the meantime, and the Commission was endorsed with the signature of the new Secretary of State, Sir Malcolm Rifkind.

*   *   *

My official calls and appointments were many and various and, of course, included numerous FCO and ODA officials, including David Wright, my opposite number in The Prince of Wales Private Office in the late 1980s, who had become an FCO Deputy Under Secretary; the Permanent Under Secretary and head of the Diplomatic Service (PUS), Sir John Coles, who had been the second Head of South Asian Department to whom I had worked in the late 1970s; and Dorothy Syme, Head of Medical & Welfare Department, who had been a colleague in Nicosia in 1971 – 1973. I also met a number of MPs and members of the House of Lords, who were part of the parliamentary groups with interests in St Helena and the South Atlantic, most notably Lord Holderness. As Richard Wood and former Conservative MP for Bridlington, Lord Holderness had been the Minister for Overseas Development from 1970 - 1974, and had developed a special interest in St Helena being the only Minister to have visited the Island. Lord Holderness' contemporary was Lynda Chalker who was the Minister at the ODA from 1989 – 1997, becoming Baroness Chalker in 1992 after loosing her seat as an MP in the General Election of that year. I called on her on 11th July and found her to be very interested in the Island and its economy and gained support from her to attempt better scheduling of the Island's lifeline, the *Royal Mail Ship St Helena.*

As Governor Gallwey had written in 1908, "...*that* sine qua non *to progress, namely capital is almost entirely conspicuous by its absence in St Helena.*" There was no retail Bank on the Island, even in 1995, although a Government Savings Bank (similar to the twentieth century British Post Office Saving Bank) held Government funds and took deposits from individuals. Briefly, between 1864 and 1865, the Standard Bank of South Africa had established a branch, but commercial conditions forced its closure. Since then no other banking company had seen an opportunity to open a high street branch on the Island.

In 1993 talks had begun between St Helena Government officials and the Bank of Nova Scotia. Callum Johnson, a senior executive of the Bank, had taken a personal interest in removing what he too thought was a real barrier to the development of a healthy private sector in St Helena. A retail bank would provide retail and loan facilities. With advice from London, the necessary local legislation had been enacted. I was in the middle of my briefing calls and thus fortuitously on hand when the next of a series of meetings was arranged. On 2nd June I took part in the discussions between FCO, ODA, and Bank of England officials with Callum Johnson representing the Bank of Nova Scotia. The meeting concluded with agreement that neither the Bank nor the Government of St Helena (whose word I gave) would be involved in any form of offshore banking. All that remained was for an agreed form of words for the Banking Licence and the Bank could be in operation in St Helena within the year.

I felt a great sense of achievement. This was probably the most important development in the Island's recent economic history and a significant bargaining point with Councillors who might be back-sliding from their commitment to reducing the dependence of the Island's labour force on

Government employ. It was certainly a very positive factor that I could bring to the table in my early discussions in St Helena.

It was quite obvious that with no airport and no other regular means of communication that the service provided by the Island's ship, the *Royal Mail Ship St Helena* fondly known as the *RMS*, was of vital importance, not only to the economy, but also to the people for whom the ship exercised a significant psychological value. Shipping was a major issue. Indeed it was recognised as so important an issue that the St Helena Government's decisions in shipping matters were reserved to the Governor. The St Helena Line Ltd, a company registered at the same address as the Crown Agents, held the legal title to the *RMS* on behalf of the St Helena Government, which had "the beneficial ownership" of the vessel. I was to spend a whole day in June with the organisation at its headquarters in Sutton concentrating primarily on the Crown Agents' relationship with the Island's ship and its operation.

The Crown Agents for Overseas Governments and Administrations was an autonomous statutory corporation that conducted financial transactions for the British colonies, transferring and accounting for grants made to them by the Treasury. It purchased supplies, recruited staff, and carried out miscellaneous other projects for other Governments, (like the road and bridge building schemes in South Yemen with which we had been associated in the early 1980s) and including the issue of currency notes and postage stamps. In the 1980s, with changes in HMG's international aid strategy, the Crown Agents became increasingly involved in matters of aid management. The 'new' *RMS St Helena* had been procured through funding from the overseas development budget; and the Crown Agents, therefore, were deemed ideally suited to oversee the operation of the vessel to ensure 'value for money' on behalf of HMG and the UK taxpayer. The directors of St Helena Line Ltd included a senior Crown Agents official and a shipping consultant, Peter Motion.

St Helena Line Ltd did not, however, run the ship. A contract to manage the operation of the *St Helena* had been awarded to Curnow Shipping Ltd, a Cornish company then based at Porthleven. The background to access to St Helena and the part played by the *RMS* and Curnow Shipping is covered in Chapter Eleven of my book, *"Quincentenary"*, covering 500 years of the Island's history. However, in addition to the need to work closely with St Helena Line Ltd, it was important to forge a working relationship with the ship's managers. I had met Andrew Bell, the managing director, as part of the briefing programme in London when he had entertained me to lunch at the Institute of Directors on 1st June.

To meet the company's management Sandi and I travelled down to Cornwall to stay with friends outside Newquay for a few days. We called on Curnow Shipping at Porthleven on 21st July meeting Andrew Bell, the managing director, and Chris Gardner the finance director, who introduced us to the company and its workings. Thereafter we were to have a very close relationship with both men as we jointly endeavoured to improve the service to the Island despite the best efforts of the Crown Agents to stymie us. Two weeks later we had the opportunity to go aboard the *RMS* during its call at Cardiff when we delivered our car as cargo for St Helena and put a trunk and my sword and uniform on board to be off-loaded at St Helena for us. Andrew Bell was there to welcome us and we met and had lunch on board with the Master, Captain Martin Smith, who would be in command when we travelled to the Island a month hence. There were two complete crews for the ship and these served on board for about three months at a time: we would meet the other Master, Captain David Roberts, later.

Having been in the Scouting movement for many years from the age of eight, through Cubs, Scouts, Senior Scouts and Rovers, and even assisting in running a Troop when it was between Scout leaders, it was an odd feeling to find myself at Baden-Powell House in Queen's Gate on 1st June 1995 being installed as Chief Scout of St Helena. I met Garth Morrison, then the Scout Association Chief Scout; picked up a few tips together with directions to the Scout Shop in Buckingham Place Road, where I could purchase items of uniform should I so wish. I left the building with the Warrant that he had presented to me in my brief case. Another piece of the complicated human jigsaw that formed the *persona* of the Governor of St Helena fell into place. At the same time Sandi, who would become President of the Guides Association on St Helena, visited the Guides Association in

Buckingham Palace Road to find out more about Guiding internationally.

The Island's Chief Justice, Geoffrey Martin, fitted in a call on me at the FCO on 2nd June; and the Attorney General, David Jeremiah, who was on UK leave at the time called on 11th July. The former Governor, Alan Hoole called for an interesting discussion on 12th and I also met with Julian Cairns-Wicks, a Member of the Legislative Council (MLC) of St Helena who was on leave from the Island. Corinda Essex, then on a degree course in England, was another caller who later returned to take up the post of Head of the Development Department in St Helena.

Finally, having said farewell to family and friends we flew to Cape Town on British Airways flight BA 57 on the evening of 30th August. En route our cabin steward asked us where we were going. When he learnt that we were going to St Helena and found out where it was he slipped away and returned with two bottles of champagne, saying that he thought we might need them! I had some official calls to make – the Embassy, situated in Cape Town for the southern summer, and the Consulate-General, where I found my old chum from Colonial Office days, Les Buchanan. The Consulate-General gave a lot of back up to the colonial administration in Jamestown, arranging hospital appointments; convalescent accommodation; the purchase of air tickets for Saint Helenians; and supplies procurement for Government departments on the Island. Les and his secretary, Wendy Smith, were to become the source of a lot of personal back up over the following four years. Les and his wife Louisa introduced us to Cape Town and kindly entertained us to lunch at one of the most popular restaurants - the Cellars-Hohenort Hotel in the Constantia Valley on the slopes of Table Mountain. We also made our number with the St Helena Line office, which was to become another source of support in Cape Town; and did a bit of last minute shopping before it was time to board the *RMS St Helena* berthed at Duncan Dock.

CHAPTER TWO

Off to St Helena Island

It was neatly choreographed so that as we arrived at the ship's side in Duncan Dock at 2 p.m. the Governor's flag was broken out on the cross trees and Capt Martin Smith welcomed us aboard personally. No sooner had we been ushered to our cabin than there was a knock on the door and the Anglican Bishop of St Helena, the Right Rev John Ruston, OGS, introduced himself. He was off the island on leave. He wanted also to introduce the clergyman who would be in charge on the island as Vicar-General (when we both arrived there), the Rev Brian Hart. Both men were members of the Oratory of the Good Shepherd, a celibate Anglican religious order. John Ruston was an ascetic and pious man who lived up to the Rule of the Oratory to live a life of prayer, discipline and pastoral concern. By contrast, Brian, a former teacher from Bondi in Australia, and the same age as me, seemed to be following the Rule of the oratory requiring celibacy almost as a penance, although he meticulously followed the injunction to make a regular account of spending in the diocese. The diocese of St Helena came under the Archbishop of Cape Town, then the renowned churchman Desmond Tutu.

Also on that voyage from Cape Town to Jamestown were a young couple, members of another church – the New Apostolic Church in South Africa. This was a new one on us, but we learnt that the New Apostolic Church was based on a belief that Jesus would rule bodily on earth for 1,000 years; and that it was a breakaway protestant version of the European Catholic Apostolic Church. It seems that most of its doctrines are close to Protestantism but the hierarchy and organization more akin to the Roman Catholic Church. The New Apostolics consider their Church to be the re-established continuation of the early Christian church and that its leaders are the successors to the twelve apostles. I do not know, but given the racial problems in apartheid South Africa it appeared that the New Apostolic Church in South Africa might have been a home for some of the so-called Cape

Coloured population of the Cape. He, his wife and their parents, whom we met later, were what had been referred to in the apartheid years as Cape Coloured; and so too were all the members of the Church that we met subsequently.

There were some Church members on St Helena and the South African Apostles had arranged for a church to be built there for them. Baron Gaskin was to be the first incumbent vicar now that the church had been completed and he, together with his wife Nerine, had been sent to minister there. They were about the same age as our own children and we were of a similar age to their parents. This was their first time away from South Africa and as outsider-newcomers we somehow drifted together after Sandi had taken Nerine 'under her wing' during the voyage to the Island. We probably kept each other sane during the time that they spent on the Island. They felt unable to mix socially – something to do with their religion I believe - and we came to spend most Friday nights together, either at Plantation House or their 'vicarage', soon after we had settled into our Island lives.

As I recorded in my First Impressions Despatch to the Foreign Secretary in October 1995, one could perhaps be forgiven for believing that it was possible to imagine how Napoleon Buonaparte might have felt in 1815 when he first set eyes on the steep cliffs surrounding the fortress island that was to become his prison.

The *RMS St Helena* had approached the island sailing along the east coast as dawn broke. There were no lights to be seen anywhere: there was no evidence of any life on the apparently barren rock we were slowly passing. Not until we rounded the unmarked north-easterly point of the island, and a little later Rupert's Bay opened up before us, did the first light appear – a rather rudimentary navigation light looking like a light bulb on the end of pole. Minutes later the *RMS*, as she was affectionately known by all Saint Helenians – or Saints for short - came at last within sight of the twinkling lights of Jamestown in the lightening day. At 7 o'clock in the morning of Friday 8th September the chain roared through the hawse pipe as the anchor dropped into the still waters of James Bay; and the slow moving ship came to a halt at 15°55´ South - 5°43´ West after five days at sea. Sandi, then on the ship's bridge, duly blew the ship's horn to announce the *RMS*'s safe arrival on Voyage 27N.

It is no exaggeration to say that *RMS St Helena's* schedule was a matter of universal interest on the island whose name she proudly bore. The *RMS* felt almost a part of the Island. A part that sailed away every so often, and returned on an irregular and in 1995 an as yet imperfect schedule, creating an air of excitement throughout St Helena on each and every 'Ship Day'. This tenuous link with the outside world emphasised the island's physical remoteness. The *RMS* was, I recognised, a crucial element in the Island's economic and social fabric and, until St Helena could become financially self sufficient, one that demanded priority in terms of its funding and sympathetic management.

On reaching the St Helena anchorage there was no mistaking that one had arrived in a British Territory. As it was a 'Ship Day' the Union flag flew proudly from the fort high on Ladder Hill above Jamestown, while another customarily flew daily on the Castle alongside the wharf where the Government secretariat, the Council Chamber and the office of the island's Governor are to be found. It is at once familiar and yet alien. Bright bougainvillea drapes itself around and above a public seat along the sea front; hibiscus vie with roses for attention, while through the gate in the defensive wall into the lower town is the oldest Anglican church in the southern hemisphere. A street of Georgian buildings leads the eye up what could be main street in any English seaside village. To add to the illusion, the Post Office-red Royal Mail van with its E II R cipher (complete with the GPO exhortation – betraying its second-hand British origin - to 'use the postcode') will have picked up the in-coming mail bags from the quay and delivered them to the Post Office: police officers, in their British style uniforms directing traffic and answering the visitors' requests for directions, are almost indistinguishable from any 'Bobby' on the beat in Britain.

On our own arrival the first boat out to the *RMS* carried Customs officials and the St Helena Government Chief Secretary, John Perrott, and his wife, together with the Chief of Police, Gerry Henry (who at that time also filled the rôle of aide-de-camp (adc) to the Governor), together with the Governor's official driver, Patrick Young. John Perrott, whose substantive appointment was as Chief Secretary, had been Acting Governor in the period since my successor Alan Hoole had left the Island some months earlier. The formalities of introductions over, Gerry Henry and Patrick Young went off to arrange for our baggage to go ashore, while we went to the Dining Room to discuss the day ahead over breakfast. As we did so, an attack of nerves about the task I was taking on hit me and I had rapidly to retreat to our bathroom. Fortunately my anxiety lasted only moments and with no ill effects. We were soon discussing the programme of events that would surround our arrival and my inauguration as the twenty-ninth Governor of St Helena under the Crown.

Everything was carefully planned and followed a well, if infrequently, rehearsed format. The Chief Secretary first asked to see my Commission of appointment and, after checking it, retained a copy that would eventually find its way into the St Helena Archive. We then went over the day's formalities, starting with our first meeting as soon as we stepped ashore. We were to be greeted by the Vicar-General, who had gone ashore in the first boat, and who would represent the absent Bishop, second only to the Governor in the Island's official protocol list. Next were the Speaker of the Legislative Council and Members of the Executive Council, other Legislative Council members (MLCs) and the Sheriff. Next I was reminded that we would be expected back into Jamestown for 2 p.m. when the Sheriff would read the Island's Address of Welcome. I had, of course been forewarned of this and prepared my response while en route for St Helena.

We were very conscious of the tricky disembarkation at the pier-head. John Massingham, Governor in the 1980s, had famously been captured on film in full uniform and up to his knees in a wave that had engulfed him when he went to greet Prince Andrew in April 1984. Now the sea was quite calm, but the movement of the boat, the slippery steps and a hundred pairs of eyes would make it a nervous moment. I would not be wearing uniform, which I took as a good omen.

It all went like clockwork, Patrick Young lent a hand at just the right moment and Sandi and I were ashore. Welcome to St Helena! The smiling, familiar face of Brian Hart greeted us and handed us to John Perrott to effect the introductions. Virtually all of the members of the Legislative Council were there and having a word to say to each of them was pretty time-consuming. It seemed to take forever before Gerry

Henry motioned towards the gleaming black Jaguar saloon where Patrick was holding open the offside door for me to get in. Gerry Henry did the same for Sandi before slipping into the front passenger seat for our first sight of Jamestown and St Helena. There were scores of bystanders, all of whom stared at us almost vacantly and without a wave among them. Indeed we had waves only from those expatriate passengers who had travelled with us on the ship and were making their way on foot from the Customs House to the Consulate Hotel and the Wellington House guesthouse on the High Street. Welcome to St Helena!

Our route took us along the wharf under the curtain wall of the Castle, with its ancient cannons and through the Town Gates into the Grand Parade, immediately recognisable as the same parade ground featured in a series of old prints of the Island that we had seen before our departure. To the right of the gates, on the seaward side was the Island's cenotaph honouring the war dead. On the left, as we went through the Grand Parade and passed the Castle entrance, the Supreme Court was pointed out to us – we would be there later for the inauguration ceremony. Almost opposite was the church of St James, reputed to be the oldest Anglican church in the Southern Hemisphere. Then we continued up through the town with the bare rocky cliffs of James Valley towering above us; up the valley side to the top of Ladder Hill; through the settlement known as Half Tree Hollow; past Bishopsholme and Red Gate to the white gate-houses of Plantation House – White Gate; and finally pulled up outside the fine looking Georgian house that was to be our home for the duration of my appointment.

A full description of the house appears in *Quincentenary* along with a detailed account of the Island's history as a dependency, first of the English East India Company and then of the British Government. Suffice it to say that the house, set in 100 acres of arable and wooded land, dated from times when the Governor's self-sufficiency was much more important than it had become in the age of the speedier and refrigerated transport links of the twentieth century. Nevertheless, there was an apparently generous number of house staff, managed by Patrick Young in his other rôle – as Comptroller of the Household. He introduced us to the cook and assistant cook, the three parlour maids, laundress, handyman and two gardeners.

Neither of us felt like lunch, but we ate some toast to keep us going for the afternoon. My uniform had been sent on in advance of our arrival at St Helena and Patrick now retrieved the newly pressed tunic and trousers; helmet, to which he had already affixed the plumes of swans feathers; and my sword, and laid them out for me. Sitting in the Jaguar with one's sword was going to be a tight squeeze. No wonder, I thought, the Governors in the Falkland Islands and Gibraltar used London taxis as their flag car. Sandi was dressed in the hat and striking gold silk outfit that she had worn to meet The Queen. Superintendent Henry returned to the house, and we were ready. In the meantime Patrick had explained that the current custom was that the police superintendent, Gerry Henry, was known as the uniformed adc and attended the Governor when the latter wore uniform; when the Governor attended official functions other than in uniform, then he, Patrick, acted as adc. This seemed needlessly complicated and the Chief of Police was really far too senior for such a rôle, so once he retired we obtained a uniform for Patrick and he became my sole adc, as well as driver and the Plantation House Comptroller.

So, it was Gerry Henry who was at my side when we arrived back on the steps of the Supreme Court on Grand Parade at 2 o'clock that afternoon. The many uniformed contingents then on parade were called to attention, salutes all round; and the first of many renditions of the National Anthem that we would receive over the forthcoming years was played by The St Helena Band. In St Helena the Governor's inauguration is conducted outdoors, on the steps of the Supreme Court, where the public may clearly see the proceedings from the Grand Parade. On that September day the Chief Secretary and his wife, the Vicar-General and the Sheriff, Pat Musk, were waiting for us on the steps, as were most if not all of the members of the Island's Legislative Council. A table covered with a large Union flag, on which stood a small lectern and a microphone, was placed between the two large cannons that flanked the entrance to the Court at the top of the steps.

John Perrot and his wife, Wendy, came down the steps to greet us and then stood either side of us once we had moved into position behind the table. The Sheriff was on John's right and Brian Hart, the Vicar-General, on Wendy's left. We were ready!

The Chief Secretary read out The Queen's Commission appointing me as Governor and Commander-in-Chief. Following this he presented the Sheriff, who administered the Oath of Affirmation of Allegiance to Her Majesty Queen Elizabeth the Second, Her Heirs and Successors; and then the Oath of Affirmation for the Execution of the Office of Governor. It was then the turn of the Sheriff to read an Address of Welcome. I had had a message whilst on passage from Cape Town conveying the text of the Address and had prepared a formal reply that I read out (Appendix i).

I took advantage of the opportunity given by a captive audience, which included the Island's legislators, to make the point that economic dependency was not really an option for the future and that their Government's rôle was not to manage business or to control enterprise, but to act as a facilitator, creating an economic environment to enable dynamic growth to flourish; our aim had to be to create the opportunities that the twenty-first century was bound to bring. Did I hear the sound of lead balloons crashing to earth among the legislators gathered further along the steps? Given the way that our later efforts to make St Helena a more viable entity were resisted by members of both the Executive and Legislative Councils, I may well have. But, the St Helena Band bursting into a verse of the National Anthem to indicate the formality of inauguration had been completed would, in any case, have drowned out that metaphorical sound.

I was then invited to inspect the uniformed contingents drawn up before the steps on the Grand Parade: the Police, Firemen, Nurses, Boy Scouts, Girl Guides and Brownies, Church Lads Brigade. The St Helena Band played throughout. It took far longer than it should have done before the Parade Commander, Police Inspector Derek Thomas, escorted me back to the steps where my long-suffering wife and companions had, in the meantime, stood quietly. There should have been a small guard of honour to inspect, but somehow this had been overlooked and I had inspected everyone that day on parade and spoken to many of them! The contingents then marched off towards the Town Gates to re-form and march back past the däis where I took the salute as the contingents and bands marched happily up the High Street.

We had not finished, however. The next part of the programme allowed the Island to meet their new Governor and his Lady in the Council Chamber of the Castle. So saying, accompanied by the Chief Secretary, we repaired to the Castle. Starting with the Vicar-General the senior officials and members of the Government, together with the managing directors of the State owned enterprises, justices of the peace and other notables, including the captain of the *RMS*, and their wives, shook hands and filed past us. A few members of the public followed this parade of the protocol list before overload and exhaustion set in. Even then we had not really finished as, we had been informed, we were to host a reception that evening to meet (once more) officials, legislators and senior Saint Helenians in our own home. It does not take much to imagine just how tired we were by the time that the last guests had left around nine o'clock that evening.

We were able to enjoy a rather more relaxed weekend, broken only by the visit of, Mrs Georgina Benjamin, a member of the Executive Council (c.f. Cabinet in the British political system) wishing to discuss matters in her portfolio before leaving on the *RMS* for a period in the United Kingdom. Nevertheless, I had plenty to think about. I had learnt in London that a Governor was not a Head of Mission in the same way that an Ambassador or High Commissioner was. I was to find out just how different those rôles were in practice. I was now technically on secondment to the Government of St Helena, although I was still subject to Diplomatic Service Regulations and the Foreign & Commonwealth Office paid my salary and allowances.

*   *   *

The St Helena Constitution recognised that the Governor was both The Queen's representative, and represented The Queen: he was neither a civil servant nor senior official - the powers of The Crown were embodied in him. He was also, however, the personal representative of the Sovereign and Head of State in St Helena and its Dependencies. In practice the position was similar to that of the President in the French constitutional structure – Head of State and Head of

Government – but, in St Helena's case, with no choice in selecting the Government he led. Further, his position crossed the division of powers customary in the Westminster-style of government model, i.e. between the executive and administrative arms of government, by being fully responsible for the public service; and overlapped the judicial arm by virtue of being, *ex-officio*, a Justice of the Supreme Court and being responsible for personally selecting and appointing magistrates who sat as Justices of the Peace. The Chief Justice, and any other Judges required, were appointed by Letters Patent upon the recommendation of the Governor. The Governor no longer sat in criminal or civil cases, but I did nonetheless have to perform some routine administrative judicial functions in the absence of the Chief Justice.

St Helena had no political parties: the twelve elected members of the Legislative Council (LegCo) considered themselves to be independent. The Constitution provided for an Executive Council allowing for upto five "Unofficial Members". The Chairmen of the five Council Committees (Health, Public Works etc) were elected by their Legislative Council peers; and those Chairmen became the "Unofficial Members", i.e. elected MLCs, of the Executive Council (ExCo). There were three "Official Members" (*ex-officios*) of ExCo, the Chief Secretary, and Financial Secretary who had votes, and the Attorney General who did not. These latter three officials were recruited and paid by HMG through the ODA.

The Governor held certain reserved powers relating to the public service, finance and shipping. Otherwise, the model of governance for which the St Helena Constitution Order, 1988 provided was one where Executive Council (with its majority of elected politicians) advised the Governor on issues that came before the Council. It was not a matter of the Governor saying this is what we do and that was that. It was, however, the Governor's prerogative to decide what was on the agenda to come before ExCo – the Government Cabinet in all but name. After discussion it was then possible to proceed in any one of three ways: for the Governor to sum up and declare unanimity on an issue ("Council advised and the Governor agreed" as the minutes would show); to put the matter to a show of hands (in which neither he nor the Attorney General had a vote); or to come to the conclusion that there was sufficient conflict of views to defer a decision until civil servants could come forward with more to inform a decision. Thus, with judicious persuasion it was usually possible to achieve the ends we sought.

Although I knew that I could rely upon a sense of unanimity from the three *ex-officios* once a course of action had been agreed, I was to become less certain about the elected members of ExCo. What had not been obvious from reading the files in a far-distant office in London was that, contrary to the belief held by officials in London, the elected representatives of the people of St Helena had but the flimsiest belief in the policies that they purported to support. According to my reading the Government of St Helena had embarked on a policy of "public sector reform", but I had already heard that some members of ExCo had openly dissented with the policy that they had adopted as Government. Collective responsibility on Westminster lines, I was soon to learn, was an alien concept.

Nevertheless, since I had started to think about how I should reply to the Address of Welcome as we sailed towards the Island, I had begun to think in earnest what I wanted to achieve during my appointment. There had been no specific guidance or instruction from Ministers in London; nor direction by the Department about what I might be expected to accomplish: nothing other than the subliminal message that perhaps I should not subject the department responsible to any scrutiny from within the FCO because of what was happening, or not being done, in St Helena. On the other hand, to make the job personally relevant, I needed some sort of long-term goal, an aspiration, for my gubernatorial term in St Helena. My exchanges with the Adam Smith Institute in London had been more than useful, they had been key to understanding what was needed in an island with a pronounced dependency culture and few, if any, viable natural resources. I concluded, therefore, that I would inform the FCO that my aim would be:-

'To work closely with the elected representatives to create the conditions in which St Helena and Its Dependencies can meet both the challenges and opportunities of the twenty-first century – seeking sustainable economic growth and conditions of

economic prosperity in which every Islander has the
opportunity to share – while ensuring that the
principles of good government are fully met.'

I never received a response or any reaction to my proposed aim, or as management-speak would call it, Mission Statement, but the following pages will, I hope, explain in some way whether and how it was met.

*   *   *

What was immediately obvious was that I was no longer a diplomat, but a politician. From a career of offering, hopefully sensible and sound advice to senior officials and politicians, I was now to be the recipient of such advice and ultimately responsible for possibly life-changing decisions affecting a community that had had no choice whatsoever in putting me in that position. I recalled my often vigorous philosophical political discussions with the Trinidadian politician Basdeo Panday: by contrast his opposite number Michael Manning didn't 'do' philosophical and had seemed to live in a 'policy free zone' when Leader of the Opposition himself. I could see that it was going to be important to explain to an unsophisticated Saint Helenian public, used to Government occupying the commanding heights of the economy, what our ultimate aim was and how we expected to achieve it. Despite the constitutional responsibility of the elected representatives to make the political decisions and enact the legislation, I realised that it would be my determination and personal engagement that would have the most influence on the Government's economic programme and its success. A big ask: and a situation with which a British diplomat was rarely faced. I hoped that I was up to the challenge.

To support me in meeting this challenge I fortunately had a first rate team of officials, senior among whom was the Chief Secretary. The Office of the Chief Secretary was headed by the St Helena Government Deputy Secretary, Ethel Yon, who ran this secretariat, the function of which was to directly support the office of Governor and co-ordinate Government policy across the board. Ethel Yon was the most senior Saint Helenian civil servant and an experienced and skilled bureaucrat occupying a position somewhat, but not quite,

43

similar to the Cabinet Secretary in the British Government machine. She attended, but did not take part in the meetings of the Executive Council. Then there was our local 'Chancellor of the Exchequer', the Financial Secretary, Bob Perrott (no relation to John); and the Attorney General David Jeremiah. In addition to these officials I could call upon the Government Economist Mark George and the Head of the Audit Department who was an accountant formerly with Price Waterhouse who had both economics and management skills – Ken Jones. These five individuals, who had been recruited by and were paid by the Overseas Development Administration, together with Ethel Yon came to form an informal advisory group that would be joined by other heads of department, public works, planning etc when wider discussion required.

As important as all these bodies were in the formulation and implementation of our policies the most important in running the Governor's official life was without doubt the Personal Assistant to the Governor, Joan Yon. In her forties, single, living with her mother in Barrack Square in Lower Jamestown, and leader of the Jamestown Brownies, Joan was an extremely conscientious and very protective secretary and, of course, knew virtually everybody on the Island. And it was to Joan that I looked in formulating a programme of first calls to get to know my public service, and the businesses and individuals in St Helena who made the Island tick.

As a British colony St Helena had developed a system based on the Westminster model of government, except that at this stage in its political maturity it had a unicameral legislature – the Legislative Council (LegCo) – and that in addition to those members elected by universal suffrage there were three aforementioned unelected members who sat *ex-officio* their appointments. Those three officials sat also in the Executive Council (ExCo) together with five elected MLCs as the nearest equivalent to Cabinet and a ministerial Government. LegCo met when it was necessary, but at least once a year, when any legislation agreed by ExCo would be debated and (hopefully) passed into law as an Ordinance (c.f. Act of Parliament). ExCo customarily met fortnightly on a Tuesday.

Around that open pattern I built a further regular pattern of meetings with the Chief Secretary each morning at 9 a.m.;

with the Chief of Police (who was responsible directly to me as the Police Force was not subject to political or bureaucratic oversight); and with the Financial Secretary on a regular weekly basis. The balance of my Governmental and official programmes were arranged to ensure that these important elements were retained.

CHAPTER THREE

First Impressions of St Helena

It was the invariable custom in Her Majesty's Diplomatic Service of the 20th Century that all Heads of Mission (Ambassadors and High Commissioners, together with Governors and the Permanent Representatives to the International Organisations) should write a brief but formal Despatch to the Secretary of State at the Foreign & Commonwealth Office shortly after arrival *en poste* conveying what were known as 'First Impressions'.

I was to be no exception and so wrote my first Despatch from The Castle at Jamestown on 6th October 1995 drawing the attention of those in London to the blindingly obvious fact that St Helena and Its Dependencies were small and remote and that the link to the outside world provided by the *Royal Mail Ship St Helena* was of paramount importance. We British, I noted, are ourselves an island race and although I had served on islands across the world none were such a speck in the vastness of the South Atlantic Ocean as St Helena, which as the eighteenth century geographer Herman Moll had described it - as being *"Further from the Continent than any other island in the known World."* Its linked Dependencies of Ascension Island and the Tristan da Cunha Group were spread over more than 2,000 miles of the South Atlantic Ocean. St Helena was so remote that Ascension Island, with the only airfield, was about 700 miles away and Cape Town some 1,700 nautical miles and five days away by ship. The only method of arrival was by sea.

History, I emphasised, had played a very important part in the way that the Colony was governed and in forming the attitude of its people to both their governance and the collective will to break out of the historic mould.

With a confidence, that events would later show to be misplaced, I maintained that attitudes were slowly being transformed and a will to experiment with change was growing. Nevertheless, I qualified my optimism by pointing out that not all the conditions were yet right: the education system required serious attention; the concerns of elected

Councillors about the Constitution had to be met; and among other non-economic imperatives, the legal system needed strengthening by the appointment of a Public Solicitor.

However, I went on, within its constraints the system of governance worked, but the twentieth century had largely passed St Helena by and it was thus unreasonable to expect major economic structural adjustment to be achieved in a short space of time (and certainly not before 2000). Basically, I explained, St Helena lacked a means with which to earn a livelihood. Nevertheless, I affirmed, the problem was being addressed even though the path towards a solution was steep and difficult. But in the meantime, HMG's financial support would continue to be essential. My aim, I wrote, was to prepare the ground for St Helena to take what advantage it could from the opportunities that the twenty-first century would offer. I also outlined the four major issues that needed a solution.

Whether my first impressions were accurate, or even near the truth, I leave for the reader to decide.

*   *   *

In more detail I wrote that during the days of sail there were many hundreds of ships calling at St Helena annually to take on water and other fresh supplies, while throughout the inter-war years the Union Castle mail service to the Cape continued a vital link to the outside world. Now calls were down to a mere handful. The last Union Castle liner called at St Helena in 1977, prompting the first of many re-thinks on access to this remote island and, giving birth to the concept of a vessel dedicated to serving St Helena. The second ship in the twentieth century to bear the island's name, the *Royal Mail Ship St Helena* was launched in 1990 and plied between Cardiff and the islands of Ascension and St Helena, and on to Cape Town; with an annual trip to Tristan da Cunha in the Southern Summer.

The *RMS* as the Saints affectionately knew her, played an important part in the lives of the islands and islanders of these Dependencies; and the vessel's scheduling was a matter of universal interest. The *RMS* was, therefore, a crucial element in the Island's economic and social fabric and, until such time as St Helena was financially self-sufficient was one which remained a priority in terms of funding and sympathetic management.

A strong sense of history surrounds the new Governor of the Colony. My offices were situated in the Castle, over the ramparts of which I viewed the quayside and anchorage of James Bay. Four Georgian cannons point their warning muzzles out to sea. I entered through an archway, over which the East India Company Coat of Arms is still emblazoned in full colour, while only a few feet away is Capt Dutton's original inscription recording the building of this fort in 1659. The inner courtyard offers the protection of a further artillery piece. Here, and at Plantation House, the country house built for the Governor in 1791-92, are kept voluminous colonial and East India Company records, together with many fine prints and etchings; portraits of Queen Victoria and Prince Albert, and our Royal Family throughout subsequent Reigns; and historical maps (one even signed by Napoleon, arguably the island's most famous resident).

These images and the fragments of the East India Company archives help to put into perspective some of those aspects of government, which at first sight seem strangely out of place. The company and its Court of Directors in London closely regulated and controlled all activity in their settlement, reaching far into the lives of each of its inhabitants, interfering in areas of social and economic activity that even Her Majesty's Government of Victorian England eschewed. This history of tight control from London helped to explain the widespread belief in St Helena that it was part of the natural scheme of things for major activities and services to be undertaken by the Government.

This belief, it seemed, was not only held by Councilors (who felt that in such capacity they had the additional right to be directly involved - some would say meddle - in the day to day matters of running the machinery of Government and staffing Departments), but also by a not insignificant proportion of the general public, who might have been heard to say that Saints are in any case unable to engage successfully in entrepreneurial activities. It is a fact that within this very small economy it had certainly been recent experience that the Government had been the sole major investor and hence the only employer of any real significance. Even the one extant trading company, Solomons, was then 84% Government owned; and there was no Company Law on the Statute Book to regulate the formation of indigenous joint stock enterprises. There was no commercial Bank.

I made the point that of Britain's remaining Dependencies St Helena alone was reliant upon a Grant-in-Aid from Her Majesty's Government in the United Kingdom to balance expenditure and those revenues the Government of St Helena was able to generate. This, I feared had led to a general feeling of expectation (especially among the island's politicians) that the British Government would fund all growth, meet all unexpected losses and ensure that the standard of living was maintained. Many, indeed I ventured to say most, recent written sources on St Helena opine that the island and its people had been forgotten and shabbily treated by the British Government. This is perhaps because that is what many Saints had told those writers, without necessarily thinking it through. It was certainly not the case, as I was well aware. In 1995 both Wings of the Department (the FCO proper and the Overseas Development Administration) spent considerably more time, effort and Aid resources per St Helenian capita than on virtually any other country in the whole world. St Helena nevertheless remained a Dependency, and was likely to do so far into the foreseeable future.

I said that my conclusion that the inherited belief that Britain will (or ought to) provide might be directly attributable to the overburdening weight of history and the influence of the East India Company. That, I subsequently learnt, was far from an original or unique impression. As Governor Gallwey, writing in 1908 as a preface to a locally published edition of the Honourable East India Company's "St Helena Records", had observed:-

"The apathetic nature of the Islanders is the growth of generations and is entirely due to their bringing up. You cannot reasonably hope to change the nature of a community at one fell swoop. It must take time. Again, that sine qua non *to progress, namely capital, is almost entirely conspicuous by its absence in St Helena. Handicapped as they are,*

The East India Company, I went on to explain, exercised its influence for more than 175 years from 1659 until the Crown took over the Administration. It is not fanciful to suggest that little actually changed even then. Almost 90 years had passed since Governor Gallwey's critical comments, and yet only in 1995 were there perhaps the first signs of evolutionary change becoming evident. The struggle to close the gap between an eighteenth century sense of complete dependence and the Business School model of a modern State had, I confidently predicted, begun. With a series of contributions from London the Government of St Helena was embarked on a policy of public sector reform. The policy was not yet owned in its entirety by all the politicians, but I detected an encouraging degree of support for the process by those who were likely to be the most affected - the public service. Progress had been achieved in producing departmental business plans for the next financial year that showed both an understanding of the concept and a determination to put it into practice. I reported that there was a most satisfactory degree of public acceptance that new methods and disciplines were needed. But, in a society where the Government control of so many elements of life had been perfectly acceptable, where unemployment was already a potential social problem, and the economy remained so very small we had to take each step with infinite care.

Turning to education I noted that some more effort would be required in producing properly trained young people. The Government had adopted the British national curriculum, but I had learnt that weaknesses had been detected in the education system's delivery at secondary level. Much of the dismally poor record lay at the door of a delivery system in which there were just far too many poorly qualified teachers. But there was another factor peculiar to St Helena that played its part: children lacked motivation because there was very little incentive for outstanding performance. Job prospects for young people were poor. Few students stayed on to take 'A' levels despite a financial inducement, because for the most part those additional academic qualifications provided little advantage in the local job market. For that reason anxieties over British nationality, and future access to the United Kingdom assumed a significant importance in the mind of every citizen. It had become quite clear that some outlet for talent, academic advancement and simple career/employment prospects had become a matter of priority.

I thought that the Island's Councillors believed this as much as I did. However, I noted that they also believed that the Colony's current constitutional arrangements needed to be changed, and not necessarily to facilitate the transition to a market economy of the twenty-first century. Nothing, of course, is ever perfect. But there seemed to be a degree of confusion amongst them over quite what the Constitution provided and how it should best work. The fact that it did not specifically make allowance for several of the hobby-horses mounted by individual Councillors, or for other views voiced during an earlier consultation exercise but not (for whatever reason) given provision, is offered as proof that the 1988 Constitution Order is flawed. By omitting *"the reasonable suggestions"* of Saints, they argue, it cannot therefore be satisfactory and work to St Helena's benefit! A Councillor will argue in the same breath a need to move to a ministerial system of government and then that all the elected representatives should be involved in making all the decisions, effectively removing any distinction between Executive and Legislative Councils. Even those Councillors who were part of the Government, through sitting as elected members in the Executive Council, frequently acted as though they formed the Opposition, treating the *ex-officio* members as though they alone were the Government, to thwart at every turn. Such confused thinking is not easily despatched, I opined, but hoped that with help from the Commonwealth Parliamentary Association that we might make some progress.

Perhaps of more direct concern, although remarkably not an issue for any of our Councillors at that point in time, was the fact that in effect St Helena was a one-man legal jurisdiction. There was no access for the public to legal advice or a lawyer independent of Government. A real conflict of interest existed. For example, where the Attorney General attempted to provide legal services to both Government and the public. At first sight this state of affairs appeared to be most unsafe in principle. Fortunately, and surprisingly so far as I could ascertain, no serious harm had yet been occasioned. But it was as unacceptable to believe that unqualified staff in the Legal & Lands Department and Lay Advocates provided a proper alternative to professionals, as it would be to accept untrained personnel giving medical advice and treatment to patients at the hospital. There was, it seemed therefore, to be both room and need for a further legal entity in the form of a Public Solicitor. Addressing this lacuna in the legal infrastructure was another priority that I added to those I had already enumerated.

In a small country it is inevitable that a few individuals will occupy a number of key roles in Government, business and society, and so it was in St Helena. The twelve elected Councillors of the Legislative Council made up between them the membership of the five major Committees established to oversee Government business, and sit also on the other public boards and committees. The three Lay Advocates in the legal system were, respectively, the Speaker of the Legislative Council and two Councillors, both also members of ExCo. The strands of familial relationship twist and turn through every walk of life and all of its friendships and feuds. The system worked, but it still needed us to help it do so.

Over the years St Helena's isolation has played a crucial part in forging its identity. The capital, Jamestown, with its many fine Georgian buildings and the Governor's residence, Plantation House, symbolised the unspoilt nature of this island. Uninhabited until the first European settlers, Britons in the service of the East India Company formed the nucleus of a population which was later expanded by the arrival of soldiers, slaves and indentured workers from the furthest ends of John Company's trading routes in the East. St Helena's geographical position had nonetheless preserved a Britishness of the people of this island. Their family values were strong and sense of community important. They had created a society in which there was no evident racism, no drugs and with serious crime virtually unknown. AIDS was non-existent. If St Helena and its people displayed many of the values of the nineteen fifties now nostalgically evoked by those in Britain critical of society in the nineties, it was hard to understand how British officials could be so impatient at the way in which the St Helena Government was struggling to adapt to the pragmatic financial imperatives of the current era. And, all the more difficult to comprehend against a background where Ministers in Britain had recently cast doubt upon the ability of the historic county of Rutland, with 33,000 souls, to govern itself (as it formed too small a unit to make satisfactory arrangements for the delivery of local services), that officials, in a remoter context, should recommend that this small country of less than six thousand inhabitants might make significant divestments of its public sector in a much shorter time scale than that which it took Her Majesty's Government in the United Kingdom to achieve a less dramatic structural adjustment. St Helena had a significantly larger proportion of the working population employed in the public sector. In 1994 just over 70% of those in work in St Helena were directly or indirectly employed by Government. There had, nonetheless, been a general decline in public sector employment over the more recent years and only buoyant employment prospects elsewhere had mitigated its effect locally. Between 1990/1991 and September 1995 the number of Saints employed abroad had increased by over a quarter. But, any suggestion that depopulation (mooted in 1993); or that the responsibility for creating employment opportunities should be transferred to Australia, South Africa or the Gulf States (as the British Aid Mission report of 1994 mooted) were assuredly too simplistic.

St Helena's principal resource is its people. There are no deposits of exploitable minerals, no oil, and the harsh terrain and poor soils of the lower lying areas are a severe constraint on the development of agriculture. Indeed, some 75 % of the land area is classified as barren with only about 15% of the land under any cultivation. The seas around the island have no abundant stocks of fish, although there is a small domestic fishing industry; and foreign licensed fishing had fortuitously added up to £1m to Government revenues in some good years.

In each of the recent years, I wrote, St Helena had experienced negative growth of about 1% per annum. The domestic economic base was, therefore, very limited and likely to remain so for the foreseeable future. Less than half of GDP was generated locally, the balance being financed by the British Grant-in-Aid and remittances from workers overseas. The objective, shared by the Governments of the United Kingdom and of St Helena, to achieve financial independence, was - while utterly laudable - one so far away from achievement as to question whether it was appropriate to gear the British aid strategy towards its attainment in the twentieth century or indeed very early in the twenty-first.

As I began summing up, I made the point that the basic difficulty was that St Helena really lacked a credible means with which to earn a livelihood. We therefore faced a series of apparently intractable problems: the need to develop an enterprise culture; to encourage moves from the public to the private sector without pushing unemployment to unacceptable levels; and improving the economy of an island that had few local resources. On the plus side, the establishment of the St Helena Development Agency had been a small step on a steep uphill path along which it was difficult yet to chart a definable way - and impossible to see how we might achieve the ultimate goal. It was encouraging that in December 1987 Ministers had confirmed that the reasonable needs of the Dependent Territories would continue to be a first charge on Aid Funds. Without this promise of support for St Helena, the outlook would have been terminally gloomy. As it was, the prospects for financial self-sufficiency were far from auspicious. Nonetheless, I had been much encouraged by ministerial expressions of support and the response of officials in London, and in Jamestown, to the idea of a more transparent financial relationship between our two Governments.

Finally and in the absence of any guidance from London, I reported that I saw my mission as Governor of St Helena as one to prepare the ground for the Government and people of St Helena to take advantage of the opportunities that would be offered by the twenty-first century: to enable that small country to take a proactive rôle rather than continually have to react to the political and economic expediencies of external forces. My time I believed would be taken up with four major issues, namely public sector reform; the need to further stimulate the creation of a private sector in the economy and to reduce the financial dependence of St Helena upon Her Majesty's Government in the United Kingdom; the problem of access; and the interlocking fourth pillar, the question of national status.

CHAPTER FOUR

The First year: an Introduction to the Life of a Colonial Governor

It had become quite obvious to me when speaking to the head of the department in the Overseas Development Administration (the ODA, the Aid Wing of the FCO) that oversaw the aid relationship with St Helena that he and his officials were exasperated with St Helena's politicians, the Chief Secretary and to a lesser extent the departing Governor. The source of this exasperation lay in what was seen in St Helena as an inadequate and unrealistic offer of budgetary aid (the grant-in-aid of the expenses of government) that had been made by the ODA's visiting Budgetary Aid Mission in December 1994 and the ODA's immovable view that it met the Island's reasonable needs. In the ODA's analysis my Diplomatic Service colleague John Perrott, who had argued the St Helena Government's case, was the arch villain. A view that was to cloud ODA officials' judgement later and to deprive me of a Diplomatic Service deputy – but that is getting ahead of myself.

There had, thus, been a difficult few months as 1994 had advanced into 1995. The ODA, whose team it is thought very likely had the sum to be made available determined even before they left London for their 'discussions', was immovable. From the St Helena Government perspective the somewhat acrimonious exchanges between Jamestown and London, while solving nothing in the longer term, delayed the preparation of the Budget in St Helena. The argument continued until June when a Grant-in-Aid figure was imposed from London, which only increased the quite valid local perception that those in London failed to understand the context of St Helena. It was far from certain that the Appropriation Bill containing the re-worked and reduced budgetary estimates would secure a majority vote in Legislative Council – but in the end the measure was passed, although a lot of bad feeling had been generated in the process.

The ODA departmental head had paid what from ODA accounts was a successful visit to St Helena in July (1995) when he had attended an informal meeting of the Legislative Council and explained the concept of a fixed envelope of funding for all elements of St Helena's aid expenditure in which reducing expenditure in one element such as grant-in-aid could be diverted to another element such as development aid. However, when I later spoke to officials in Jamestown I learnt that the ODA had been unable (or unwilling) to share with Councillors the sum that the Aid Wing had in mind, leading MLCs to the conclusion that the concept of virement between the elements of the aid package was a confidence trick. They had petitioned the Minister for Overseas Development "*to take account of and make proper provision for the reasonable needs of St Helena when imposing the figure for Grant-in-Aid for 1995/96*". Baroness Chalker had replied (in a letter written for her by officials, of course) that it was for the St Helena Government to manage the elements of the aid package locally, but the not unreasonable response of MLCs was that when they made such determinations that were unpalatable to their ODA interlocutors their decisions were ignored.

I hoped that my assumption of office might have drawn a line under all this in Jamestown as well as in London. In any case I hoped that the occasion presented by the public response to the Sheriff's official Address of Welcome was an ideal opportunity to draw that line under the disagreements and to remind politicians and their public that the immense changes in the world since 1990 had a lesson for St Helena too. The speech, carried live on the local radio and later published verbatim in the *St Helena News* opened the public debate that was to be the coda to the four years that followed. The full text is included in Appendix ii. Briefly, however, I sought to make the point that the world had seen many changes in the years since St Helena had first been settled and that there was global recognition that the State could no longer effectively own and control the commanding heights of the economy; and thus that our aim together must be to create the conditions in which St Helena could meet the challenges and opportunities that the twenty-first century was sure to present.

What had not been obvious from reading the files in a far distant department in the Foreign Office was that the elected representatives of the people of St Helena had but the flimsiest belief in the policies that they purported to support. The legacy of tight control from London, that was such a feature of the East India Company's governance of the island, perhaps explained the inherited belief that was widespread on the island in 1995 that it was part of the natural scheme of things for major activities and services to be undertaken by the Government. In any case, a number of the elected members of Executive Council quite openly dissented with the policy of public sector reform that was beginning to take shape, despite being members of the Government whose policy it was! Collective responsibility, I was soon to learn, was an alien concept.

At that time, St Helena alone of the remaining Dependent Territories was reliant upon a grant-in-aid of the expenses of administration of the Colony from the British Government to balance expenditure and those revenues that the Government of St Helena was able to generate. This it seems had led to the general feeling of expectation, especially among the island's politicians, that the British Government would fund all growth, meet all unexpected losses and ensure that the islanders' standard of living was maintained. Nevertheless, and unacknowledged by Members of the Legislative Council (MLCs) for what it was, it was an underlying truth in the relationship between London and Jamestown that both Wings of the FCO together had spent more effort and Aid resources per capita on St Helena than virtually anywhere else in the world. St Helena was a dependency – and likely to remain so into the foreseeable future. These facts did not inhibit MLCs in expressing their belief that the Governor held too much power and that the Constitution must change to provide that the islanders should have the means to get on with running things themselves (without interference from a Governor or the Powers-that-be in London).

All these were to make the next four years the most interesting of times! The economy was in recession and had been shrinking for the previous three or four years. In the best of circumstances the domestic economic base was very limited. The outlook was of a series of apparently intractable problems - the need to develop an enterprise culture; to encourage moves from the public to the private sector without pushing up unemployment to unacceptable levels; and improving the economy of an island that had few natural or local resources.

The establishment of the St Helena Development Agency, in November 1995, marked a start on the steep uphill path towards an, as yet, invisible goal. It was the Governor's rôle to prepare the ground for St Helena to take a proactive stance, rather than continually have to react to the political and economic expediencies of external forces. The next four years would be taken up with the four major issues that I had identified in my first impressions Despatch. Along the way there were to be both success and failure, but to sum it up in a word: it was *challenging.*

Sir Peter Ramsbotham wrote in his valedictory as Governor of Bermuda that, despite having occupied important diplomatic posts (High Commissioner in Cyprus, Ambassador to the Shah's Iran in the early 1970s, and Ambassador to the United States of America), the most difficult job of his career had come at its conclusion in one of the remaining Dependent Territories. The job in St Helena is one of the most hands-on of Governors' appointments, given both the political immaturity of the elected representatives and the fact that at the end of the twentieth century the Territory still received a relatively large proportion of its budgetary requirements through a grant-in-aid of administration, for which the Governor was accountable through the Secretary of State to Parliament in London.

It had been the disagreement over the size of the grant-in-aid that had soured relations between Jamestown and London before our arrival, and it was still simmering in September 1995. A decision had been reached in London that a line should be drawn under the issue and that the St Helena Government should prepare for a Budgetary Aid Mission from the ODA in mid November 1995 to seek mutually agreed solutions to the perennial problem of financial support from HMG.

Despite the better inclinations of a number of the members, the Legislative Council had been very closely involved with drafting a 'Vision for St Helena' setting out objectives for Government, the text of which was announced on 9th November. Many MLCs were sceptical, but realising that the Overseas Development team were due on the island within days, they saw the presentational advantage that embracing it might have when the amount of aid was being discussed!

*   *   *

Before the ODA's Budgetary Aid Mission arrived I had the opportunity to visit another of my gubernatorial responsibilities, Ascension Island. The *RMS* conducted what in the terms of the Schedule was a shuttle between St Helena and Ascension after arriving at Jamestown from Cape Town and discharging passengers and cargo. The routine was to leave St Helena on the morning of Day One; arrive on the morning of Day Three; disembark those passengers for Ascension and those in transit bound for the Falkland Islands or Brize Norton via the RAF 'Airbridge'; and return to St Helena with passengers travelling in the opposite direction from late in Day Three arriving back on Day Five. Depending on its departure time from St Helena the *RMS* might sometimes have to anchor overnight at Ascension.

The *RMS* had arrived at Jamestown under the command of Capt David Roberts, Martin Smith's opposite number. Whereas Martin was jovial and somewhat piratical in appearance with a neat beard and having one good eye to which he held a monocular; David Roberts who had briefly been in the Royal Navy was a rather more austere officer who wanted everything 'tickety-boo' and for whom the ship's company had to have everything running 'just so'. We got to know them both pretty well, travelling many miles at sea with them over the four years that we lived in the South Atlantic.

On this occasion we were to be at Ascension for the inside of a day, arriving at 7 a.m. and departing again at 4 p.m.. Roger Huxley, whom I had met in London before his posting as Administrator at Ascension Island, came aboard with his wife Niddy to meet us. Sandi and I had separate programmes to acquaint ourselves as much as was possible in such a short time with the island and its occupants.

A brief history of Ascension appears as an Appendix iii. It is a dry and essentially barren volcanic outcrop with no indigenous population other than breeding seabirds and turtles. Discovered by João da Nova in 1501 it was garrisoned by the Royal Navy in 1816 to prevent it falling into the hands of the French sympathetic to Napoleon. The beginnings of its late twentieth century existence began in 1899 when the Eastern Telegraph Company established a regeneration station for its undersea cable from South Africa to Britain. The station manager was appointed resident magistrate, and responsible to the Governor of St Helena for the island's administration. The company's successor – Cable & Wireless - was still there, but the responsibility for the island's administration passed in 1964 to an Administrator appointed by the Colonial Office. At that time facilities for the Composite Signals Organisation and a relay station for the BBC Overseas Service were built on Ascension and a Users Organisation was established, including Cable & Wireless, to finance the running costs of the island. I had attended a meeting of the 'Users' at the BBC's Bush House in May; and now I met their representatives on the island.

The other 'Users', not part of this arrangement, were the military – the Americans, USAAF and contractors, and the RAF – at Wideawake Airfield; and the small Ariane rocket monitoring station operated by the European Space Agency.

The population of Ascension was all expatriate and overwhelmingly from St Helena, whose islanders made up almost three quarters of the total. Together with the employment opportunities offered by the military in the Falkland Islands since 1982, Ascension had long provided employment for Saints, and their earnings there been the means for many to buy their houses on St Helena. The Saints there were subtly different to their compatriots at home – more outward looking, mobile and entrepreneurial.

Our visit highlighted a lunch at the Administrator's Residency, a former Royal Navy sanatorium near the summit of Green Mountain, overlooking Georgetown and the anchorage. Our time on Ascension was very brief, but enough to gain a superficial impression of the island and an idea of how Roger was coping with the unusual circumstances of life on what was more akin to a somewhat authoritarian employment park than a mature democratic community. All were there as volunteers however, and this fact must account for the impression that everyone was enjoying life on what was oft termed by the residents as "Hell with the fire put out" or "Slag-heap on Sea".

*   *   *

Meanwhile back on St Helena preparations for the Budgetary Aid Mission (BAM) had progressed and we were ready for the four-man team when they paid their visit to the Island from 13th – 21st November. At the outset colleagues at the Castle and I felt quite confident that the St Helena Government case had been well drawn. Nevertheless, given the innate scepticism of the Islanders in general and the politicians in particular, we emphasised to our own officials how important it was to present a robust case.

While there were several areas of difference in perception of the impact of progress over the following financial year, at the end of the day what MLCs could accept as a satisfactory formula for bridging the gap in budgetary requirements in 1996/97 emerged in the final round of negotiation. Certainly the St Helenian side of the deal must have seemed sealed to our visitors by the adoption of the official 'Vision for St Helena' which had earlier emerged from ExCo and been articulated for MLCs by officials in the terms of *"A prosperous, peaceful and democratic society for all, achieved through sustainable development leading to a healthy and eventually financially independent Island."* I had a very experienced team of experts who could come up with such persuasive language, but could we achieve success? ExCo had been persuaded of the efficacy of setting a policy for public sector reform in terms of the financial rewards it might attract from the ODA. Legislative Council had subsequently been persuaded to endorse the policy of public sector reform, and the 'Vision', and thus the politicians were, at least on paper, seen to be solidly behind a reform agenda.

A full meeting of Legislative Council grudgingly accepted the recommendations of the Budgetary Aid Mission. Their confidence was soon to be shaken, however, as at the end of November the Bank of Nova Scotia withdrew its application for a commercial banking licence, citing bureaucratic obstacles (i.e. the failure of the Foreign & Commonwealth Office to allow the Banking Ordinance - the terms of which officials there had earlier agreed upon when the legislation was in draft; and which had been the subject of further detailed discussion between officials, the Bank and me before my departure from London – and the FCO's failure to come up with acceptable terms for a Licence). The fact that two years had passed since the application was first made had also meant that other and better commercial opportunities had arisen for the bank elsewhere.

'Public sector reform' would be the main item of Government business during the forthcoming year. Fortunately, as an administration, we were supported by another of the ODA's fundings - for a Change Adviser – who would be committed to visiting and advising St Helena over the next twelve months. But a lot hung in the balance, especially given the tendency for elected members of ExCo to agree to something under the cloak of anonymity provided by the proceedings of the Executive Council and to speak out against the same proposal in public to their constituents, i.e. *"Don't blame me, it was the others"* or, more likely, *"...the Governor."*

Even before the ODA's BAM team had packed their bags to leave, Remembrance Day was upon us. On Saturday, which happened to be 11th November the, what I was to learn was, traditional 'Night to Remember' was staged at the secondary school in Jamestown. Well supported, it mirrored in its small way the by then well established Royal British Legion evening at the Royal Albert Hall in London, complete with its net of blooms, in this case bougainvillea rather than poppies, to be released over the audience as a finale. It was all rather well done. Remembrance Sunday was a uniform engagement at the Jamestown Cenotaph on the sea front. The Bishop of St Helena conducted the Service; the St Helena band was in attendance as was the marching band of the Scouts together with all the other uniformed organisations on St Helena supplemented by a good turn out by members of the public. Saints had given their lives in both World Wars and so the ceremony had its relevance to the islanders and their lives.

*   *   *

The year ended, however, with Sandi flat on her back with a troublesome sciatic nerve that gave her severe back pains. She listened to the noises of the traditional Plantation

Christmas Fête held on the paddock in front of the house where that year a visitor on the *RMS* entertained the crowd to a display of fire eating. The occasion was one for 'all the fun of the fair' and for the craft group that met at Plantation House to sell their wares for charities. Fortunately Sandi had recovered sufficiently to take part in the round of parties marking the Christmas festival, including that at Plantation House around a fine Christmas tree that Patrick had arranged to be delivered by the Agriculture & Forestry Department at nearby Scotland, and which the staff decorated.

Being public figures, indeed the most high profile and august, on the Island meant that we were 'on duty' virtually 24/7. We did try to keep Sundays as days on which we did not, as a rule, take on any public engagements. Remembrance Sunday was, of course, an exception and although we usually were able to keep Christmas Day private too we were required to do a round of the 'Homes': Sundale, in Half Tree Hollow, which catered for the mentally handicapped; the Jamestown Hospital; The Haven, the old people's home, also in Jamestown; and Barnview, the children's home. For each the Plantation House cook would bake a large Christmas fruit cake, which we would then deliver on Christmas Eve and visit the patients/in-mates. Looking back it seems like a rather patrician and somewhat condescending act but no doubt the origins lay far back in time and by the late 1990s it had become something of a tradition. Also something of a tradition, and reflecting the difficulty that the Islanders had in being able to get away for a break, was the public service 'block-leave', a compulsory week off work, encompassing Christmas and New Year. In 1995 the St Helena Government shut down on Friday 22nd December until 2nd January – a period of 10 days.

We had long arranged to spend Christmas dinner at Plantation House with the young Apostolics that we had met on the *RMS*, with whom we had forged an early friendship, but we also had the first of the tiny handful of visitors from the outside world and our past. A Diplomatic Service colleague, Simon Butt, who was able to take leave at just the right time, came to St Helena for a week that fuelled a passionate interest in Napoleon and Napoleonia that survives to this day. As a resourceful young diplomat he travelled with a dinner jacket and black tie, so with the ladies in their finery the Plantation House staff served us with a traditional Christmas dinner after which we had a relaxed evening around the log fire while Nerine entertained us on the piano.

The piano had been a stroke of genius by Sandi. As part of the standard briefing programme for a Head of Mission my HOMS minder had included a visit to the FCO department dealing with accommodation. Ambassadors and High Commissioners were often notorious for re-equipping and redecorating official Residences to complement their notions of their importance. I had struggled against this, what I had seen as unnecessary expenditure, previously, but here I had been invited to uplift the inventory at my Residence to be, it seemed, as my right! At the time I tried to point out that 'Government House' in St Helena actually belonged to the Government of St Helena. I assumed this would exclude it from any FCO schemes, but that the files showed that no funds had been spent on the Governor's residence seemed to mean that I had an almost free hand to spend – with no sum being suggested as a limit. As it happened the expenditure that the FCO agreed to was eventually spread over several years and we saw little of the outcomes to the schemes for redecoration and refurbishment of furniture and fittings that Sandi chose. The re-tiling of the roof in Welsh slate was completed only in time for the Millennium, but the music centre and piano that we requested were supplied very soon after our arrival.

Another hitherto unexpected influence that Heads of Mission were able to bring to bear within the FCO's administration lay in the field of communications. Again, a morning with the appropriate departmental head within the communications division at Hanslope Park, the former Diplomatic Wireless Service (DWS) transmitting and receiving station had been included in my briefing programme. I learnt that St Helena had simple telex and was unable to receive classified telegraphic communications. Having started my diplomatic career in Colonial Office communications I had taken an interest in the work of and equipment used by DWS personnel in the Posts in which I had served; and from Aden onwards I had in any case been the line manager at Post responsible for them. The dissolution of the DWS as newer satellite equipment became available, which was operated by non-technical FCO members of staff had had a significant impact on staffing overseas. This new generation equipment, with its roof-top satellite dish, had been installed at the new High Commission building at Port of Spain and had been operated by my PA. Once again it came as a bit of a shock to find that I only needed to say what I wanted and it was done. The new communications equipment came with an installation and training team of two the next time the *RMS* called after our arrival. It meant that St Helena suddenly received far more telegraphic traffic than ever before – but I was in the FCO loop as none of my predecessors ever could have been.

*　　　　　*　　　　　*

As the New Year approached I turned my thoughts to the customary Head of Mission review of the year past. Aid was the major topic of 1995 both for my predecessor and for me. What I thought ought to prove a satisfactory formula for bridging the 'aid gap' had emerged in the final round of negotiation with the Overseas Development Administration's Budgetary Aid Mission in November. In his own Despatch reviewing 1994 my predecessor had written that modern banking legislation had been passed in consultation with the Bank of Nova Scotia and that he looked forward to commercial banking being established on St Helena. However, I had to record, the process had become entangled with bureaucratic obstacles raised in London between the passage of the legislation and licensing and the Bank had of necessity to withdraw its application. St Helena no longer had the prospect of a commercial bank enabling locals access to business banking and loans for entrepreneurial activities. A bank remained central to St Helena's development potential, but I noted that the establishment of the Development Agency, with limited loan facilities, had been a step in the right direction prior to a fully-fledged bank being attracted to set up shop on the island.

As a major milestone for 1995, I pointed up the adoption by our politicians of the 'Vision for St Helena' and the Government having set its policy of Public Sector Reform. It would definitely form a major element of Government activity in 1996, but I didn't say that I knew not how successful it would be given the half-hearted support of the politicians. The trustees of the Commonwealth Parliamentary Association had approved financial support in the year to come for a review of constitutional and parliamentary matters, which I hoped would enable Legislative Councillors better to understand their rôle and that of the Governor while examining the relative rôles of the Councillors and Committees and the St Helena Constitution Order, 1988. I had hopes that this would jolly the Councillors along and better inform them at the same time so that we might get down to some serious work in attempting to attain the 'Vision'.

CHAPTER FIVE

The Idea of an International Yacht Race is born; and our first Visit to Tristan da Cunha

The Governor of St Helena is not only Governor of Ascension Island, but has also been Governor of Tristan da Cunha since 1938 when it was declared a Dependency of St Helena. The island lies about 1,500 miles south of St Helena and 1,750 miles almost due west of Cape Town. Like St Helena and Ascension, Tristan da Cunha was discovered during the great age of Portuguese discovery - by Tristão da Cunha - in 1506. Appendix iv briefly outlines the island's history. As in the case of Ascension, Tristan was settled in 1816 by a British garrison to deter French intervention in Napoleon's imprisonment at St Helena. In the 1960s it was perhaps more widely known than either St Helena or Ascension as the whole population was evacuated following a volcanic eruption in 1961 and temporarily settled at Calshot in Hampshire. The evacuee's desire to return and their resettlement of the island two years later gives an indication of the islander's strength of character and community.

There is no direct commercial link between St Helena and Tristan da Cunha, and for the most part the island has to rely on the two South African fishing vessels, under a fisheries contract in Tristanian waters, to convey passengers and goods between the settlement of Edinburgh-of-the-Seven Seas and Cape Town. A further annual visit was made by the South African polar research vessel the *SA Aghulas*, which brought freight and the occasional passenger during its voyage to the South African Weather Station on Gough Island 200 miles to the south. To cater for a cruise market and generate extra much needed income the *RMS*, introduced into service in 1990, included an annual voyage from Cape Town to Tristan da Cunha. This provided the way for the Governor to visit this southern outpost of the British Colony of St Helena & Its Dependencies. It had one slight drawback, however: the round trip, via Cape Town, took the best part of four weeks. Nonetheless, it was a 'must do'.

The *RMS* under the command of Capt David Roberts had arrived at Jamestown on 11th January and, as custom dictated, he called on me at my office in the Castle bursting with an idea that he had had while berthed in Duncan Dock in Cape Town. He had been on the bridge of the *RMS* as the fleet of yachts competing in the Cape to Rio Race (now known as the South Atlantic Yacht Race) had sailed past from the yacht marina towards the open sea. *"Why not have a Cape to St Helena yacht race?"* he had mused. The notion appealed to me too, not only could it be developed into a worthwhile event in its own right it could be good publicity for the Island's tourism as well. The concept of the yacht race, which later became the 'Governor's Cup Race', was born: there was an Admiral's Cup Race (a biennial event organised by the Royal Ocean Racing Club), *"So, why not a Governor's Cup"* I had suggested. The label stuck and the Governor's Special Fund (otherwise known as 'the Governor's cocoa tin') purchased the crystal trophy.

In a port like Jamestown, with no berthing facilities, the weather played a critical part in loading and unloading any ships that called. It was not uncommon for a cruise liner to make a scheduled call but fail to land any passengers on account of sea conditions. Landing conditions could be quite difficult, even in the best of times, as Governor Massingham's drenching on the arrival of Prince Andrew in 1984 had illustrated: he missed his footing on the Steps. The mighty Atlantic rollers would roll into James Bay and often lift containers about like matchboxes on the wharf. In conditions like that it was difficult enough to move cargo, but it would normally lead to the Master of the *RMS* deciding that it was too dangerous to allow passengers ashore. That January call was one of those occasions, which was doubly unfortunate as the South African New Apostolic Church had virtually chartered the *RMS* to convey more than 100 members to St Helena for the formal opening of Baron Gaskin's church.

All was not lost, however, as the leader of the delegation, Bishop Kriel, and some of the more athletic of the members made it ashore on 12th January and were joined by a few more to enable a quite formidable, yet reduced, choir and band play at the ceremony the next day. We departed St

Helena on the *RMS* on 14th January with the ship full of 'New Apostolics' and their music for a quite unusual cruise to Cape Town during which David Roberts and I developed the embryonic plans for the Governor's Cup Race. The voyage was remarkable for even more than those two developments in that it also introduced us to our first experience of mobile telephone technology. As the ship approached the South African coast, miles north of Cape Town, probably in the vicinity of Walvis Bay, passengers started to congregate on the aft deck with handsets clamped to their ears calling to others that they had 'a signal'. By the time we had passed Saldanha Bay and were in sight of Table Mountain what seemed like the whole complement of passengers was busy talking to relatives and friends ashore.

The telephonic announcement of our imminent arrival meant that by the time the *RMS* was inching into Duncan Dock the quayside was crowded with New Apostolic church members. Hymns of thanksgiving for a safe voyage/arrival sprang up spontaneously from ship and shore. The embarked band broke out with the 'new' South African national anthem – '*Nkosi sikelel' iAfrika*' (The Call of South Africa) – which was taken up by the couple of hundred voices gathered there to fantastic effect. Then, to cap that, they played '*God Save The Queen*' when, if our eyes hadn't been brimming with tears already, they certainly became so.

Our new friends wanted to whisk us off, but business called. St Helena Line Ltd (aka the Crown Agents) had floated a new Schedule for the *RMS* to which I had some fundamental objections in the terms of the service that would have resulted. David Roberts, articulating Curnow Shipping's views, also found difficulties in putting the suggested Schedule into effect. During the voyage south from St Helena he had helped me revise the draft in a way that met all our joint objections. But that was not the only reason St Helena Line in London were incurring the expense of sending the Board member and shipping consultant Peter Motion to Cape Town to parley with me: London wanted to ease Curnow Shipping out of the contract to run the *RMS*. I had no inkling of this in advance but had no difficulty in firmly resisting Peter Motion's proposals, despite the delicious lunch at a Waterfront hotel, his smooth manner and the well disguised knife in Curnow Shipping's ribs: I had gained a lot of experience and insight to the company over the period since Sandi and I had met with Andrew Bell and Chris Gardner in Porthleven several months earlier.

I had already recognised that it was imperative to ensure that all the arrangements for satisfactorily securing the Island's life-line were in place and that the new management contract was particularly important in the light of the new Shipping Schedule that we hoped to have in place from early in May. The new Schedule for the *RMS* would allow for more calls at Cape Town, with a corresponding reduction in the long periods when the ship was away sailing to and from the United Kingdom. There was, nevertheless, a dichotomy: the long cruises to and from Cardiff brought a strong passenger revenue stream (but not necessarily tourists to the Island in volume) and freight revenues were buoyed up by local sourcing of supplies direct from the UK; while the short term growth in tourism, with its obvious economic benefits to St Helena, were destined to come from South Africa. With the ship being in the Southern Hemisphere for longer periods access for Saints themselves as well as visitors would be significantly increased via Ascension as well as Cape Town. I firmly believed that fly-sail holidays through Cape Town would also prove popular, as was happening elsewhere. Tourism was a potential growth industry and in my view it was worth any extra costs to the shipping subsidy (*"by managing locally the elements within the ODA's Aid envelope"*) to build up extra local earning power – creating jobs, income and taxes! It was a bit of a step in the dark then – unprecedented for St Helena. But it I was convinced it was both logical and in the Island's best interests. It was no time to be timid. It seemed right at the time and I think history may well have proved it to be so.

With that sorted and St Helena Line in no doubt about my views on the Schedule and the Shipping Contract we returned to Duncan Dock to board the *St Helena*. The ship had been running behind schedule for a while and that call at Cape Town had been cut from two nights to a day to enable it to catch up with the published timetable. Leaving at around 4 p.m. for our voyage to Tristan da Cunha it was immediately noticeable that our passengers had changed from a high-spirited musical group of mainly Cape Coloured South Africans to an eclectic mix of mainly elderly white middle class travellers. One stood out from the crowd, Warren Searle: a South African and retired former Shell executive who gave daily lectures on the bird life that might be encountered along the line of our voyage. He was an interesting man who had once flown Sunderland flying boats. We saw him quite regularly and remained in touch until his death in the early 2000s.

As mention above, Tristan da Cunha, like Ascension Island, had no indigenous population until garrisoned in 1816. Although the garrison was withdrawn in late 1817 one soldier, Corporal William Glass, opted to make his future life there: he had married a Cape Coloured lady, Maria Leenders, in South Africa and apartheid, although not official policy, was alive and thriving. He and his wife returned to the island and William and Maria's descendants remain there to this day. A twentieth-century Glass, James, was Chief Islander in the latter half of the 1990s. The population was a little under 300 and comprised members of only six other families, namely Repetto, Lavarello, Green (anglicised from the Dutch Groen), Swain, Hagen, and Rogers.

Tristan da Cunha is an almost perfect volcanic cone with its peak some 6,750 feet above sea level. Approaching the island as dawn broke was what must be one of the world's most splendid natural spectacles. The sun, initially far below the horizon, behind the RMS, gradually began to paint the topmost parts of the previously invisible peak in a soft pink glow as daylight gradually strengthened. Slowly, and like a gigantic film set, the cone changed colour bit by bit as we watched – from the rosy blush of dawn to a sunlit hue of brightest green illuminating its thick cover of vegetation. As the morning light increased a wreath of cloud began to circle the slopes, and a wind blown plume of cloud seemed to issue like a reminder of the volcano's smoking origins. That first sight of the island, appearing to rise out of the very depths of the South Atlantic Ocean, has remained with us ever since.

A sailor's privilege? Perhaps. In any case it is only the sailor, or those who come by ship, who can experience Tristan da Cunha, as there is no airfield and no other way of reaching the island other than by sea. The island's economy was heavily dependent upon its fishery resources and especially the export of Tristan crayfish. The fishery resource was exploited in co-operation with the islanders by a South

African company under contract to the Tristan da Cunha Government and provided the Government's main revenues. The crayfish, or lobster tails, maintained a premium price in the international market place.

An increasing number of cruise ships had started to call at Tristan da Cunha, but the only regular liner service was provided by the *RMS St Helena* which had a three day call at Tristan da Cunha. However, even in the southern summer when she normally called, the weather could not always be relied upon to allow passengers ashore on each of the days. On these occasions the ship slipped away to anchor in the shelter of either Nightingale or Inaccessible Island both some 30 miles from the anchorage at the settlement of Edinburgh-of-the Seven Seas on Tristan da Cunha. These two uninhabited islands are home to hundreds of thousands of sea birds, penguins and seals. In January and February the seashore is lined with scores of moulting rockhopper penguins looking like a welcoming party of nightclub bouncers. Seals bask in the sheltered bays and their pups, like tiny puppy-dogs, roll around in the rock pools unfazed by human intrusions. Here large areas of the sea itself appear in the bright sunshine to be paved with shiny cobbles, only to be revealed on closer inspection to be hundreds of thousands of resting shearwaters. They, like the skuas, petrels and stately albatross, all breed on these islands and provide a day long and absorbing flying-display for us rather more earthbound mortals.

The yellow nosed albatross breeds on Tristan da Cunha's Base, the land at the foot of the mountain atop the 2,000 ft cliffs, which tower over the settlement of Edinburgh. It was named for the eponymous Duke and son of Queen Victoria who, as a naval officer, visited in 1867. The Village, as it is more commonly called, is situated on the only habitable area of land at the north-western corner of the island and which appears to have been formed by a large landslip from the cliffs above. No more than a half mile wide for most of its extent and some three or four miles in length this area of land forms the settlement and its main agricultural resource for crops and grazing. For the visitor it provides a fascinating glimpse of a world far removed from the industrialised and consumer oriented 21st century of shopping malls and motorcar dominated existence in which most of us are accustomed to live. Nevertheless, some fifty years ago, in 1963, a generation of Tristanians chose their way of life over what the outside world had to offer following their evacuation to Britain in 1961. The volcanic eruption in 1961 and the publicity surrounding the islanders' resettlement certainly increased public awareness of Tristan da Cunha. It is no longer a philatelist's speciality interest. Nevertheless, Tristanians have always been careful in protecting their environment and never sought to attract mass tourism

Calshot Harbour, built after the re-settlement of Tristan da Cunha following the volcanic eruption of 1961 had obliterated the traditional landing, now nestles beneath the cliffs below the Village and is the visitor's point of entry after disembarking the *St Helena* in the anchorage by launch. Most of the visitors make straight for the Handicraft Shop where hand-knitted woollens and other local handicrafts are popular purchases. But a pullover or sweater from Tristan da Cunha really is different, not simply for its design but because, as with all the other knitted items available here, the wool from island sheep has been processed completely by hand on the island. Most of the island ladies card and spin their own wool after the shearing in the Spring and, although knitting is very much a cottage industry, selling the finished goods to visitors is a useful additional income for them as well as providing a sought after souvenir for the tourist. These and other traditional skills are still alive and well on Tristan da Cunha.

The fishing concession; the need to provide island services; and increasing tourism had broken down the early subsistence economy of the island and introduced a wage-based economy, imported foodstuffs and other goods. Nevertheless, the traditions of a self-sufficient community die hard and, as there are no contractors, builders or plumbers in business, families helped one another with the essentials of house maintenance and building a home for young marrieds. Each family had its own sheep; a cow; and plot to grow vegetables at the Potato Patches west of the Village. And yet progress to some is measured by the fact that in 1995 the island's senior citizens were able to travel the two miles to work at the 'Patches' by a Government owned mini-bus rather than walk, as formerly.

Nonetheless, the day still started for many of the island's womenfolk by a walk to the pasture to milk the family cow before going off to work in the Administration (the *H'admin*) or the island's single store, to teach, or perhaps to spend time with family and elders and work on the next piece of knitting. The weather dominates life on Tristan da Cunha. It can change very quickly and every islander was an amateur forecaster, able to judge whether the apparently balmy breeze and sunshine might enable them to sail to Nightingale for the weekend or turn into a raging gale. In the season, if the weather looked at all promising, community leaders decided that it was to be a 'fishing day'. Tools were downed at the Public Works Department and elsewhere while the men took their boats out to lay pots for crayfish and to put out a line for some fish for the table. For those of us softened by the conveniences of our consumer society life seemed hard on Tristan da Cunha, but it had produced a close-knit community of amazingly resilient and hard-working people who repaid our visits with warmth, hospitality and humour.

Only Sandi and I (as Governor and the First Lady) were officially allowed to stay ashore while the *RMS* lay off Calshot Harbour. We were housed in one of the Government's Guest Houses, referred to as the 'Governor's House'. The Administrator, Brendan Dalley was a fisheries expert first and foremost and he, his wife Eileen, and Jimmy Glass arranged comprehensive programmes for both Sandi and me. However, that first year was a special visit for a number of reasons, not only was it our first, but it also provided an opportunity to present the insignia of his award of an MBE to Lewis Glass, the Village policeman and to host a Reception to celebrate that and meet a number of Tristanians all at one go. My full uniform was packed and Patrick, who had apparently been accustomed to accompanying my predecessor, was with us and able to look after my uniform. He brought it ashore so that I could change and officiate at the gathering congregated in the garden of the Administrator's Residence. It proved to be a great photo opportunity for many of the passengers ashore from the *RMS*, but it was, in fact, the only time that I thought it necessary to appear on the island in uniform: it is hardly the most comfortable of outfits!

Sandi milked cows, carded and spun wool and generally learnt how a Tristanian lady worked so hard domestically. I, on the other hand, toured the Government Departments and facilities and the crayfish processing plant. I also talked Jimmy Glass in taking me up to 'The Base' – the sloping plateau around the volcanic cone above the 2,000 feet high cliffs that circle the island. It was a stiff climb and Jimmy carried a sheep over his shoulder for the last part of the ascent. Patrick gamely accompanied me up. From our vantage point high above sea level Capt Smith reported by radio that the weather was getting up and he was retreating to the shelter of Inaccessible Island. We three then descended swiftly down the red shale slope east of the Potato Patches, which felt like downhill skiing without skis! The *RMS* had disappeared from the anchorage by the time we had returned to 'the Village'.

Sandi and I met lots of Tristanians, dined in their homes and joined them at the Edinburgh Hall, the social centre of the island life. Part of the rationale for such a visit was to give an explanation for HMG's policies – the issue of British nationality was a recurring theme; to address the Island Council; and to learn how the Governor could assist in implementing the Island Council's own policies. One matter in which I was involved from early on was the process of seeking the award of a Coat of Arms for the Territory separate from those of St Helena. Sadly this process, involving the College of Arms in London, took a very long time and it was not until 2002, long after I had left the Service, that the evolving design was approved and granted to the island's Government.

CHAPTER SIX

1996: Reality and an Unprecedented Disturbance

The return from Tristan da Cunha and our call at Cape Town was both good and bad. We met my old colleague Les Buchannan and his wife and we dined them; and lunched with Bishop Kriel and Baron Gaskin's parents at Ons Huisie, a famous seaside seafood restaurant at Bloubergstrand on the coast north of Cape Town: but a medical check arranged for Sandi, who was still suffering from back pains, revealed that she might have had a kidney stone. The hospital suggested an immediate operation. However, deciding to return home for a second opinion under the FCO Medical Adviser's auspices, Sandi was booked on Saturday's British Airways flight to London, while the *RMS* and I sailed for St Helena without her at 4 p.m. on 3rd February.

The five days at sea gave me pause to think about the months ahead. Hopefully the political process could be managed so that the public service reform programme would not be de-railed by those MLCs who, despite having agreed to it, were in reality opposed to change. To assist those same MLCs, whose belief that the Governor had too much power I have mentioned above, I had supported an approach to the Trustees of the Commonwealth Parliamentary Association (CPA) to conduct a review of constitutional and parliamentary matters in St Helena. The CPA had agreed to financial support and I had sought back-up funding from the FCO's Good Government Fund. If two experienced Commonwealth politicians could work with MLCs and help them to understand their constitutional rights and parliamentary responsibilities perhaps Legislative Councillors and particularly ExCo might work better for the Island's good. St Helena was a very immature parliamentary democracy, but the Constitution – The St Helena Constitution Order, 1988 - had been in force for less than 10 years and was a robust piece of legislation giving elected members considerable powers. It was nowhere near its 'use by date'. Indeed many, if not most, of the MLCs quite simply failed to see the degree of political independence from the Governor (HMG or The Crown), or the extent of their ability to run their own Government and shape its policies, that it gave them. Thus, the idea of independent and outside experts coming to assist MLCs to examine Legislative Council procedures, Standing Orders and Council Committee Rules, as well as examining in particular the rôle and responsibilities of the Governor, Executive and Legislative Councils and Council Committees appealed to me.

Public sector reform was but one element of the process needed to stimulate the economy. There were two other aspects, the most important of which had been the establishment of retail banking facilities by the Bank of Nova Scotia. Since the meeting in June, which I, and others, had taken as the green light to proceed with the Banking Licence – the Banking Ordinance had already been enacted – the process had become entangled in bureaucratic obstacles raised in London, which had eventually prompted the Bank to withdraw the licence application at the end of November 1995. Things had moved on in the world of banking in the two years since the invitation to establish on St Helena had been made and other investment opportunities were available to the Bank. End of a dream; but also a severe blow to St Helena's economic development: a commercial bank offering retail services and loan facilities to business was an indispensable and essential ingredient in the development we wished to see in the private sector.

However, emerging in 1994 from another of the numerous visits by 'experts' had been the establishment of the St Helena Development Agency (SHDA) to use Aid funding to develop the private sector by supporting the creation of small businesses. It had had some success in this, and was moving to promote the tourism potential of St Helena. To build on this I felt we needed to 'put St Helena on the map'. I had encouraged the FCO to think about a ministerial visit and suggested that another Royal Visit would be more than welcome in that context. As it transpired no such visits would happen on my watch. But St Helena did get its publicity: in April, covering the invasion of the Governor's

Office by an unruly mob; and at the end of year in respect of the Governor's Cup Race. More about both of which below.

*   *   *

A great feature of travelling on the *RMS* was that there would always be at least one really interesting passenger. On that voyage back to St Helena in early February 1996 it was no exception. His Honour Judge Stephen Tumin travelled with us. Judge Tumin, had been Her Majesty's Chief Inspector of Prisons from 1987 to 1995 and had received the 1995 Perrie Award for excellence in prison practice. In addition to his inspectorate duties in England and Wales, he had regularly inspected in Northern Ireland, the British West Indies, and other countries, and conducted enquiries into prison troubles. By 1996 he had retired from his inspectorate duties and was taking a cruise from Cape Town to Cardiff on the *St Helena.* I spent a number of fascinating hours with him on board the *RMS* and, as he was to spend a week on the Island, invited him to visit HMP Jamestown and let me know what he thought. His views on what was billed as the smallest prison in the world were favourable, which was perhaps fortunate given the official dinner that I held at Plantation House in his honour before he departed! He died after a distinguished life in 2003.

Shortly after my return to St Helena we lost the Attorney General, David Jeremiah at the end of his appointment. David was very musical and played with a group of likeminded ex-patriates under the name of the Hillbillies. His partner, Joy, was also an accomplished musician and under the direction of Eric George, a former school music teacher, they gave orchestral performances. And, over the years we hosted a number of recitals by the St Helena Ensemble at Plantation House. Both Sandi and I engaged Eric as a music teacher – Sandi for the piano and to teach me to play the guitar, and later the clarinet. David Jeremiah's musical farewell was held at the local bar and restaurant, Anne's Place, when all the guests were asked to take their own musical instruments. I barely knew where the chords were on my guitar, but with help from and a practice with Tony Cowan, one of the Hillbillies, also shortly to leave, I too strummed along in the jam session that evening.

Sandi arrived back on St Helena via the RAF Airbridge and Ascension on 21st March, the kidney stone having sorted itself naturally. Also on that sailing of the *RMS* were the CPA's 'eminent politicians', the Speaker of the antipodean Norfolk Island House of Assembly, the Hon David Buffett, and Jurat Eric Potter from the Channel Island of Jersey; the newly appointed FCO desk officer for St Helena, Ric Nye; and, as it happened, the ODA funded Change Adviser on one of her regular visits. All these latter visitors created a busy period of work and official entertainment for us. To add to this, the Chief Justice, Judge Geoffrey Martin, accompanied by his wife Marie arrived on 28th March.

The Chief Secretary, John Perrott, and his wife departed for leave in the UK on the 29th March, leaving the top management team temporarily weakened. Ethel Yon was capable of carrying out the day-to-day functions of the Chief Secretary, but already had a rôle in the team and could not replace John's input. Further, no successor for the Attorney General, who at that time was the only legally qualified body on the Island, had yet been identified; and the then Financial Secretary Bob Perrott (no relation to John) was winding down prior to his own departure,

Official life went on, however. I attended the formal opening of the Supreme Court Session and we got to know Marie and Geoff Martin quite well during that stay on St Helena. Geoff was also to help me in my quest to establish a Public Solicitor on the Island. Until then St Helena had managed as a one-man legal jurisdiction without access for the public to legal advice or a lawyer independent of Government. There was a real conflict of interest. At first sight I found this state of affairs quite horrifying and felt it was most unsafe in principle. Fortunately, and quite surprisingly, no serious harm or miscarriage of justice seemed yet to have occurred. But it was, in my view, unacceptable. We did succeed in the establishment of a further, independent, legal body in time, and eventually, also with Geoff Martin's considerable assistance, successfully addressed the other legal lacuna – that the Court of Appeal sat in London rather than St Helena.

Arriving on the southbound shuttle from Ascension on 18th April was the Government's new Financial Secretary Matthew Young, together with his wife Sheila. Matt had been a financial officer with the Strathclyde Council in Scotland and was new to overseas service. However, this was irrelevant as he quickly showed himself to be on top of the brief and he became a close and trusted colleague, friend, and tennis partner and opponent. He was also an important member of the group of senior officials who helped to develop policies for the St Helena Government. But the events that unwound less than an hour after he had made his first call on me the next morning were to test us all.

The ODA funded Change Adviser had been going about her visits to Government Departments, attending meetings of Council Committees and discussions with officials: her rôle to identify areas in which economies and privatisations might be achieved. This was, doubtless unsettling to Saints unwilling to countenance change – *"we've never done it that way before"* – was a common, if not always voiced, response. Unemployment at around 15%, lack of resources and increasing poverty were fertile ground for those who wished to derail the public sector reform programme, or to simply create trouble for the St Helena Government. Nevertheless and recognising the problems that poverty could be storing up for the future, the Government had, with some professional input from another ODA funded adviser, set a review of child and other benefits in hand. However, on the eve of the conclusions being submitted by the relevant Committee to the Executive Council for agreement, a Legislative Councillor sought to force the issue with a demand for increased benefits. This self-proclaimed champion of the poor was Councillor Bobby Robertson, a retired ex-patriate Scotsman married to an islander. According to Island lore he was said to have single-handedly brought the entire workforce of British Steel's Scunthorpe Works out on strike. As a member of Legislative Council, this one-time militant had used his entitlement to airtime on Radio St Helena to agitate against the Government's social policies. He capped this by calling for a major demonstration outside the Social Services Department on 19th April 1996.

There was a noisy but peaceful protest outside the Department, after which the demonstrators retreated to one of the pubs in town to slake their thirst – much, it was later alleged, at Councillor Robertson's expense. Around 12:30 p.m. and having cranked up the level of emotion, Robertson led a procession numbering about a hundred to the Castle, where he demanded that they should see the Governor. The Government offices in the Castle were virtually deserted, as it was by then lunchtime. I was there and having a sandwich lunch, so agreed to see them. I descended to the Castle courtyard where we had an orderly, if lively, meeting. However, after having addressed their concerns for some twenty minutes, the frustration and resentment simmering just below the surface erupted as I turned to retrace my steps into the Castle having exhausted all the arguments. The angry crowd surged up the staircase and swept me forward into the Castle and my office at the head of the staircase.

A mob of about sixty assorted islanders and Cllr Robertson swarmed into my office, where several of the well-known ne'er-do-wells from Longwood let off steam, harangued and sought to intimidate me. Councillor Robertson egged on the mob. He even suggested that if they received no satisfaction from the Governor then they should go back into the town and take what they wanted from the shops! Several threats of physical violence were made – "We've killed more than one Governor in the past, we could do it again"! Indeed, one female protestor got hold of my tie and yanked it above my head to show how easy it could be to lynch me by hanging! The Police were stood by in anti-Riot gear and took some persuasion not to deploy it for real in my office. After using their powers of persuasion on the acting Chief of Police, I was joined by two of the island's most senior public servants, Ethel Yon then acting as Chief Secretary in John Perrott's absence on leave, and Ivy Ellick, who was Head of Personnel but acting as Deputy Secretary. They put themselves in considerable danger by joining me and refusing to leave. The confrontation, which certainly had its ugly moments, nevertheless provided a unique opportunity to speak about the reality of Government policies to an audience that would hardly have bothered to 'tune in' on any other occasion. Whether it did any good or not it is difficult to say, but it did seem to help to defuse a situation which Robertson was less and less able to control. In one of those 'it can only happen in St Helena' paradoxes, Robertson was a member of the Social Services Committee whose recommendation for an increase in the level of benefits was to go before Executive Council on the following Tuesday – four days hence!

The occupation lasted a little over three hours. Nothing like it had happened in living memory. Fortunately there was no damage to persons or property, but the ugly event left its scar on those most closely involved. The less than generous might have concluded that the timing of the demonstration (*The Daily Telegraph*, to the chagrin of the FCO, reported it as a riot) had been chosen with care. The departure of the Attorney General and the Chief Secretary in March, and the incumbent Financial Secretary on the *RMS* that morning on leave, had certainly left the senior management team under-strength. But Robertson, in his rôle as a Councillor and Chair of the Social Services Committee, had known that the conclusions and recommendations of the review of benefits had been accepted by his Council Committee and that the new benefit rates, after being rubber-stamped by ExCo, would be paid from the next week. It was impossible, therefore to regard him as anything other than a deliberate troublemaker. Whether he would have been able to claim to be responsible for making Government increase the benefit rates is, of course, doubtful. That may well have been his motive, but the events, which he had conspired to stage-manage, I think actually precluded that result.

The demonstrators, although leaving peacefully, did so with the vocalised threat that further direct action could be expected if nothing was done to resolve their grievances over the inadequate social security benefits. An arson attack on Plantation House was threatened. Clearly the Administration needed to demonstrate that control had not slipped into the hands of "Red" Bobby Robertson. The Police were instructed to maintain a high profile while tempers were given a chance to cool over the weekend. At the same time I conferred with the senior management team and consulted Executive Council members informally. We agreed that I would broadcast a message addressing the issue over Radio St Helena on Monday.

The message, which was broadcast live to a quiet and somewhat shamefaced island on 22nd April, made the points that neither elected members of the Island's Councils nor senior officials were unaware of the cases of hardship that existed; that despite the pressure put on the Governor on the previous Friday neither he nor officials were empowered to make changes in the rates of social security – this was a matter for the Social Services Committee, which was mainly comprised of MLCs; that Government could only pay benefits that it could afford; that, nonetheless MLCs had welcomed the recommendations of the recent review of social service benefits; and that it was expected that the Government would be able to put in place the first of the financial recommendations as early as the week following. Finally, it was necessary to add a reminder how counterproductive it could be to take the law into one's own hands and the address ended with the thought that:

> "...To tackle unemployment we must create more jobs. For more jobs to be created we need more tourists to visit the island and overseas investors to help us set up more business activity. What are they going to think about St Helena as a destination in which to spend money if they learn that people here are prepared to take the law into their own hands when they don't get their own way?...."

Nevertheless, this explosion of feeling underlined for us all that Government had to ensure that it was seen to be putting policies in place to deal with the simmering resentment brought about by lack of employment opportunities and the general level of poverty. The roots of the problem, of course, lay in the uneconomic nature of the island and the negative growth imposed by reducing the real levels of Budgetary Aid, as well as the deficiencies of the island's social security system which, although having many positive elements, was designed to follow technical rules and procedures drawn up in the United Kingdom and which were perhaps unsuited to St Helena's circumstances.

*   *   *

As a condition of continued disbursement of the aid package, the St Helena Government was required to report back to the ODA by the mid-point in the financial year on the progress made in meeting the targets agreed with the 1995 Budgetary Aid Mission (BAM). Continuing and concentrated efforts were made across the Administration to ensure that Government as a whole was making progress and, as a result, we were able to successfully report that not only had the targets set by the BAM been met but that significant progress in planning for the new activities outlined in this interim report had been made. These activities would utilise the savings which we expected to accrue in the 1996/97 financial year, as well those that we planned for realisation in the following three full financial years. We were already forward planning for the next visit by a team from the ODA, which in normal circumstances could be expected in November.

In the meantime, the calendar with its fixed quota of events, Commonwealth Day, The Queen's Birthday, St Helena Day etc ticked over as it had for countless years. I was invited, as a newcomer, to present a weekly half-hour programme of music *"From my Collection"* on the radio station for a month. I joined the cricket community of St Helena and we were invited to various local social functions. We occasionally joined groups attending community events across the Island. At one such, not that long after our arrival, I was surprised to find, in an island of less than 6,000 souls and only 47 square miles, how one could remain 'unknown' to the general public outside Jamestown. We had been at a dance at the Blue Hill Community Centre and I had repaired to the Gents. A fellow occupant turned to notice the stranger and said *"Who be you?"* I told him and batted the question back, to which he replied *"I be Chuck and Chew"* and that he visited Plantation House each week. He did so as an operative in one of the Island's two refuse collection vehicles, emblazoned with the sign – 'Chuck and Chew'! We also did a fair amount of travelling around to see all aspects of the Island.

The *RMS* came and went on its new Schedule from 9th May; and Curnow Shipping Ltd retained the shipping management contract. Despite both my arguments in early January and a messy and unnecessarily complicated attempt to remove the company by splitting the contract into two parts in the hope that a larger company of international ship managers made a bid or bids, which could then be argued to be better value, none did! Curnow Shipping won the day.

To provide the optimum access (for tourism and for Saints to come and go to work in Ascension and the Falkland

Islands) it had been agreed that it was in the Island's interests were the *RMS* to have fewer calls in the UK, so allowing the vessel to remain in the South Atlantic longer: the aim to reduce this to one, or even no calls had been floated to me when I had called on the Minister, Baroness Chalker, in July the previous year. Subsequently, together with the re-scheduling which reduced the number of calls in the UK from six to four a year, we had agreed to re-examine the scheduling to assess the options to further reduce the number of times the *RMS* returned to Cardiff. It was disappointing then to learn that St Helena Line had engaged consultants to review the options before the new scheduling had been tried and tested and which failed to address the issues of access to St Helena. Curnow Shipping had a vast experience of St Helena, its people and its trade and served the Island well. I cannot to this day understand what it was that drove what posed as a shipping company - St Helena Line – in Sutton, Surrey to try to prise their excellent management of the Island's Lifeline away from Curnow Shipping, as they eventually did in the early 2000s by raising false accusations of accounting irregularities. Nevertheless, I found my special responsibility for shipping to be one of the more interesting aspects of my rôle as Governor of St Helena. As David Roberts once put it when we boarded and my flag flew from the crosstrees, *"Your yacht awaits, Sir"* The Queen no longer had Her yacht: *HMY Britannia* was decommissioned on 11th December 1997!

I also found the constitutional responsibility for the Police very interesting and was pleased that I could get the FCO's Police Adviser (a relic from Colonial Office days – the job not the incumbent I hasten to add) to visit and advise me on the St Helena Police Force. The rôle of Governor was both symbolic and bureaucratic and, in St Helena, was absorbingly hands-on. I had visited every Police Station on the Island, each of the Government Departments and their outlying parts, and we had got to know Michel Martineau, the Honorary French Consul who was the *conservateur* of the Napoleonic sites on St Helena and lived at Longwood House, Napoleon Buonparte's island home during his incarceration between 1816 and his death in 1821. Our early voyage fellow passenger, Brian Hart, had attached himself as my Personal Chaplain and moved into the vicarage nearby, which made it a very convenient stroll when he felt like company, a chat and a glass of whisky!

We had, of course, done lots more than the words above convey by the time that we boarded the *RMS* bound for Cape Town and some UK leave. We had *inter alia* visited the young David Henry busy trying to re-establish coffee on the Island, played cricket and established ourselves in our rôles as patrons and presidents of St Helenian societies and the Scouts and Guides, attended camps of the latter and the Church Lads Brigade, and even found that we had been able to make a few local friends (well perhaps very good acquaintances). Sandi said that she always knew when the Government was in bad odour, because when she went into Jamestown people turned away and did not acknowledge her! Perhaps the only real friend that we made and she was far more Sandi's friend than mine at the time, was Dot Leo. Dot, of 'Dot's Café' in the market, was always the same, always had a kind or encouraging word for Sandi while knowing just about everything that was going on – or as they had it in St Helena "*What street say*" i.e. the local gossip.

We left for a leave break on the *St Helena* on 23rd June and David Roberts briefed me on the progress that he had made in getting a Cape to St Helena yacht race up and running. The Royal Cape Yacht Club were interested and, while in Cape Town, we gave a presentation on the ideas we had to a meeting of members and some journalists before Sandi and I travelled on to London, home and some leave on 29th June. If I had learnt one thing during that first period in St Helena, it was that in the political context that I then found myself, the essence of good management was most definitely to make the right decisions, not those which might be most popular!

CHAPTER SEVEN

A Word in your ear, Sir

Before departing St Helena on leave, and in keeping with the Diplomatic Service custom of highlighting the issues in play in the territory for the Department to digest before my arrival, I wrote a think piece, which I entitled "*St Helena: a Twentieth Century anomaly*". It was of the utmost importance, I believed, for the Government of St Helena (my Government!), for officials in London, and incidentally for me also as the interlocutor, to set out in detail the issues upon which we all needed to concentrate. Thus, I hoped that those in London who needed to understand them might do so.

The words of the former Foreign Secretary, Lord Carrington, used in his Chatham House lecture of 25th March 1982, now seemed very apposite to me sitting in my office in the Castle at Jamestown in the middle of June 1996:-

> "*We have, in short, to avoid the dangerous policies of believing, either that any instability anywhere in the world is a threat to our interests, or that there are little countries far away to which we never need pay attention.*"

I used them to head my Despatch: a Foreign Office custom.

In summary, I wrote to suggest that with action in hand to re-assess the political and the aid relationships with St Helena it was apposite to consider the issues we faced. St Helena's geographical position dictated its settlement and occupation. After it was brought under the direct governance of the Crown this geographical position became a liability rather than an asset. Flax was the backbone of the economy until the mid-1960s, but the Island offered few advantages for alternative agricultural production and it had no other natural resource than its people. The economy had been shrinking as a result of the reduction of British financial assistance; there was no conventional private sector to take up the slack; and poverty and despair were growing. The Government of St Helena recognised the realities and had embarked upon an ambitious programme of structural adjustment. This was showing the first signs of success, but it did not create employment. The British Government formerly acknowledged the uneconomic nature of the Island and assisted accordingly. This had now changed, and United Kingdom Aid support had declined substantially over the previous 5 years. St Helena's programme of structural adjustment was continuing (and producing results), but the Government needed help to carry it through.

In detail, I started by stating that at a time when the Aid Wing was prepared to negotiate a Country Policy Plan for St Helena and a three-year Aid commitment for the years 1997/98 - 1999/2000; and the Diplomatic Wing proposed to devise a medium term strategy for St Helena to be in place before the end of 1996 it was apposite to consider the two important issues which I had earlier identified as being among those facing the Governor in those last years of the 20th Century. These were: 'public sector reform'; and the need to further stimulate the creation of a private sector in the economy and to reduce the financial dependence of St Helena upon Her Majesty's Government in the United Kingdom.

After an unbroken period of 162 years of administration of the Island by the Honourable East India Company under a Charter from King Charles II granted in December 1673, St Helena was brought under the direct government of the Crown on 22nd April 1834. At that time the annual expenditure amounted to some £90,000 (£18.4m at 1996 prices). In the late 17th Century the Island had become established as a base and refreshment centre for the fleets of the East India Company; and St Helena's importance grew with the growth of operations of the Company in the East Indies to reach its peak between the mid-18th and early 19th Centuries. However, the technical innovations of the Victorian age destroyed the Island's importance for shipping: steamships and refrigeration made it possible for ships to by-pass the Island; and even more significant was the opening of the Suez Canal, which meant that the main shipping routes from Europe to the Far East were no longer by way of the

South Atlantic. As the Island's importance as a re-victualing centre declined, a search began for a viable industry to support the Island economy.

In 1874 the first New Zealand flax (*phormium tenax*) was introduced. Although at first the experiment offered little hope of commercial success, foundering through the thoughtless siting of the first mill on the Jamestown seafront: after a second attempt (when mills were built in the outlying districts in the interior) the flax industry took off in 1907. Hemp became the principal export of the Colony and the growing and manufacture of it the main industry. The industry's fortunes, and thus those of the Island too, fluctuated wildly in response to world demand, with the periods of maximum prosperity occurring during the two World Wars and the Korean War. The flax crop, which for half a century was the main agricultural product, died a quick death. It was killed by a combination of falling world prices and demand; the high costs of production; and the increasing use of artificial fibres. In its heyday the fibre industry employed between 250 and 400 Saints, and was thus the major source of employment. The St Helena Government had for a number of years guaranteed a price of £78 per ton, but the market price was for most of that time below the guaranteed price, and subsidies cost the Government heavily. The cost of production had risen to about £100 per ton by the end of 1967: so far above the world price as to ensure the collapse of the industry on the Island. The last mill closed down in September 1966, leaving the large flax acreage unproductive. As there seemed to be no hope of re-establishing the production of what was St Helena's only exportable commodity, it became desirable to eliminate the useless *phormium tenax* and replace it with pasture and forest. This process is still continuing, although a considerable acreage remains on the more isolated and exposed slopes where endemic vegetation was grubbed out in the early years of the 20th Century to make way for the flax.

Production from the arable land, pasture and forest, was currently aimed at making the Island as self-supporting as possible, as it was accepted that St Helena in its limited circumstances was unable to produce an exportable commodity which could compete on world markets with modern production techniques in other more favoured environments. The import substitution goal was, however, still far out of reach and unlikely to be attained until large-scale irrigation is available to supplement St Helena's very erratic rainfall. Even today, I noted, the Island's agricultural production was dependent on rainfall, and this inevitably resulted in seasonal gluts and shortages. Taken together with disease and other predators the short term prospects were far from good, and with some 75% of the land area being classified as barren there was not a great deal of potential. In the 1990s St Helena imported approximately £1.75m worth of food each year.

The Island's principal resource was and remains its people. There are no deposits of exploitable minerals, no oil, and its isolation puts a severe constraint on the viability of any prospective processing or assembly operation. St Helena did not have a private sector in any sense that would be generally understood. There was a small amount of direct production in agriculture and fisheries; some construction; a rather larger retail sector than was easily sustainable; and small-scale tourism and craft enterprises. The most recent figures showed that private sector employment accounted for some 37% of those in work: the balance being employed in the public sector. These statistics had also to be considered in the context of the registered unemployment rate of 15%: over 350 persons (including those on community or work-fare relief). Fortunately offshore employment in Ascension Island and the Falkland Islands had remained buoyant and provided over 1,000 jobs, which absorbed something in the region of 28% of the total working population of St Helenians.

The economy was in recession and had been shrinking quickly, mainly as a result of the reduction in the real value of the United Kingdom Aid programme. Indeed, in line with the pressure on these funds, the St Helena Government introduced another deflationary Budget in March 1996. The Budget confirmed the cash limits imposed on Government expenditure, which were a means of containing an increase in Grant-in-Aid rather than any attempt to contain Government expenditure *per se*. The impact of the cash limits was to reduce the real value of Government expenditure in 1996/97 by some 6%, the forecast rate of inflation. Under the constraints imposed by a grant-aided budget it could do nothing for the supply side of the economy.

Since the St Helena economy was dominated by the public sector, changes in the size of the Budget had direct as well as indirect consequences upon economic growth, the net result being that as the size of Government contracted the private sector did not move in to replace it, nor be the source of economic growth, as it was neither large enough nor sufficiently vigorous to stimulate economic growth on its own. Even the most optimistic projections showed that the private sector could, at best, generate 150 new jobs by 2000/2001. Unfortunately additions to the labour force (school-leavers, returnees etc.) were estimated to be more than that. Stagnant taxation revenues, coupled with declining interest in portfolio investment and falling UK aid, meant that the sources available for financing Government expenditure were declining, which in turn meant that an important source of economic growth on the Island (i.e. Government expenditure) was contracting. This reduction in the real level of Government expenditure was on its own estimated to reduce national income by approximately 4% in 1996/97, marginally above the contraction experienced in 1994/95.

Reduced Government expenditure in St Helena arose not from a policy of introducing tax breaks, or a deliberate intention to reduce public expenditure, but from declining non-Island revenue sources. In other words, low levels of public expenditure in St Helena did not equate to more resources left in the private sector. Thus, in a situation that would normally demand a reflationary budget aimed at putting to work the growing number of unemployed and to increase the size and vigour of the private sector, the imposition of budgetary aid conditionality, by capping expenditure, produced the opposite effect.

The deflationary spiral was tightening and there were signs of deepening recession in the economy. Poverty was growing; debt increasing; and there was a rising sense of despair in the population at large. Tensions that had been simmering for some time had boiled over on 19th April with the near riot in Jamestown and an attack on the police at Longwood a week later. The storm clouds forecast over the past 2 years were now overhead. A re-evaluation was required before ODA officials came to negotiate over the detail of the budgetary and aid relationship, which we hoped to put in place for the period 1997/98 - 1999/2000. We must, I emphasised to my colleagues in London, reach common ground on the economic realities, and the assumptions based thereon made by the St Helena Government in its fiscal and budgetary projections. Too often, it seemed, that these were dismissed or ignored in order to fit in with the vastly different metropolitan economic assumptions that had become a *sine qua non* of British economic modelling. Despite all the surface similarities, it was nevertheless a fact that none of the routine economic assumptions made in respect of the domestic British economy could be readily adapted to the circumstances of St Helena. The sad fact was, however one looked at it, St Helena was an uneconomic entity. Nonetheless, the Government of St Helena recognised that it was incumbent upon it to 'do something about it'.

Indeed, we took this need very seriously. We recognised on the one hand that it was essential to increase the efficiency of Government and the services it delivered; to get better value for money; and to stop doing what was not relevant to Government. In response we had embarked upon 'the public sector reform programme'. On the other hand, was the necessity for the creation of a private sector in St Helena where effectively none had existed beforehand. Neither of those processes was easy, but the St Helena Government was committed to them despite the extraordinarily difficult circumstances of St Helena. However I restated, we needed the firm hand of partnership with Her Majesty's Government in the United Kingdom to achieve what many would consider to be the impossible.

We recognised the extent of the historic level of financial assistance to which successive British Governments had committed to St Helena. However, some 15 years earlier there had been a clear and unambiguous agreement that the Island was uneconomic. The result of successive budgetary aid negotiations throughout the first half of the 1980s was, while paying attention to the functioning and efficiency of the Administration, to acknowledge this total lack of conventional employment prospects and to assist the Government of St Helena in expanding public sector jobs. Concurrent advice was that this guaranteed employment policy impacted on private sector employment, but also recognised that the work-fare scheme then in force paid such low wages that this was not a really serious problem with respect to crowding out the private sector. In addition, during this period development aid was increased significantly with the purpose of improving the social infrastructure with the concomitant result that the total Aid figure rose significantly in cash and real terms between 1981/82 and 1985/86.

As structural adjustment in the United Kingdom itself impacted harder on the economy the more *laissez faire* attitude in the metropolitan economy triggered a move away from the support of the historic mutual acceptance of the fundamental uneconomic nature of the Island. Indeed by 1990, and with no indication as to what prospects existed for a private sector, we had moved apart to a position where the St Helena Government was left in no doubt that public expenditure had *"in future to be related more to what its economy can afford, and the importance of public sector pay and productivity not worsening the prospects for private sector growth"*. Although development aid continued for a while at levels close to £2.5m per annum, 1990 marked an important structural shift in United Kingdom aid and strong downward pressure on the element to fund the budget gap between public expenditure and those revenues that the Government of St Helena was able to generate. A further shift in philosophy, in 1991, advanced the argument that economic self-sufficiency should be the objective of the St Helena Government, and that to secure this end a 3-year reducing Grant-in-Aid was the best incentive and motivation for efficiency savings to provide a better environment for the private sector. The assumption took root that public sector resources could be transferred to the private sector without, unfortunately, recognising that there was no private sector in the conventional sense.

In reviewing these arguments with the benefit of hindsight, the inevitable conclusion was that this policy shift represented an act of faith in London, rather than anything more certain. The claim to potential for (and of) private sector growth was predicted on *inter alia*, the introduction of a weekly service by sea to Ascension Island (at 706 miles distant the nearest airhead); the establishment of a domestic commercial bank; and the introduction of a portable pension scheme. For one reason or another outside St Helena's control, none of these came to pass. Although a fourth assumption, the establishment of a development agency did materialise by the end of October 1995. Even then, its Terms of Reference needed to be revisited to strengthen its rôle in developing the necessary entrepreneurial culture in St Helena and a domestically based private sector.

Thus, in the 10 years between 1985 and 1995 we saw a complete turn-a-round in the philosophy behind the British Aid programme from supporting Government activities to a belief that not only could the private sector develop but also that in future financial support would be directed to private sector development. The belief that the State should occupy the commanding heights of the economy was current in the United Kingdom for less than 40 years. In the case of St Helena the Government, and the East India Company before it, had occupied what limited heights there are in this economy for nearly 350 years: some legacy! Nevertheless, and despite a perception in London that there was a reluctance to bring about the structural shift from public to private sector, which had become the core of the aid policy, the Government of St Helena had risen manfully to this most unaccustomed challenge.

I had to dispel the impression that the St Helena Government was opposed to the notion that the Island should strive to develop a viable economy with a greater degree of financial independence from the United Kingdom. Indeed, at least on the surface the opposite was true, as the adoption of the 'Vision for St Helena' and the reform policies that supported it amply illustrated. St Helena (not simply the Administration) had accepted the need to shift resources from the public sector to create a private sector. The policies, which were beginning to emerge from the wide-ranging programme of public sector reform, demonstrated the priorities the Government had to actively shrink the former and expand the latter, by transferring public sector activities to the private sector through privatisation and contracting out. A reduction in public expenditure was already being achieved through optimising the range of services provided by Government: through realising substantial efficiency savings; and through increasing charges to reflect the true cost of service provision. There was more, much more, to do;

but in such a micro-economy the law of diminishing returns would inevitably set in within the next three years.

Throughout the previous year officials had been examining some twenty specific areas of Government activity accounting for more than 50% of Government expenditure. The purpose of each review, or 'business case', was to determine whether the target service should continue to be provided by the public sector and, if not, to determine how it should be transferred to the private sector. Where services were to remain in the public sector, measures to ensure that the services were provided efficiently and effectively had been identified. This process was successful, and I was confident that we would meet the budgetary aid conditionality in respect of efficiency savings for the 1996/97 financial year.

Detailed projections had been completed to cover the subsequent three-year period, which was to be the subject of our Country Policy Plan and anticipated three-year aid support package. These budgetary projections included ambitious targets for further savings as the programme of public sector reform accelerated. We believed the targets to be reasonable, but their achievement far from easy. The net overall effect would anticipate a modest increase in the current level of support from Her Majesty's Government in the United Kingdom, but below the recent historic base line (e.g. £9m per annum in the early 1990s). The target was to ensure that the Grant-in-Aid, as a percentage of the overall package did not increase beyond its current level; and that this element of local revenues did not also increase beyond its current level. This would, nevertheless, require a commitment to a minimum of £26.5m in the aid framework for the next three years.

In my Despatch No 17 of 6th October 1995 (First Impressions) I had referred to the doubt cast upon the ability of the historic county of Rutland, with a population of 13,000 souls, to administer itself as it formed too small a unit to make satisfactory arrangements for the delivery of local services. St Helena, with a resident population of some 5,500, could hardly compare with the county of Rutland, either in terms of size, wealth, or natural resources. However, the Government of this fragment of rock in the middle of the South Atlantic Ocean was expected to provide all services commonly found in an independent country, save for a defence force and a foreign service. Her Majesty's Government in the United Kingdom currently paid a greater proportion of the running costs of Local Authorities in Britain by means of a central-Government grant than was reflected in the Grant-in-Aid to St Helena. At the same time officials in London sought to micro-manage the economy of this Colony, imposing often-impossible strictures upon its economic management. We had no problems with accountability, but we did have a problem with the ever decreasing assistance in real terms when there was no other source of financial support.

I concluded by noting that St Helena carried a very heavy historic burden. Nonetheless, the Government of St Helena was committed to implementing change. But we needed both the British Government's help to do so and a recommitment to meet the reasonable needs of the Island. We saw those needs as a realistic appraisal of the aid framework figure for the period 1997/98 - 1999/2000; and a relatively insubstantial but very important Transitional Aid package to absorb the increasing unemployment resulting from the budgetary measures that we were obliged to implement and the shake-out from the public sector as a result of our structural adjustment.

CHAPTER EIGHT

Maintaining a Balance for 1996 – and the First Race for the Governor's Cup

It was, of course, impossible to avoid St Helena intruding into our leave break in the summer of 1996. Indeed it was absolutely necessary that I had some consultation with both the political and aid sides of the Office. After all it was why I had addressed the current issues on the Island in my recent Despatch and detailed in the previous chapter. In any case and as part of the normal process, the FCO expected that I would call to give a first-hand account of developments. Not least as the South Atlantic & Antarctic Department had been irked by the press references, particularly in *The Daily Telegraph*, to the occupation of my office by Councillor Robertson's mob on 19th April as *"a riot"*, even though my reporting both telephonically and by later telegram had been much more measured and factual. The problem for the FCO, where questions had been asked of the department, was that a well-known and reputable journalist – Simon Winchester - had written the article that appeared in *The Daily Telegraph.*

The background to this was that the author of the 1985 book, *Outposts: Journeys to the Surviving Relics of the British Empire*, later republished as *The Sun Never Sets*, happened to have stepped ashore from the vessel *Akademik Boris Petrov* at Jamestown on 27th March. He called on me and said that he was updating his knowledge of the remaining colonies, although he volunteered that he had been refused permission to land at Tristan da Cunha – something to do with what he had written about Tristan or the Tristanians the last time he was that way! Perhaps I should have taken the hint!

However, I wanted to make sure that this time he had the facts about St Helena straight! He had earlier concluded that there was an *"...evident lack of caring, or prescience, or sympathetic understanding that too often seems to characterise Britain's dealings with her final Imperial fragments...*". But it was not as Simon Winchester had written, that a decision was taken in London in the early 1980s "*...taking the daily running of the island away from the Foreign Office*" – in spite of the hopes he and others professed that this might improve matters. It was, rather, the misinterpretation of the FCO's pre-occupation with the Falkland Islands following the Argentine invasion, admittedly coupled with a lack of focus on matters Saint Helenian – the island was not causing any problems on Foreign & Commonwealth Office desks. Further, the responsibility for Budgetary Aid – and hence the responsibility for certifying the (Colonial) Account – had been transferred to the Aid Wing of the FCO (the ODA) with effect from the 1972/73 financial year. Nevertheless, in this atmosphere of insouciance, it was indeed true to an extent that ODA officials seemed to have been able to set an agenda for the Territory, which Diplomatic Wing inertia seemed to have accepted quite happily.

We had passed an agreeable hour or two chatting in the study at Plantation House about St Helena 'today'. I felt, then, that I knew him, and he me. So, when he telephoned after being alerted to the incident on 19th April, I was happy to talk to him about it "*off the record*". He did later apologise for putting words in my mouth for *The Daily Telegraph* readers that I had certainly never said nor even thought at the time. But, it was a useful lesson, nonetheless: there was no real interest in administering the colonies. It was an FCO policy *cul-de-sac*; and the main concern that my colleagues back in the Foreign Office had had was that no one should rock the boat and cause difficult questions to be asked of them from on high. I had been mildly chastised for not consulting enough – I took it to mean with legislators locally, but it was only much later, on the cusp of retirement, that I realised that the departmental head had meant my (lack of) consultation with his department. Although the desk officer was keen and had kept himself well informed, the inertia from above was dispiriting and draining of initiative. I had some long and often pointless discussions with so-called colleagues in the Office settling virtually nothing at all. The underlying coda being that I shouldn't allow matters in St Helena to become headlines in the UK.

I called on Baroness Chalker once more but was unable to elicit even the vaguest suggestion that a more generous approach to St Helena's problems might result from the next round of aid discussions. Nevertheless, she still seemed disposed to allow us to manage the Shipping Schedule better by keeping the *RMS* in the South Atlantic longer and reducing the calls in the UK. This was almost the opposite of what my exchanges with the Crown Agents acting in the capacity of managers of the St Helena Line had produced. I felt that officials in South London believed that I was an obstruction to their aim to keep the service profitable. On my Government's behalf I sought the best possible service for St Helena and Ascension Island, which I recognised was incompatible with the Crown Agent's financial imperatives. But I was confident that the undertaking by the ODA to allow virement between one head of expenditure and another under the total aid package gave us the incentive to make the service better and the means with which to pay a bit more for it.

I also called on Sir Malcolm Rifkind, Secretary of State for Foreign & Commonwealth Affairs, to whom I had officially written my word for his ear (Chapter Seven). He didn't seem particularly well briefed on the minutiae of my Despatch, but responded to my arguments for amending nationality legislation, which had deprived Saints of their full rights to British citizenship and was yet another brake on economic development. "*We must do something about it,*" he had said. However, before the Conservative Government could consider getting around to doing anything concrete about it, had they even intended to do so, the Party was defeated at the general election in May the following year, 1997.

All this allowed little time to truly enjoy a relaxing holiday but, nevertheless, I returned to my desk in the Castle with promises that I took to mean that those in London would do better. On the Island I wanted to give as much support as I could to the Development Agency to grow a private sector. In St Helena this was a difficult enough task: as I had reported at length to the FCO on many occasions. St Helena was nothing if not something of a twentieth century anomaly, an uneconomic entity, as I had pointed out to the Foreign Secretary in my Despatch of 14th June. It was remote and lacked easy access; there were no deposits of exploitable minerals or hydro-carbons; 75% of the land area was classified as barren and rainfall was erratic and unreliable; inshore fishing resources were limited; and there was a only a small private sector accounting for less than 40% of those in employment. There was a small amount of direct production in agriculture and fisheries, but the Island was far from self-sufficient and about £1¾m worth of food was imported annually. On the positive side, offshore employment and crewing the *St Helena* provided well over 1,000 jobs engaging up to 30% of the working age population, resulting in remittances into the local economy of over £1 million a year.

I had a simple message in my annual review of 1996: although the year had been dominated once again by the aid relationship negotiations had ended successfully with an agreed settlement. I also pointed out that the difficulties in April had to some extent been compensated for by helpful advice from the Commonwealth Parliamentary Association, although at the year's end it had been followed up by neither a Report, nor much increased understanding on the part of our Legislative Councillors.

It seemed to my management team and me that officials in London were continually attempting to micro-manage St Helena's economy with little regard to the context. This placed often impossible strictures upon its economic management. We, as officials within Government had no problems with accountability, but St Helena did have a problem with the ever-decreasing assistance in real terms when there was no other source of financial support. Hardly surprisingly this elicited no response from London, but given the team's performance in 1995, it should have informed the ODA indirectly that we would again be ready to robustly argue the case for what we saw as St Helena's reasonable needs.

Our core policy - the public sector reform programme - was aimed at achieving a massive restructuring of the economy: shrinking the public sector, which indisputably occupied 'the commanding heights of the economy'. This entailed the transfer of assets and functions into the private sector and creating small scale business. Despite a few 'good news stories', the policy was meeting strong resistance. This was noticeably the case with the Island's politicians, who had ostensibly approved the policy and signed up for it and the 'Vision for St Helena'. Government, i.e. officials and politicians together, had agreed with the ODA's Budgetary Aid Mission in late 1995 that we would implement the restructuring as a condition of the aid package. We knew that we would be tested on the Government's commitment when the next aid mission visited to assess progress and the future structure of aid. Preparation for the 1996 Aid Mission would inevitably occupy a significant amount of our time.

In the meantime, the customary round of official engagements continued. We paid a further visit to Ascension Island when we were able to spend the night with the Huxleys at the Residency on Green Mountain. Later in the year we lunched aboard the German frigate *Schleswig Holstein*; had drinks on *MV Explorer*; and were helicoptered out to lunch on board *HMS Endurance*. This was the polar exploration vessel that supported the British Antarctic Survey in Antarctica and carried out hydrographic surveys. It had been the British Government's withdrawal of the former *Endurance* that had led the Argentines to believe HMG's commitment to the Falkland Islands had weakened and prompted the invasion of the British Dependency in 1982.

As the time approached we learnt that the ODA intended that their visit, to take place towards the end of the year, should take a slightly different form. It was to be an 'Aid Planning Mission (APM)'. St Helena was apparently being rewarded: perhaps we were no longer third class! As part of the conditionality of the 1995 aid settlement we had agreed that the St Helena Government would conduct a thorough strategic economic review and produce a Country Policy Plan – an ODA term for a framework into which future economic policies could be integrated. We were to be judged by the level of agreement that the ODA had with our plan. Full marks would mean success, and that we would be negotiating an aid package to cover a three-year period. Less than that and any aid package would be geared to tighter control from London and an agreement to cover only the next financial year.

A core of senior officials co-ordinated the work of the Government Economist and the departments to enable Matt Young, the Financial Secretary, to pull together all the strands in a financial review to submit to the Aid Planning

Mission. This was to form the basis of the Government's bid for its three-year package of financial assistance - comprising budgetary support; technical co-operation spending (i.e. the expenditure on salaries etc for the Chief Secretary, Financial Secretary, Attorney General and other ex-patriates); development project funding; and the shipping subsidy. The senior management team and other officials worked very hard to project a positive view of St Helena to counter the apparent lack of understanding in London of the Island's context and its unique economic situation, and the lack of recognition of the Administration's commitment to the programme of structural adjustment upon which the St Helena Government had embarked.

It was an uphill struggle with St Helena's politicians in their aid-dependent cocoon, who had little grasp of the political and economic realities of government. They floundered and flatly refused even to try to come to terms with the demands of a new age. They held to the belief that it was the Government's rôle to run the economy; and that it was the British Government's responsibility to make up any shortfall in the St Helena Government's income.

Nevertheless, we had prepared well and were ready to receive the Aid Planning Mission, which was to visit the Island from 6th – 13th November. The seriousness with which the ODA were seeking a fresh start was underlined for us by the fact that Mike Bawden, an experienced former colonial official, had been appointed to lead the Aid team rather than the senior ODA official. However, even while the team were at sea en route to the Island I received intelligence from the *RMS St Helena* (from what the newspapers call a very reliable source) of the lines upon which the BAM approach was evolving. It was not good news for the Island. A plan had been cooked up in London that would, in effect, ignore any case that we made: a non-negotiable sum was to be put on the table on the Mission's arrival. The visitors would thus occupy the high ground in our exchanges and there would be no meaningful negotiation. It was, of course, quite reasonable for the ODA's bean counters to suggest a sum with which they might feel comfortable. Indeed, it would have been odd if the APM did not have a 'ball park' figure as guidance. But, this information, which retrospect confirmed as accurate, implied that the ODA would 'play hard ball' in the belief that they could face down we whom they saw as antagonistic to the aid relationship. I realised that it was going to be very important to get off on the right foot with the visiting team as soon as they hit the quayside.

So, in keeping with the aim of presenting a strong case and without divulging to anyone that I might have been forewarned, we - the senior management team - devised a strategy to set the scene and open the dialogue on our terms rather than be put in the disadvantageous position of having to respond to the visitors' opening gambit. I called together the small group of senior officials that had been steering the process of structural reform and preparing the Country Policy Plan. We clearly needed to be on the front foot from the moment the APM arrived and to gain the high ground for St Helena. Otherwise we would be in the position of supplicant rather than partner: a rôle the ODA seemed obviously to prefer for the St Helena side. I suggested that we scrap the initial meetings planned for the first day's programme and give a presentation, with flip charts etc, to the mission members at Plantation House, a little less formal - with comfortable chairs, coffee and biscuits etc. - than locating the discussions as originally planned in the Council Chamber. Not quite neutral territory, but sufficiently removed from Government Offices to have an impact of its own. I would make an introductory statement, John Perrott would make a presentation on public sector reform, and other key figures in the senior management team would speak on finance, the economy, Country Policy Plan, staffing and the labour market etc. We would then invite the APM to conduct its mission. In this way we had our say, before they could present theirs. Tactically this worked, as neither the leader nor any member of his team made any substantive response; and we were led to believe that they might have gone away to regroup and rethink!

Although I received The ODA's head of department and the mission leader, Mike Bawden, at a brief courtesy call at the Castle immediately after their disembarkation, we did indeed seize the initiative. We had prepared well, even having a full-scale rehearsal of the presentation the afternoon before the visitors arrived to iron out any potential glitches.

The discussions between Government officials at all levels and with the Councillors were held in a positive and friendly atmosphere. Although there remained several points of difference between the two sides there was a great deal of common ground and openness on both sides. The visitors were steered towards a belief that St Helena's politicians would adhere to the programme that we had laid out; and acknowledged that within the constraints of the small island economy in which it was placed that a considerable amount had already been achieved or was in the process of being achieved.

This was, in all respects, a very sympathetically managed Aid review and found much common ground upon which the relationship might have been built. However, the politicians were not entirely convinced. Their political commitment to more rigorous financial control and to public sector reform were questionable to say the least, whatever officials might have believed, or hoped.

The St Helena Government's submission postulated a financial commitment of some £30 million from the British Government over the three year period 1997/98 – 1999/2000, of which £13·8m was the sum needed for budgetary support. The outcome on 12th November was an offer of £26m over the three years of the Country Policy Plan. This was accompanied by a proposed change in the ODA policy to the provisions for capital expenditure for repairs and renewals, allowing the Government to draw down on previously earmarked Reserves. This was a welcome attempt to strike a balance between increasing Budgetary Aid and enabling significant elements of the St Helena Government's proposals to be implemented as our plans predicated, albeit at a longer term domestic expense. Much of this compromise was the direct result of very diligent negotiation by Mike Bawden. For the St Helena Government the ODA offer was disappointing in absolute terms, but it represented a significant shift by the visitors from their opening position and recognised the strength of our case. Privately, Mike Bawden later confided to me that neither he nor his fellow team members had experienced such a well-prepared Government and well argued case. He had, he confided, never seen such a professional presentation of a country's case for Aid and that it had convinced him to move away from any preconceived financial plan for St Helena; and, moreover – and more importantly - to persuade his colleagues to abandon their set ODA brief. Perhaps a matter of it all having been in the preparation and the detail? I was more than thankful for the early intelligence that I had received from the *RMS*.

The result would face us with significant challenges in identifying additional savings and opportunities for increased revenues; and the immediately evident downside was that the 1997 Budget would inevitably be deflationary. But, even though reluctantly and after serious persuasion, the elected members accepted the package; and we had a financial framework set for the following three years.

Arriving with the APM on 6th November had been two FCO officials: the Assistant Head of South Atlantic & Antarctic Department; and one of the FCO's Legal Advisers. We accommodated both at Plantation House and the SAAD Assistant had attended our presentation to the APM and tracked the ODA visitors for much of the time that he was with us. He was a decidedly odd character and his behaviour as a guest at Plantation House was even odder. However, during our first opportunity for a discussion of St Helena/FCO issues well after the presentation and not long before he departed St Helena he handed me the CVs of the three Diplomatic Service candidates for the vacancy that would occur when John Perrott came to the end of his appointment in March 1998. I studied them them carefully and conveyed my views on the suitability of the candidates to the FCO Personnel Department, as I was asked, in the diplomatic bag leaving on the *RMS* with our visitors.

However, without discussion or forewarning of any kind, while in transit at Ascension Island he faxed a copy of a letter that he had written to London *"agreeing with the ODA"* (whose departmental Head had failed to raise the subject with me) that the Chief Secretary post should be filled by a recruitment process conducted by the ODA. It was true that the Chief Secretary's salary and allowances had been paid from ODA funds – a throw back to Colonial Office days – but since the demise of the Colonial Service the position as the Governor's deputy had been filled, quite naturally, by the Diplomatic Service. The ODA's man had, it seemed, put the time at sea en route for Ascension to good use! My telephonic intervention with my erstwhile Diplomatic Service colleague before he departed Ascension Island for Brize Norton was to no avail – <u>he</u> had made the recommendation to the FCO and that was that. Perhaps it was a case of the Aid Wing seeking a score of ODA 1, St Helena 1, rather than the score being 0 – 1?

To cut a long story short, I was too late and my arguments for reinstating the *status quo ante* were only received in London after the decision had been agreed. The only concession offered was that the ODA recruitment process would be timed so that I could participate in the interviews when I was next on UK leave in the following May. The ODA would have an officer responsible to that Department, and not to the FCO, able to insidiously introduce issues on their behalf and breaking the direct chain of FCO command.

*   *   *

We left St Helena on the *RMS* ourselves before all the elements of the above saga could be played out: the first race for the Governor's Cup was due to be staged.

The Start at Cape Town's Table Bay was scheduled for 8th December and the *RMS* arrived at Duncan Dock promptly at 6 a.m. that morning. The passengers were disembarked and the crew then set about preparing the *St Helena* for the vessel's part in the proceedings. Tables and chairs were set out on the sundeck and everything was polished, tickety-boo and to David Roberts' satisfaction. I had invited the South African President, Nelson Mandela, to be aboard and start the Race. He had graciously declined but delegated fellow Robben Island prisoner and Sports Minister, Steve Tshwete, to represent him. Dressed in full uniform, with Sandi, she and I, together with Capt Roberts, greeted the Minister and the hundred guests we had invited on board at noon for lunch and the Start of the first Race for the Governor's Cup.

The Race was designed from the outset to cater for all classes of yacht, from the out-and-out racing yacht, mono and multi-hulls, to the more sedate cruising boat with family embarked. As I remarked at the Start of the inaugural event, we hoped that the race would "*encourage a new generation of travellers*" to St Helena. The island needed to develop its niche in the tourist market. The exposure that the media coverage of an international event would give to St Helena as a viable tourist destination, and of the ship and its service to the island were, we considered, incalculable.

The *RMS St Helena,* which was to be the Start Boat for the Race, slowly edged out of the Dock into Table Bay. There was time for drinks, a few speeches and a buffet lunch for the assembled guests before the *RMS* was manoeuvred into position for the start of the Race at 3p.m.. Steve Tshwete came to the bridge and sounded the ship's horn and the Race was started. Then, after following the fleet up the channel between Robben Island and the coast for a while, the *RMS* returned to Duncan Dock, discharged its day-trippers, and resumed its normal schedule of loading cargo, minor maintenance and refuelling for the return journey. That journey, however, was to prove rather different to the normal voyages as the *RMS* was also to fulfil the rôle of Race Guard Ship, keeping tabs, through regular scheduled radio contact, with the Race fleet. We also carried a large contingent of Race officials and families and friends of the participating crews.

Before we left Cape Town, however, I had two items of business. The world famous Archbishop of Cape Town, Desmond Tutu, had retired and there was a new incumbent whom John Ruston, the Anglican Bishop of St Helena, had encouraged me to invite to the Island on a pastoral visit – St Helena lay within the archbishopric of Cape Town. I called at Bishop's Court in the eponymous leafy south Cape Town suburb, the official residence of the Most Reverend Njongonkulu Ndungane the recently installed Archbishop. A humorous man, reminiscent of Archbishop Tutu, greeted me and bade me *"Take a pew."* I duly issued the invitation to visit St Helena and we chatted for what seemed like ages and, when I said that I ought to leave as he must be busy, he replied, *"Oh no! Everyone knows that clergymen only work on Sundays."*

From the quiet, wealthy suburb with its peaceful views of Table Mountain I hurried to the hustle of the fish-docks to talk to Premier Fishing, the company which then held the Tristan fishing contract. Brendan Dalley, the Administrator of Tristan da Cunha, had alerted me that bids would soon be invited for the contract that had been held for many years by the Cape Town based company; and not having met me, the company now wished to put in a good word for themselves as it would be a gubernatorial responsibility to implement a new contract.

The Race had already attracted the attention of the media and during earlier stopovers in Cape Town I had given interviews to Talk Radio 702. On this occasion *The Cape Times* and Brendan Boyle of Reuters sought interviews, which despite my experience with Simon Winchester and his *Daily Telegraph* article I was happy to give, to promote both the Race and tourism for St Helena and Tristan da Cunha.

Sandi and I lunched with David Roberts at the Royal Cape Yacht Club, almost hidden away at the far eastern end of Duncan Dock, as guests of the Club before the *RMS* sailed that afternoon. The RCYC Commodore, Paul Maré and his crew partner, Lindsay Birch, were racing their yacht *Maji Moto II* on its way to St Helena. Their wives, Adéle and Kate, were sharing a cabin and travelling with the officials and other families of yacht crew members to be in St Helena for their arrival. Adéle and Kate had made sure that they wouldn't get thirsty on the voyage by packing their cabin with cases of wine! These two families became firm friends as our visits to Cape Town continued over the following years. Also among the RCYC members travelling to St Helena was Nina MacLennan, Canadian by nationality but, who had been married to a keen South African sailor, and who would later play an important part in launching recreational sailing in St Helena.

It was business as normal once we returned to St Helena, with its round of ExCo and other meetings. But something was quite different in Jamestown in that week leading up to Christmas. The South African visitors, swelling in number as succeeding yachts arrived at the Finish Line, created a festive atmosphere and filled the shops, pubs and eating-places in a way not seen for years, so we were told. So, from such relatively small beginnings was the thought planted in Saint Helenian minds that perhaps tourism might be a good idea, after all. Our Plantation House Christmas Party became a Cocktails and Carols event supported by the sound equipment from the Radio Station. But, in the background Sandi had a major worry – organising the function that we had planned for the 100 South African visitors and those on the Island involved in local arrangements for the Race: the Governor's Cup Ball.

Not only did Patrick, the Plantation House Comptroller, have to beg and borrow a marquee, tables and chairs from the local school, and other equipment; our chef had upped and gone to the Falkland Islands; and the Agriculture & Forestry Department was refusing to allow the importation of all the salad stuffs, fruit and vegetables that Sandi had procured in Cape Town. There was no phytosanitary certificate. The Head of the Agriculture & Fisheries Department (a UK-based expatriate on ODA contract terms) threatened to dump the whole shipment into the harbour if one was not produced – 'just obeying the rules', of course! Nevertheless, the *RMS* came to our rescue and the Purser's office, which had the right contacts in Cape Town, ensured that we had the certificate faxed to St Helena in time to prevent the wanton destruction of the fresh produce that could not have been purchased on the Island.

It was all very well having saved the fresh produce, Sandi had purchased half a dozen frozen turkeys and, of course, there were other dishes that needed to be cooked; and there was no chef and no immediate way out. However, the alternate chef on the *RMS* was on leave and on St Helena. But, when asked he declined to take on the job. Sandi used all her powers of persuasion, appealing to his pride in St Helena before he, somewhat grudgingly, took on the work. Nevertheless, once he got stuck into the job, he excelled; and the spread laid out on the dining room table was simply stupendous and it's equal probably never before having been seen at Plantation House.

The meal was a success and, as the dancing started after dinner, Sandi was able to agree with Patrick that they had together succeeded in pulling off a fantastic coup – a triumphant accomplishment! And I think that everyone concerned would have agreed that it was a major success, giving that inaugural Race for the Governor's Cup a tremendous launch. The lesson was also learnt, however, that it was a pretty well unrepeatable achievement. That the next morning's routine Christmas Eve visits to the hospital and Government Homes with the Christmas cakes was an anti-climax was perhaps an understatement! Although that evening's presentation of the trophy's and prizes from the steps of the Supreme Court to the yachtsmen renewed the casual festive air, that had been so evident since the 'yachties' had first arrived on 15th December with the *RMS*.

Part of the attraction of the involvement of the *RMS* in the Race was the ability it had to return to Cape Town with a lot of the participating yachts as deck cargo. In a race, which left the participants with a return leg against the prevailing wind and currents, it was a significant time saver – as a later anecdote will illustrate.

CHAPTER NINE

1997: A Year of Change

We departed St Helena for our second visit to Tristan da Cunha on 30th December 1996, but not before what I later saw was a seminal moment in getting sailing started in St Helena. The Governor's Cup yachties had arranged a light-hearted race, which although being billed as a round-the-island race, because of the prevailing winds was a course of a few miles along the coast west of Jamestown and back. The genius of the idea was, however, that they invited whomsoever wished to join the crews to come along. It attracted the support of lots of young people: the joy of whom the aforementioned Nina MacLennan had later picked up on. During the return voyage to Cape Town on the *RMS* she pledged £1,000 were I able to get more funding together to purchase a couple of dinghies to start training young sailors in St Helena. Over-nighting in Cape Town on 4th January allowed us to be lunched at RCYC where I was invited to become an honorary member – for as long as the Governor's Cup remained in the trophy cabinet and the Race continued to be run under the auspices of the RCYC. This provided the ideal opportunity to make my first enquiries about dinghies for a sail-training project on St Helena.

The *RMS*, now with a change of command and Martin Smith at the helm, arrived off Edinburgh-of-the-Seven-Seas in the early hours of 10th January. Patrick had accompanied us once more and our programme followed much the same pattern as it had in 1996. However, since that visit the fisheries patrol vessel that had been acquired with assistance from UK Aid funds was operational. The vessel was similar to the medium sized RNLI lifeboats around Britain's shores. The Tristan Island Council had identified the requirement for a fully seaworthy vessel that could cover the area around the three major islands of the Tristan group – the blind side of Tristan da Cunha itself, and around the coasts of Nightingale and Inaccessible Islands. Gough Island, some 200 miles south of Edinburgh, was too far away to patrol. The

Administrator, Brendan Dalley, was a fisheries expert himself. When we discussed the capabilities of, and use to which, the vessel was being put, a brief demonstration seemed the best solution.

To this end Patrick and I with Jimmy Glass, Brendan Dalley and several Tristanians as supernumerary crew departed Calshot Harbour to visit Nightingale Island, about 30 miles distant. Tristanians had traditionally maintained a number of small huts on Nightingale in which they stayed on expeditions when they went to extract the oil from Shearwaters: a custom similar to the inhabitants of the Furneaux Group of Islands off Tasmania. It was an exhilarating dash across the open sea in the powerful patrol vessel before we anchored and a party went ashore in the RIB that was carried onboard. As we approached the rocky shore a line of moulting rockhopper penguins awaited us, like a row of nightclub bouncers dressed in dinner jackets. They separated to let us through and we tramped up to the plateau on the top of the island, which was the breeding ground for the yellow nosed albatrosses. The albatross nest on a pot-shaped mud pile. They fly far out to sea for food - squid, fish and krill. Their chicks - the size of a turkey – are left alone on the muddy tower. On their return the wind whistles through the wing feathers of these majestic adult birds like a jet turbine heralding their arrival as they glide in to land

On the lower slopes of the island there are hundreds of holes in the ground, which one has to be careful to avoid as twisting or breaking an ankle in that remote location could be a problem. The holes are the nesting burrows of Shearwaters, who spend most of their day out at sea only coming back to roost at night.

We returned to our boat as the *RMS* was circumnavigating the island for the benefit of the passengers onboard before heading back to Cape Town. The fisheries patrol vessel headed out to meet the *RMS*, then in a display of machismo the coxswain ramped up the power. We did a pass down the side of the *St Helena* fore to aft, with most of us crammed in the aft cockpit waving and hanging on as best we could. The boat was then taken around the lee side of the *RMS* as she slowed to a halt. The boat was manoeuvred alongside so that we could board via the Jacobs ladder slung over the ship's side. It was a most exhilarating day, which was capped when looking into the sun and seeing the cobbled effect created by the thousands of shearwaters sitting on the surface of the sea

*　　　　　*　　　　　*

Two days out from Tristan da Cunha the radio operator who, from the *RMS* as guard ship to the Race fleet, had acted as the daily contact between the yachts sailing to St Helena during the Governor's Cup Race, picked up a call from one of the boats sailing home to Cape Town. The yacht had run out of fuel, its food and water were running low and the man and wife crew had run out of cigarettes! After establishing their position, Capt Smith made a rendezvous with them for later that evening when the ship would transfer some stores sufficient to get them home. A jerry-can of diesel would allow them to make some headway against a troublesome headwind. The problem with sailing the reverse course to the direct track from Cape Town to St Helena was that the South-east Trade Winds and the Benguela Current flowed north-westwards from the Cape and were virtually impossible to sail against. This was why the East Indiamen of the East India Company had sailed almost to Brazil before, at around the latitude of 30° South, they had turned east to sail with the current and friendlier winds to round the Cape of Good Hope on their way to India and the East Indies.

The rendezvous was made in the dark and the searchlight from the *RMS* picked out the sail of the yacht wallowing in the Atlantic swells. A line was shot to the waiting yacht and a package was tied together and fixed to a life jacket and swung over the side as the *RMS* came alongside. Shouted greetings were lost in the wind, but we watched the light on the life jacket dipping and rising until the whole package was safely retrieved and landed aboard the yacht. Sandi and I hurried to the radio room to speak to the two lonely sailors, who, of course, we had met during their time on St Helena. Our conversation was broken off after they had promised to buy beers for everyone when they returned to Cape Town. That, however, took longer than they had estimated, or hoped, as we only briefly caught sight of them tiredly making for Duncan Dock half an hour after the *RMS* had set course for St Helena after our South African call some four days later on the afternoon of 18th January, 21 days after they had left St Helena's James Bay.

On our earlier arrival at Cape Town we had been invited by Paul and Adéle Maré to spend the weekend at Langebaan, on the coast north of Cape Town in the holiday home they shared with the Kate and Lindsay Birch overlooking the lagoon. It was a super, relaxing, break away from all to do with St Helena, but we had to return in mid afternoon the next day as the British High Commissioner had arranged a post-Yacht Race Reception. Some of the sponsors of the Race had additional prizes to distribute, which they wanted me to present. Maeve Fort, the High Commissioner, had readily fallen in with the idea as it had come with the endorsement of the British company, Massey Ferguson, who had been the sponsor of the winning yacht.

Later, Sandi learnt that her mother was very ill and she returned once more to England to be at her side. The Consulate General arranged the ticketing and she left Cape Town on 20th January. The benefits of a relaxing weekend by the blue lagoon were forgotten when she realised that her ticket was on the *RMS* as it pulled away from Duncan Dock. Kate Birch fortunately came to the rescue; and it was something of a relief to be on the *RMS* once more bound for St Helena, albeit on my own.

At sea we encountered *HM Bark Endeavour,* said by the director of the Australian National Maritime Museum to be *"the most authentic replica ship in existence".* The modern day *Endeavour* was under the command of a 'tall ships' acquaintance of Capt Martin Smith, Chris Blake, and en route to a call at St Helena from 26 - 28th January. The eighteenth century bark *Endeavour* had been a three masted 550 ton converted coal carrier commanded by Lt James Cook of His Majesty King George III's Royal Navy. Capt Cook, as he became known, sailed to the South Seas, discovering New Zealand and charted the coasts of the North and South Islands. He also charted the east coast of Australia from Point Hicks in the south (Victoria) to Cape York in today's Queensland. Cook's voyage was one of the epic journeys of discovery. It was the first to fix longitudinal positions with any degree of accuracy and, thus, accurately chart a substantial part of the Australian coastline; and to fix the continent in relation to other known waters, e.g. in the East Indies, which he also visited during the course of his voyage.

The original *Endeavour* called at St Helena in May 1771 and the log reads:

> "*Wednesday 1st. Winds SE. Fresh trade and pleasant weather. At 6 in the AM Saw the Island of St Helena bearing West distant about 8 or 9 Leagues. At Noon anchored in the Road before St James Fort in 24 fathom water. Found riding here His Majesty's ship Portland, Sloop Swallow and 12 sail of Indiamen...*"

Cook departed for home on the following Sunday in company with *HMS Portland* and the laden East India Company merchantmen. He returned briefly to the island again in command of the ships *Resolution* and *Adventure* in 1775 after his voyage to search for a north-west passage to the Indies.

Cook's voyage to Australia and his landing at Botany Bay are seminal events in Australian history, and the link that the 20th Century *HM Bark Endeavour* forms in the Anglo-Australian relationship is real and enduring. The British Government had felt it right to make a contribution to the celebrations in Australia and New Zealand of the bi-centenary of Captain Cook's historic voyage and commissioned the National Maritime Museum at Greenwich to produce two models of *Endeavour*. The models were 5' 9" in height, and 6' 6" in length. The New Zealand model was presented in 1969. The anniversary of the landing in Australia's Botany Bay fell on 29th April 1970; and the Australian Government decided that the presentation of their model should take place at the National Library at Canberra and that The Queen should unveil it during Her Majesty's visit to Australia that year.

In 1987 the trustees of the Australian National Maritime Museum proposed that a full-scale floating museum replica of *Endeavour* should be built, and the Bond Corporation offered to take on the project as a bicentennial gift to the people of Australia. Work began in January 1988 and the keel was laid in October of that year. Financial problems plagued the project and the sponsors had to withdraw, and eventually a charitable trust was set up to complete it. The replica *Endeavour* was launched in December 1993 and, after gaining operational experience in Australian waters, sailed from Freemantle on 16th October 1996 bound for James Cook's home port of Whitby in north-east England, via Plymouth.

During the short time that we passed *Endeavour*, then under full sail on the South-east Trade Wind, I took a number of photographs, copies of which Martin Smith later passed on to Chris Blake who had them uploaded to the web site that the Endeavour Trust was maintaining to follow the voyage from Freemantle. On 27th January, at Jamestown, Chris Blake invited us aboard to tour the ship; and marvel at the lack of room that Capt Cook and his crew would have had on their eighteenth century journeys of discovery. *Endeavour* departed St Helena the next evening, arriving back in England in time for Easter.

*   *   *

There had been an element of drama during my absence in Tristan da Cunha and South Africa. During the period that Government closed over the Christmas and New Year break one of the Councillors – Eric George – whose grasp of hand I once described as being stronger than his grasp of a situation - had sought a judicial review of the Aid Agreement and the utilisation of the Reserves in partial funding of the period between 1997 and 2000 to which he had himself given his approval in November. However, he had made his application to the Chief Justice, Geoffrey Martin, who had no difficulty in refusing leave because the order was sought over a matter within the jurisdiction of the English Courts, not those of St Helena.

If that was the bad, it was only to get worse! Towards the end of January the Councillor who was Chair of the Employment and Social Services Committee resigned her seat in the Legislative Council leaving the Social Services seat in ExCo vacant. The Constitution provided that the Chairman should be elected by the membership of LegCo (MLCs). This led the self-proclaimed hero of 19th April 1996 to scent an opportunity to take over the Department; and he duly got the support of his fellow MLCs and was nominated to fill the position. However, I was not bound to accept the nomination, and did not do so on the grounds that it was not in the public interest so to do. Perhaps quite understandably that led to a period of political tension.

I invited another member of the Legislative Council, a mature and experienced lady who had at one time held the self-same Chair, to accept the appointment. Her acceptance of the position led to the resignation of another MLC, also an ExCo member in his position as Chair of the Public Works Committee, Bill Drabble, on the grounds that he could not accept her appointment: not that it was in his gift, or otherwise, to accept or decline the appointment of another member of the Executive Council. He then walked out of the ExCo meeting. Later, and after the meeting, Eric George announced that he too had resigned. But his resignation was for no given or apparent reason. He possibly felt up-staged by his colleague and sought to occupy an overt position of opposition in the run-up to an election due towards the end of the year. Being opposed to the Governor, the Castle and the Administration would, perversely, garner him votes and ensure his return to Government as a member of ExCo. It could only happen in St Helena, surely!

After consulting the Speaker I called a Sitting of LegCo to seek nominations for the vacated Council Committee Chairs. But the boys had smelt blood and Cllr Drabble successfully sabotaged the nomination process. Whereupon, a Motion calling for an early General Election was proposed and carried. The rebels were positively glowing with pride at upsetting the political process and business of Government. However, the successful Motion had provided me with the opportunity to choose the day for the election with more than customary notice before my planned departure for Ascension and London. I shouldn't have been surprised that this led to stories of constitutional crisis appearing in the UK press fed, certainly by Bill Drabble for one, who had links with one particularly disagreeable MP at Westminster.

Sandi finally arrived back at St Helena on 6th March 1997 only to learn, once she was safely back at Plantation House, that her mother had died the day previously: a devastating blow. She had thought her mother's condition had stabilised and had made the decision to return in the light of there having been very little change since she had returned to

England in January. Her 'homecoming' was thus somewhat muted.

*   *   *

Meanwhile strides, however amateur they might have been, were being made to turn foreign visiting numbers into a tourism industry. The development authority (SHDA) had set up a Tourist Office from within its own budget. The Yacht Race, contrary to Island opinion beforehand, had been a success, bringing much needed extra money into the local economy. To listen to some, it would have been possible to believe that MLCs and the public generally had welcomed the idea with open arms, that the idea was home grown and the Castle had not been involved at all! But, if it had not been for the small group of dedicated public servants in the Administration we would never got official traction for it. It was certainly an effort in which a far-sighted, or perhaps loyal, few had contributed, despite many sceptics amongst them!

As part of the effort to increase tourism our discussions with St Helena Line (SHL) about the Shipping Schedule were continuing. But it was heavy weather given on the one hand Peter Motion's focus on, and preference for, the long distance cruise market, and on the other hand the Island's need to attract increased tourism, most obviously from and through southern Africa. It boiled down to a political decision. Having the ship travelling between Cardiff and Cape Town, via Ascension and St Helena, kept passenger and freight income buoyant for SHL: but plying between Cape Town, the Island and Ascension, increased access and had a greater economic impact on the Island. The solution seemed relatively simple: if necessary the shipping subsidy should increase and other elements in the aid package adjusted as a consequence. That was the best course for the Island. It was not a view popular in London, but as the frequency of calls in the UK reduced over the following years, and indeed fell to just one a year in time, I think the force of our arguments did prevail in the end. The ODA really had little other choice in the light of their fine words to the effect that the management of the aid package was the responsibility of the St Helena Government!

MLCs were still not happy about 'Shipping' being a matter reserved to the Governor. However, that didn't stop them or the public voicing the opinion that the Governor should "*do something about it*" when the occasion to intervene rose. One such occasion was the sad death of Carla Stroud, a 15 year old who had suddenly fallen inexplicably ill on 9th or 10th July. None of the three doctors resident on the Island could diagnose the cause and had recommended, as was frequently necessary, that she be evacuated on the *RMS* for treatment in the United Kingdom where the Health Department had an arrangement with an English hospital to take Saint Helenian patients who needed more advanced treatment than could be given on the Island. By good fortune the *RMS* was in port and the girl, accompanied by her mother and grandmother left on the ship the next day for Ascension.

But before they could reach Ascension and the RAF Airbridge to England, the patient died at sea, midway between the two Islands. The news quickly filtered back to St Helena, where one of the newly elected MLCs set about arranging a demonstration to 'make the Governor' turn the ship around and return with the body to St Helena for burial. I had a quick round of consultations, including with the *St Helena* and Curnow Shipping in Cornwall, to discuss the pros and cons of such a course. My inclination was not to bring the *RMS* back to the Island, distressing as that might have been for those concerned. That opinion was endorsed by those involved with the ship with whom I discussed the situation. There was a febrile mood in Jamestown, and I was very conscious of the easy way the situation had got out of hand on the 19th April the previous year. Sandi and I then went into town to see the child's grandfather, Eric Thomas, so that I could explain the circumstances to him. He immediately agreed that the ship couldn't be turned round and his friend, good old Cllr Eric George (for once), then went out to 'the street' and told them that Eric and Molly Thomas didn't want the *RMS* to return and that they should all go home – which they did!

The considerable downside to all this was that on that voyage the *RMS* was on its way back to Cardiff. This meant that the mother and grandmother had to spend five weeks on Ascension until the ship could return to St Helena with them and the body of the young girl, which had been stored in a freezer-container. Their return was a very emotional occasion. A funeral was held within the sight of the ocean at St James' church in Jamestown on 21st August immediately after the *RMS* arrived. Following which, the cortege accompanied by pupils and staff of the Prince Andrew School where she had studied, repaired to the cathedral where she was interred in the graveyard.

Meanwhile, MLCs nevertheless seemed to have high hopes that the Commonwealth Parliamentary Association visitors the previous year, Messrs Buffet and Potter, would recommend changes to the constitutional arrangements for St Helena and that the Reserved Power of Shipping would be swept away along with all the other niggles that they had about the way in which the Constitution of 1988 worked (or as they may have put it, impeded their freedom of action). However, when it did finally emerge, the report made a series of proposals for constitutional change, which failed to recognise the dependent financial relationship that St Helena had with the United Kingdom.

But the report hadn't surfaced as I set the date for the General Election for 9th July and we prepared to take a short break in the UK in the interim. However, having in their view pushed me into declaring that there would be an election and perhaps with the feeling that they now wielded some power over the Governor some of the outgoing members of the Legislative Council embarked on feeding the British press with fictitious tales of a lack of democracy, an autocratic Governor and other tendentious stories. Almost perversely we had felt a sense of oneness with the Island on 11th April, when we had been invited on board the sumptuous luxury liner *MV Crystal Symphony* with its plush restaurants, ballroom and white grand pianos. The opulence, compared with the conditions in which Saints lived was too much, and Sandi and I had declined the invitation to stay on for lunch on board. Then a completely unconnected arson attack on a police vehicle in Longwood that weekend was twisted in its relay by those trouble makers so that even the most reputable of British newspapers carried stories of a Governor fleeing an island in the throes of a constitutional crisis, burning and in revolt against him. We were, indeed, at sea en route for Ascension Island, and it took a number of telephone calls from the Residency to assuage official jitters in the FCO

– although one journalist who did manage to get through (and whom I had met when she was writing complementary tourism related words about St Helena) reported my calm and composed response to her question headlined *"Crisis. What crisis?"*

Back on St Helena, however, the damage that such distorted publicity was having on the Island's image as a peaceful and welcoming destination for tourism and a stable and attractive prospect for inward investment had been recognised. The Executive Council issued a statement on 17th April to clarify the situation, deploring the inaccuracies in articles in the British and other Press about riots and, *inter alia*, the suggestion that the Governor was fleeing from an island in crisis and turmoil. The supportive hand of my colleague, John Perrott as Acting Governor, was clearly behind this, but that the statement had issued from ExCo also indicated that the more responsible elements among MLCs were clearly lined up on the side of law and order.

The British General Election that took place on 1st May had ushered in a whole new kind of government – the New Labour project led by Tony Blair – and meant that Ministers were disengaged from the minutiae of matters Saint Helenian. Officials too were rather preoccupied, and the business of my leave was focussed on the ODA's recruitment process for a successor to John Perrott as Chief Secretary. I attended the final Board at, what had overnight and indicative of the grandiose nature of the New Labour project, become a new and independent Department for International Development (DfID). None of the candidates seemed at all suited for the rôle that they would have to assume, but it was made very clear by Desmond Curran, who was managing the process, that DfID would neither re-advertise nor invite the FCO to put forward anyone despite the FCO's internal posting process having identified a number of suitable Diplomatic Service candidates prior to the Aid Planning Mission in November the previous year: I could choose the candidate to whom I least objected! I did and made the wrong choice! But that is another story. The view that the FCO now had was that DfID paid the salary, so the choice was theirs, history and any other circumstances notwithstanding. In other words – you're on your own mate, so make the best of it.

John and Wendy Perrott left St Helena on 11th July 1997 and Ethel Yon stood in as Chief Secretary until the DfID recruited successor, Mike Clancy, arrived on 2nd October. As I mention above, he was the least poor candidate. Nonetheless, although a British civil servant, he had had a brief spell in Hong Kong and with that period of overseas experience I really hoped that we could work well together. However, he was not as able as John Perrott had been to master the brief and I soon realised that he was an effective cut-off from the rest of the Administration in the Castle. Ideas that had come from his department, and Ethel Yon in particular, he passed off as his own; but more worryingly he was failing to convey what had been agreed in our regular morning meetings either completely or until he could put a personal spin upon an agreed course of action. He was a typical product of the New Labour project – all spin and very little substance. I began to rely more heavily upon Ethel Yon as Deputy Secretary and finally had to ensure that she too was present and participated in our daily morning meeting to ensure that things did actually get done as agreed. This was far from ideal: I had to check that what I had expected to be happening actually was in train. My conclusion was that he would have had great difficulty in holding his own in the competitive bureaucratic milieu of the Diplomatic Service. But I had to manage with what I had – not what might have been!

CHAPTER TEN

Changes of Government: Home and Away

With a change in Government in London in May 1997 there was obviously no opportunity to take up the issue of citizenship again with Sir Malcolm Rifkind while I was on leave in London; and the new Secretary of State and his junior ministers were far too busy to see the Governor of three specks in the South Atlantic Ocean while taking up the reins of foreign policy. Citizenship was still a very live issue, however, for Saints.

So, on my return to St Helena I undertook to address the matter officially and comprehensively in a Despatch I headed using the Island's motto - 'Loyal and Unshakeable'. The Britishness of the people of St Helena, the second oldest remaining British colonial possession was undisputed, as was that of the Tristanians. But, of course, remote and economically dependent St Helena had rarely been a subject of great interest in the corridors of power in 20th Century London and nor had the loss of their citizenship of the United Kingdom & Colonies in 1981 caused more than a ripple on Foreign Office desks. However, with no right of abode or ability to freely seek employment in the mother country Saints had been denied the access that millions of European foreigners had acquired as of right on account of the UK's membership of the European Community. Subjecting Saint Helenians and Tristanians to immigration control had created financial implications for the United Kingdom as well as for the Islands.

There were fewer than 7,000 islanders belonging to St Helena and Its Dependencies and the people of those islands had had no other allegiance than to Britain. It was, therefore, a devastating blow when the British Nationality Act, 1981 had removed the rights of these colonial people to their United Kingdom citizenship. Had the human rights legislation introduced by the Blair Government in 1998 then been in place it may well have been struck down as being *ultra vires*. As it was, the legislation, which was primarily aimed at stemming the imagined hordes fleeing Hong Kong when it was ceded to China in 1999, also removed the close ties of nationality between the colonies and the metropolitan power. Feeling in St Helena was incandescent. Legislative Council refused to enact the legislation forced upon St Helena by London, which would give effect to the changes in national status. In response to the local mood Bishop John Ruston, formed the Bishop's Commission to report on the citizenship issue as it affected St Helena.

A great deal of what emerged from the reports of the Bishop's Commission dwelt upon the emotive and historical aspects of the island's long relationship with the English Crown and particularly the Royal Charter of Charles II. Not that such matters can be dismissed out of hand, even though they might have little legal weight in an age of political pragmatism. It was this Charter that gave comfort to Saint Helenians and which might almost be seen as the charter of the Citizenship Commission founded in 1996 after the Bishop's Commission had fulfilled its remit. It had been frequently, if erroneously, quoted in support of their thesis that native-born Saint Helenians had an indisputable claim to British citizenship because King Charles decreed so. It is easy to see how such a belief can grow out of a simple reading of the 1673 Charter as *inter alia* it declared for all islanders and their children

> "...*all liberties franchises immunities capacities and abilities of free denizens and natural subjects within any of Our Dominions to all intents and purposes as if they had been abiding and borne within this Our Kingdom of England...*"

And it was perhaps understandably difficult for the average Saint Helenian to comprehend why, without consultation in 1981, they were no longer considered to be those 'free denizens of England' that King Charles' Charter had declared them to be for posterity. There is no doubt about the authenticity of the Charter. At the time it was granted, and until 1948, the term British subject covered all those citizens of the Dominions and Colonies equally with native-born Britons.

The legislation passed in 1948 broke down this over-arching definition of nationality accorded to all subjects of the British Crown; and in 1981 it was further refined by prescribing that those British Subjects formerly Citizens of the United Kingdom and Colonies who belonged to colonial territories should become British Dependent Territory Citizens. In addition, the British Nationality Act, 1981 limited the right to live in the United Kingdom to those who became British Citizens, i.e. those with a natural tie to the metropolitan country, which effectively excluded its colonial citizens. It seemed pretty conclusive that the subsequent legislation by parliament had extinguished the rights granted under the Charter of 1673 and that no legal rights bearing on nationality remained from the Charter.

It was as incomprehensible to an outsider, as it was to a Saint Helenian, to understand just how a British Government could have continued to exclude their colonial citizens (in the face of the completely relaxed regime as regards immigration and employment offered to European Community citizens) when, as was the case of St Helena, they could demonstrate their incontrovertible allegiance to the British Crown. Nevertheless, some 165,000 British subjects, categorised as Citizens of the Dependent Territories, were denied free access to the United Kingdom: while non-English speaking Europeans with no connection with or allegiance to the United Kingdom were allowed to enter the country at will to live and work there. The Despatch had no immediate effect, but it soon became evident that I had been pushing at an almost open door.

There was fertile ground for belief that there was an injustice to be righted; and fortunately there were those in the UK ready to take up the cause. Lord Iveagh, Ned Guinness, was one of those enthused and visited St Helena later in 1997 in support of the lobby to restore full citizenship to Britain's remaining colonial citizens.

Lord Iveagh visited St Helena from 5th – 12th September 1997 in a private capacity, and spent quite a lot of time with members and supporters of the Citizenship Commission. He made a last call on me at the Castle on the morning of 12th September. His enthusiasm kept him talking there, and 'on the street' subsequently, so he had to board the RMS, which had hauled up its anchor and was on the point of departure, from a hastily hired launch and via the Jacobs ladder suspended over the side! He became a good friend of St

129

Helena and introduced a Private Member's Bill in the House of Lords to rectify the anomaly. It was unsuccessful. Together with my Despatch St Helena: "Loyal and Unshakeable" (to the new Foreign Secretary, Robin Cook), which made the case for restoring their national status to Saints, it certainly added to the pressure on the British Government to do something.

Before Lord Iveagh's visit, however, we received news by telephone early the next morning of the death of Diana, Princess of Wales. She had died on 31st August in a car accident in Paris. By the summer of 1997 St Helena's television service, provided via satellite feeds by Cable & Wireless, was well established, and we spent most of the day tearfully watching the upsetting news as it unfolded. Bishop John Ruston later discussed how we on St Helena might mark the event. He and I agreed that he should conduct a Service of Thanksgiving for her life at the cathedral the following Sunday, 7th September. The Island's St Pauls Cathedral was packed to capacity. As Governor I would, no doubt, have been expected to make an address during the service, but as someone who had known her, I also wanted to deliver my own eulogy. I found it quite a challenge to produce what I wanted to say in just a few words, but it proved even more difficult to deliver them without faltering when the time came. The Princess of Wales had touched all our lives and at that moment the whole congregation, Saints, expatriates and visitors, realised just how much she would be missed by everyone: as the outpouring of grief and the fields of bouquets outside Kensington Palace that week had already demonstrated.

Later - between 29th and 30th September - we made our by now annual official visit to Ascension. On this occasion Roger Huxley had persuaded the RAF Station commander to put out a Guard of Honour in recognition of the visit of the Governor of the island and Her Majesty's representative there. It was a bit of unexpected pomp and circumstance for what was normally a very casual and relaxed community, but fun. It was not often, indeed only very rarely, that Ascension Island saw its Governor in full uniform.

On our return journey from Ascension we found that the St Helena citizenship issue had become a UK news story. The newspaper *Mail-on-Sunday* had recognised this and had sent

Kim Wilshire, its top feature writer, and a photographer to the Island, via the RAF's Falkland's Airbridge and Ascension Island to cover the story. The two days at sea on our return journey to St Helena provided an ideal opportunity to put the citizenship into sharp focus for the UK press.

'Access' in terms of the Schedule for the *RMS* also continued to be of interest and importance. But there was also continuing interest in access by air. The 'airport issue' was one that had been on the desk of every Governor for many years. Whether St Helena should have had an airport was as an emotional issue in 1995-99. However, in the 1990s it was by no means clear that a significant number of the population would even have welcomed the construction of an airport and the introduction of an air service.

The problems, of course, were many. Firstly, St Helena is an extinct volcano formed of sheer high cliffs surrounding a mountainous land mass: there is very little flat land, even at the sea's edge. Secondly, unlike the island chains of the Caribbean, for example, it is a long way from any other land, which limits the type of aircraft that might be employed in an air service to the island on grounds of range. A short un-metalled airstrip could feasibly be built, but the type of commercial short-take-off-and-landing (STOL) aircraft that could use this sort of strip did not have the fuel capacity to safely fly to and from the island, even using the United States airfield at RAF Wideawake on Ascension Island, the nearest point of land to St Helena.

Nevertheless, during the Second World War Royal South African Air Force engineers had made a survey of St Helena to examine the feasibility of building an airfield at which maritime reconnaissance aircraft could be based to patrol the Atlantic. Their conclusion was that it was probably possible in civil engineering terms to construct an adequate runway for aircraft then in service, but that it would be both prohibitively costly to build and dangerous operationally to use. Times and aircraft performance have changed since then, but the fact remained that building an airport would be an expensive undertaking; and the additional infrastructure costs would no doubt exceed those of simply building a runway, a total running to several millions pounds sterling.

The suggestion that St Helena might have an airfield resurfaced a little more than twenty years after the Second

World War had ended, when the British Government funded a further investigation. Two feasible runway alignments were identified, but both technical and meteorological constraints argued against their adoption. The final conclusion in London, which also informed the Five Year Development Plan approved by the Minister for Overseas Development, Judith Hart, in June 1974, was that the costs of construction would be extremely high and the expenditure unlikely ever to be justified on economic grounds. The FCO's Dependent Territories' economists estimated that some £20 million at mid-1960s prices would be required – clearly an uneconomic investment given the small population (then 5,800) and the limited prospects for large-scale tourism that St Helena might offer. Indeed, a tourism consultancy commissioned at around the same time concluded that the construction of an airfield would have been unlikely to yield more than a small socio-economic benefit in relation to the estimated cost of £20m.

But still, the idea would not go away entirely. In the early 1990s Alandis (London) Ltd, a shipping company incorporated in the United Kingdom and belonging to Greek interests, registered two £100 companies in London as St Helena Airways Ltd and St Helena Airport Ltd. The stated purpose of these two companies was to be involved in the construction and running of an airport on the island and an air service to and from St Helena. However, the rather sketchy proposals that the company put to the ODA were rejected in 1994 after economic and financial appraisals showed that most, if not all, of the financial risk in the proposed venture would have fallen on the British Government. Expectations in St Helena had, in the meantime, naturally grown and the St Helena Airport/Airways companies and their island champion had a ready audience for unfounded accusations of HMG's bad faith.

For some years after this, and despite the periodic suggestions by one particular MLC, Julian Cairns-Wicks, that the St Helena Airport/Airways proposals should be revisited, the St Helena Government had concentrated its access attentions first on a so-called 'shuttle ship' to ply between the Island and Ascension, and later on the scheduling of the RMS St Helena and the need to provide safer landing conditions at the wharf for visitor, returning resident and fishermen alike. However and at the same time, an active pressure group for air access remained.

So, in 1997 the St Helena Government conducted a detailed consultation exercise setting out the pros and cons of the provision of an airport, as opposed to a replacement of the *RMS St Helena*. Every household on the Island received a questionnaire, the answers to which we hoped would give us a clear indication of Saints' views on the matter. As was so often the case on St Helena, the results were influenced by the unwillingness of many to make a decision for which they thought they might be later held responsible or for which they might be blamed. Although the returns indicated a clear majority in favour of building an airport the result represented the views of only 15% of those consulted. The consultation was thus, by the most favourable interpretation, inconclusive. Nevertheless, the 'airport saga' continued to run, as the following chapters will reveal.

*   *   *

There was a good turnout at the general election on 9th July in which a refreshing new bunch of candidates had stood. However, hopes for a progressive new legislature were dashed as not only did they, in the main, fail, but the few Unofficial Members, i.e. elected MLCs who had remained on the Executive Council, lost their seats. Councillors Eric George and William Drabble were returned by their constituents and were nominated for seats on ExCo, and Councillor Robinson was similarly nominated and found a seat as Chairman of the Public Works Committee.

Nevertheless, following the formation of a new Legislative Council I set out to establish a new relationship between MLCs and officials aimed at breaking the old belief that MLCs were elected to oppose the Administration. At the strategic level I formed a Policy Co-ordination Advisory Group to look jointly with Administration officials and the Unofficial (i.e. elected) Members of ExCo at the bigger picture and the agenda for the future. I also formed a Finance and Development Policy Group to provide a forum for Unofficial Members and appropriate senior officials to consider financial and development matters; and a Development

Forum to bring together the public and private sectors to hear and discuss the progress of the pubic sector reform programme and the priorities for the future, with the aim of getting more private sector input into the process. And, with help from another Overseas Territory, I was able to draft and publish a set of guidance for MLCs, which could have instructed them more fully of their constitutional and legislatives rules and behaviour.

It is doubtful whether this latter, or indeed any of the other matters upon which we sought to give the new LegCo guidance during a pretty intensive and comprehensive programme of seminars and instruction had much impact. MLCs continued to say publicly that decisions were made by the Administration and not by them; and continued to reiterate the call for constitutional reform to give them more power. But even though the report drafted by David Buffett and Eric Potter, when it finally arrived, seemed to offer them a series of proposals that they could make to HMG, they failed to come up with any way of taking the matter further. Yet, there was no other simple single issue that had united MLCs over the past many years than the belief that the Governor's discretionary powers, particularly those for finance and shipping, should be curtailed; and that *Ex-officio* participation in Government (i.e. ExCo) and membership of Legislative Council should cease. Given the conservative dependency culture that existed, the subliminal message of all this anti-Administration, anti-Governor (even anti-HMG) rhetoric was that MLCs saw it as a way to resist the pressure from HMG, exercised through the Governor, to introduce and follow reforming policies which might make them unpopular with their fellow citizens and constituents. Their equivocal standpoint thus made it impossible for the St Helena Government to take a view on the need or desirability for constitutional change. However, I recognised that at some time it would be necessary to address the issue to somehow enable Government to reach a formal position.

Gerry Henry the Chief of Police retired on 27th March after a period of pre-retirement leave to use up his outstanding holiday entitlement - a public service custom that is not peculiar to St Helena, it has to be added. The succession planning pointed to his successor being his half-brother Inspector Lawson Henry, who had been serving as head of the small SHPF detachment on Ascension when it might have been convenient for him to attend the police staff command course in the UK that had been set as a requirement for the Chief's job; and he had been Acting Chief of Police since the beginning of November in 1996 during Gerry Henry's absence from duty on leave until a place on the Overseas Course was available.

Lawson Henry departed on his UK training on 28th March 1997 but when he returned after several months of rubbing shoulders with other police officers, including British Inspectors, he demanded a substantial rise in the salary he would get as Superintendent and Chief of Police. He didn't accept that the Public Service Commission set the salary and that I had no say in his remuneration package as Chief of Police. Whereupon and possibly in the belief that he could call my bluff (although bluff it certainly was not) he said he would resign. I accepted his resignation. Although had he returned the next day and withdrawn it I would quite probably have acceded. However, at a simple stroke we had got rid off a bully who would have been a disaster as head of the police force. Instead, Inspector Derek Thomas, who had been standing in as Chief of Police in Lawson Henry's absence in the UK, filled the position by default. He had had less experience, didn't have Lawson Henry's seniority, and he had not therefore been a natural contender to fill the top position before Gerry Henry had retired. He had wanted a posting to Ascension Island, but the SHPF structure couldn't accommodate that and he had rather unwillingly become the Acting Chief of Police in the expectation that when Lawson Henry returned he would get the plum posting that his colleagues considered Ascension to be. Surprisingly that weighed more with him than the fact that he was now at the head of the Island's Police Force. . .

Rising unemployment meant that throughout the year all our efforts and the advice of a stream of overseas experts was concentrated on the need to expand the private sector. It was not, however, simply a matter of shedding public sector jobs into the private sector. The private sector was, of course small, and although Government did have some success in slimming the public service there was a concomitant problem of recruitment and retention across the board, and particularly in nursing and the police: employment opportunities on Ascension, and the Falkland Islands, offered higher financial rewards. Indeed Lawson Henry and his wife, who had been the Postmistress, both upped sticks and went to better paying jobs on Ascension.

By now I think that there was a realisation in London that building a strong economy and making St Helena less aid dependent needed quite a lot of help from outside. The FCO batted away at the Ministry of Defence after thirty years of procrastination about recruiting Saint Helenians on St Helena and finally overcame the last objections so that direct recruitment of Saints into the British armed forces could start. In that first year an Armed Forces recruitment team tested and interviewed forty young people and selected 24 recruits for enlistment – nine to the Royal Navy; four to the Royal Marines; and eleven to the Army. DfID funded a business adviser; and Government started negotiations with a company, Argos Helena, which was prepared to use St Helena and Saints in their fisheries business in the Southern Ocean. And another Government decision had started the process of examining the possibilities for the Government Savings Bank to be grown into a conventional 'high street retail bank'.

During my brief visit to London in the Spring the department had agreed that an invitation would be extended to the members of the new Legislative Council as part of our efforts to educate the MLCs in the Westminster system of government. The first group of six MLCs selected to take up the invitation extended by the FCO Minster with responsibility for the dependencies, now to be known as Overseas Territories, departed for London on 27th November. We hoped for the best, but feared for the worst as the participants had neither consulted with, nor sought briefing from, the Administration before they left . . .

*   *   *

Also in November *HMS Monmouth* a Type 23 frigate, accompanied by *RFA Orangeleaf*, called at St Helena en route to a six-month deployment as the Falkland Islands Guard Ship. We enjoyed another Lynx helicopter trip out to the ship in James Bay and used the opportunity offered us by the crew to photograph St Helena from the air. The Governor's

XI, which was now an established part of the cricket scene took on a team representing the combined crews of *Monmouth* and *Orangeleaf*, the result of which I no longer have a record, although my abiding memory of the match was the naval bowler apologising for getting me out when I was caught off his bowling by the wicket keeper!

I had been drawn into the cricketing fraternity early in our time on St Helena. I had been able to arrange for the MCC to provide a matting wicket for the St Helena Cricket Association, which had started the process. I was elected as President of the St Helena Cricket Association in November 1995, soon after my arrival and was the first Governor to have filled the position in living memory. I used that position, in time, to gain the International Cricket Council's acceptance of an application by the St Helena Association to join the ICC as affiliates. It took time; the help of old chums in the Trinidad & Tobago Cricket Board of Control to write an acceptable constitution; a form of sponsorship from South Africa via contact with Dr Ali Bacher; and a visit to the ICC Secretary in the Clock Tower at Lord's Cricket Ground in 1998.

I enjoyed being involved in cricket on St Helena, but on a wider international stage I am proud to note that the Island now rates its own page on the website for the International Cricket Council (ICC). There, *inter alia*, it is recorded that,

> "*In 1995, Governor David Smallman, a member of the MCC and the Queen's Park Cricket Club in the West Indies, became the president of the SHCA. It was he who was prominent in getting the association to become an Affiliate of the ICC by piggy-backing on the ACA, as he knew that the available funding of the SHCA would not allow it to become an Affiliate of its own accord. The constitution of the SHCA was finalised and adopted in November 1998.*"

It took time, however, to put everything into place and the unusual nature of the isolated Island's cricket association joining the international fold was overshadowed by Afghanistan gaining similar recognition at the same ICC meeting in 2001. Nevertheless, in April 2012 St Helena competed in its first international tournament, the ICC Africa Division 3 T20 Tournament held in South Africa. St Helena beat Mali, Gambia, Cameroon and Morocco finishing in fifth place out of eight teams. However, from small beginnings . . .

Another of the regular occasions on the Island was Radio St Helena Day. I had participated at the opening of the 1995 event, but my interest in the radio station and its programmes led to my greater involvement in the following years. Radio St Helena Day had been the idea of Jan Ekwell and Jan Tuner, two Swedish amateur short wave radio enthusiasts – radio hams – in 1990. The intention at the outset was that radio hams (DX-ers) around the world would contact the lonely South Atlantic outpost and claim a special QSL card – the acknowledgement sent between enthusiasts to confirm the contact and the details of the transmission.

So that a signal could be broadcast from the Island, Cable & Wireless on St Helena lent their 1KW short wave transmitter to the Government owned radio station for four hours once a year on a day in October. From small beginnings the programme grew so that by the late 1990s it was attracting listeners from 23 countries in Africa, the Americas and Europe. This was at a time before St Helena had e-mail, so listeners contacted the radio station to speak to the programme presenters by telephone and by fax. It was great fun, and by 1998 I was, to my great delight, co-presenting the programme.

After what we had come to learn were the customary pre-Christmas activities, we held a post-Christmas lunch party on one of the Plantation House lawns on 27th December. We were to embark on the *RMS* the next day for Cape Town and Tristan da Cunha. I had been talking to the former head-teacher at the Island's secondary school, and she had spoken about the things that she wished to do in retirement. One of those things was visiting Tristan da Cunha, where a programme of sending some pupils with potential to study for GCSEs at St Helena's Prince Andrew School had begun. *"Then why not come tomorrow?"* I suggested; and despite the imminence of the ship's departure, because St Helena was a small society, she managed to obtain a passage and be on board the next day. While she was making her arrangements the party had moved to the other lawn and started to play croquet. It was then I understood why it had been described as a vicious game. The normally quiet Bishop John revealed himself to be a ferocious player, much to everyone's surprise other than that of his sister, who was visiting at the time and knew him of old from vicarage croquet lawns.

*   *   *

The *RMS* arrived at Tristan da Cunha on the morning of 9th January 1998 where, after our two earlier visits, we now felt very much at home. There was now a new (Diplomatic Service) Administrator, Brian Baldwin, and his wife at the Residency. On this occasion I was able to visit Inaccessible Island, using the fishery patrol vessel once more. Inaccessible Island is aptly named during the days of sailing ships its steep cliffs and narrow, pebbly beaches would have made landing very difficult indeed. There was a small lower area at the eastern end of the island, but otherwise it was probably just as tricky to land on as it always had been. As with our landing on Nightingale Island the previous year, the Fisheries vessel went in quite close and the landing party were put ashore by the RIB. We saw seal pups and plenty of bird life, but what was amazing was the amount of plastic litter, bottles and small containers of household liquids with Portuguese writing, which had obviously come on the wind and currents from Brazil. There was also an array of plastic fishing gear, including storage boxes that had either been jettisoned or washed overboard in the mid Atlantic. We were picked up once again by the passing *RMS* St Helena.

Capt Smith suggested that during the return voyage to Cape Town the *RMS* should make a first foray for the ship into the Roaring Forties and give us a sight of Gough Island, the furthermost southerly island of the Tristan da Cunha Colony Group. A British island, but with no permanent population, that had a meteorological station maintained by the South African National Antarctic Programme since 1956. Although it had been there for over forty years, Capt Smith thought that no-one from the sovereign power had ever been there, and certainly not in recent years.

Thus, we circled Gough Island some 200 miles south of the islands of the Tristan da Cunha Group. The sight of the green and uninhabited island – well, uninhabited apart from the handful of South Africans manning the weather station –

caused me to wonder whether any of the island's Governors had ever set foot there. But that, as they say, is another story, the answer to which will be revealed in due course.

On our return to Cape Town we met friends who were then in South Africa and had dined with them at the renowned restaurant of the winery hotel, Spier, near Stellenbosch. I was also able to get in an afternoon's racing the Royal Cape Yacht Club in our chum's boat, *Maji Moto II*, on Saturday before we joined our ship's captain, David Roberts, for sundowners at RCYC. The next day we departed Duncan Dock again, to enter what was to all intents and purposes the last chapter of our time on the island of St Helena.

CHAPTER ELEVEN

Misplaced confidence?

I had signed off my annual Review for 1997 before leaving once more for Tristan da Cunha. The year had opened in my absence at Tristan da Cunha with the somewhat ridiculous call by a member of the Executive Council for a judicial review of the November 1997 Aid Agreement with HMG to which he had been party. There had followed an uncomfortable four months with that member of ExCo in outright opposition to the Government of which he was a member. The Constitution gave the Governor no power to dismiss or effectively discipline a member of ExCo and nor was it at all easy to bring any pressure upon this one to resign as he totally failed to comprehend how anachronistic was his position.

Politics, I thus wrote to the Foreign Secretary, had dominated 1997 with the challenges to agreed Government policies by members of the Government. Later, resignations and the General Election seemed to have cleared the air a little but not that much as the old faces were re-elected and went on to be appointed to the Executive Council. Legislative Council members continued to see constitutional change as the solution to their issues. However and despite the growing problem of unemployment, I sought in that Annual Review to assure those in London that we gave priority to developing a private sector and maximising off-shore employment opportunities. I looked forward with optimism to 1998, a year in which I believed that the St Helena Government could live up to its part in the Aid Agreement Package. However, arrival back on the Island on 23rd January 1998 was, in retrospect, the start of yet another political era in St Helena's relationship with authority.

We had travelled north with a small group of ODA officials, who comprised a review team – to check up on the Government's progress in implementing the reforms that we had put forward in the Country Policy Plan; and which we had agreed with the APM during their visit in the previous November. At the conclusion of this visit the Government signed a joint Aide Memoire recalling the progress that had been made and the matters to be addressed over the forthcoming period. ExCo had agreed to the terms of the Aide Memoire at a meeting with the visitors from DfID and these were endorsed at a full meeting of the Legislative Council on 30th January, shortly before the review team left the Island.

In the Westminster system of government a Government is normally able to command a majority in the legislature to ensure the passage of its legislation. Because of the political significance of financial measures, a Government defeated on a money bill is generally expected to resign. Constitutional development in the United Kingdom Overseas Territories has been related to this pattern; and care has always been taken to make provisions to ensure the passage of financial legislation. In general this has been provided by control of a majority in the legislature: initially a majority of *ex-officios*; then a majority comprising both officials and elected (Unofficial) members, until the *ex-officios* can be phased out as elected members assume responsibility for the Executive, with the necessary support in the legislature - usually through the growth of a party system of representation. Because of the importance of the Executive retaining control of the Budget, the transitional stages of constitutional development in the Dependencies have always been backed up by reserve provisions in the Constitution covering the whole or certain areas of government, but especially finance. These provisions usually empowered the Governor to enact legislation without the consent of the legislature or, in some cases, only after that consent has been withheld. Obviously such Reserve Powers can only be used sparingly, since their use implies a political conflict

Although 1998 started well, with a successful week of discussions with the team from DfID, the seeds of conflict had been sown, unbeknown either to senior officials or me. The fact that the Unofficial members of ExCo had subscribed unanimously to the joint Aide Memoire of agreement with DfID; and that Legislative Council, when consulted informally at the end of the review visit, had no substantive comment, led us to believe that the island's politicians had, indeed and as they said, been carried along.

However, we had not been aware of how strongly held was the belief of the six MLCs who had been received in London soon after the General Election in 1997, that they had forged a direct link to sympathetic Ministers in London to whom they could appeal over the heads of the Governor and FCO officials. Further, Councillor Eric George had gone on to meet the new Secretary of State at the Dependent Territories Association Conference in London during February, when he had no doubt mistaken Robin Cook's words of encouragement as a sign that E George had a direct line to the Foreign Secretary. This emboldened him, without resigning from the Government, to oppose the Budget proposals tabled in ExCo on 10th March. Nevertheless, the Financial Secretary introduced the Appropriation Bill to the Legislative Council on 20th March. This would give effect to the Estimates of Recurrent Revenue and Expenditure and the Development Fund Estimates for 1998/1999. However, the first reading of the Bill was defeated by a margin of 7 votes to 4. There followed a period in which senior officials, both formally and informally, sought to ensure MLCs understood the import of their actions. But, when Legislative Council reconvened on 23rd March Eric George, in a show of bravado, led the move for a formal vote against the Appropriation Bill. It was carried and the Budget legislation was defeated once more.

London had been pleased to learn of the agreement reached at the end of the Aid review in January, and furthermore had signalled the political will in London to fund the expected deficit in the 1998/1999 Budget. Rejection of the Budget proposed by the Appropriation Bill implicitly challenged the agreement that Ministers had endorsed. Both they and officials in London, and we in St Helena, were alarmed at the implications of such a rejection.

I consulted Executive Council three times over the next two days, and held two informal meetings of the whole Legislative Council to find a way forward. Although our ExCo deliberations were not able to sway Eric George from his position of outright opposition he did agree to abstain on the issue (rather than resign his portfolio). We also regained support from the other dissident, Cllr Robertson, and it appeared that together with support from a sufficient number of other MLCs it was likely that if a further Bill were presented to LegCo it might secure a First Reading. The advice of ExCo was still that there remained a risk of the

Budget failing to gain approval, but to represent the budgetary proposals in a new Bill was a risk worth taking. The only contrary view to this line within ExCo was Eric George. He now opined that the democratic process had run its course, and that the only alternative now open was to use the Governor's Reserve Powers to enact the Bill using a declaration under Sec 34 of the Constitution. He was, however, in a minority of one at this stage; and all the other members of ExCo advised that any other course, for example under Sec 10 of the Finance Ordinance, was inappropriate.

A new Bill was duly presented to LegCo on 30th March. However, those MLCs who had indicated that they would vote in favour of the new legislation only five days earlier, voted against the Bill in its First Reading. I called an emergency meeting of ExCo that afternoon, when all the Unofficial members of ExCo, including Eric George, advised me that the only course now open to save the Budget was indeed to enact the Bill under the provisions of the aforementioned Sec 34 of the Constitution. The powers accorded to the Governor under that Section are for him to act in his discretion, that is, without necessarily consulting with or taking advice from his Executive Council. However, in the light of the important nature of the legislation and the very serious problem that its failure in the legislature posed, I thought it only right and proper to consult once again to ascertain the views of what was a parallel to the Cabinet in a more sophisticated jurisdiction – Executive Council. I also wished to ascertain their level of support for any action that I took thereafter. As a result, with their unequivocal advice to follow the course that I did, I acted on the understanding that I had the unanimous and unqualified support of all in the Executive Council, including the elected members, to use the Reserved Powers to enact the Appropriation Bill, 1998.

Notwithstanding this careful approach to a difficult situation all five Unofficial Members of ExCo were later to be signatory to a letter of protest to the Foreign Secretary at my action! The letter to the Secretary of State, whose support Eric George must have assumed, was issued under a letter-heading of "Elected Members of the Legislative Council" which implicitly meant it was not the text of a LegCo Motion and thus enjoyed the formal support of the Legislative Council. Furthermore, it also bore the signature of Eric

George, who twice had advised me to enact the legislation by the method to which he was now objecting The letter was also signed by the three other MLCs in ExCo, who had also so advised me on 30th March! Surely, it could only happen in St Helena!

The letter, signed by 11 MLCs, was addressed to me as Governor and stated, *"We the undersigned Elected Members do hereby object to the need for the declaration made [by the Governor] under Section 34 of the St Helena Constitution."* Describing the vote against the Appropriation Bill on 30th March as, *"the disallowance of the Appropriation Bill . . . by a majority vote"*, on the grounds that the Estimates failed to *"contain sufficient funding and safeguards to address the pressing issues which threaten the well-being of the people of St Helena,"* and that *"The enforcement of the said Bill will create a continuing deterioration of what is already an unsatisfactory situation."*

In an accompanying 'Statement' these Councillors called for *"an independent enquiry into the management and administration of this island with special reference to the Public Sector Reform Programme and Private Sector Development."* It further went on to claim that rejecting the Appropriation Bill was *"not in any way an indication of not honouring the St Helena Government's agreement of the three year aid package . . ."* but *"to signify the serious state of affairs that St Helena is at present facing"* and had they approved the Budget it would [in the eyes of their voters] *"indicate Council's approval of St Helena's rapid deterioration."* No greater indication of going back on their word could be imagined.

The response, when it came from London, was robust. But, the incident nonetheless served to demonstrate the lack of responsibility that characterised the behaviour of the overwhelming majority of the elected Members of the Legislative Council throughout the 1990s. I wonder too, how much their rôles as (unqualified) Lay Advocates gave Cllrs George and Drabble the mistaken impression that they were legal experts in arguing their demands and what they believed were their constitutional rights.

*   *   *

Despite all the roadblocks that the politicians put in the way, the drive to create a private sector continued. It had to. St Helena desperately needed a growing private sector to build an economy that could lead to sustainable growth. There had been those in London who seemed to believe it was simply a matter of saying that there should be a growing private sector and it happened. Indeed, this fundamental difference in our positions seemed to have led to a belief that we were not pulling our weight in implementing the programme that Government had set out and agreed with DfID. With this gap in our positions partly in mind it was easy from our part to welcome the suggestion by DfID for an advisory project to look into developing a private sector over a six-month period.

Far from proving that St Helena had been dragging its feet, the adviser was able to dispel some of the myths prevalent in DfID's corridors about the private sector and its capacity for development and to absorb privatisations. This business adviser actually confirmed that we were, essentially, on the right track in tackling both that and the thorny problem of the Government's 84% stake in Solomon & Co, the Island's largest non-Governmental employer and purveyor of numerous services in the retail and other fields. Perhaps our biggest success, however and a touchstone for the Island's ability to attract inward investment, was the establishment of Argos Helena Ltd, a British owned fishing company, which would in time provide a number of new jobs in St Helena for Saints. The proposal had been running for a couple of years before we finally pinned down an agreement, which was eventually signed on 19th June 1998.

The other element in the St Helena Government's push to ensure that there was a productive private sector on the Island was the issue of access. Discussions with the ODA and its successor department, the St Helena Line and Curnow Shipping, didn't move us on far through the years during which I grappled with the Schedule and the issue of the number of calls that the *RMS St Helena* should make in the United Kingdom.

I had had a clear steer from Baroness Chalker in 1995 that I should consider a Schedule with no calls, or at most one call, in the UK as the optimum at which to aim. In doing so, an increased frequency of calls between St Helena and Ascension Island would be provided which would finally despatch the unrealistic notion that some on the Island had that, in addition to the *RMS*, HMG would provide and subsidise the operation of a second vessel to service the inter-island passenger trade – optimistically known as the 'shuttle ship'. There was a strong island resistance to reducing the number of UK calls, which was emotional rather than practical: the *RMS* providing the umbilical cord to the mother-country etc.. As I have mentioned, I was quickly able to agree an interim rescheduling that reduced the number of calls at a United Kingdom port from six to four, with effect from May 1996. At the same time it was suggested that we would look at the options again after two years and use the experience to inform decisions about any new Schedule. In fact we all, the Government Economist, St Helena Line, Curnow Shipping were continually weighing the evidence – it was a critical issue as the size of the shipping subsidy determined the amount available in the other constituent parts of the aid package.

Almost inevitably, there was a knee jerk Saint Helenian reaction to something new. However, once it became clear that more calls at St Helena for departure to Ascension or Cape Town was indeed the advantage that had been promised for it, objection to the new sailing Schedule for the RMS dissolved. In the meantime tourism began to take a firm root and the economic benefits of further amending the Schedule to enable the service to be based entirely in the South Atlantic became more evident. Instead of problems internally the problem became one of trying to keep DfID on side in respect of the size of the shipping subsidy. Although access by sea was, of course, not the only long-term option that was up for discussion. Building an airport and introducing an air service had long been an unresolved issue as the Consultation of 1997 had illustrated.

*   *   *

Bearing in mind St Helena's lack of aviation history, it might have struck as odd that an RAF sub-aqua team should have chosen the Island as a venue for a visit, or to give it its correct form – an adventurous training exercise. A member of the RAF Sub Aqua Association had visited St Helena whilst on leave some time in 1996 or 1997 and had dived in James

Bay where the remains of wrecks from the earliest days of the East India Company's use of the Island were evident. There were also wrecks of more modern provenance, including the *RFA Darkdale*, sunk by enemy submarine action on 22nd November 1941. A team of officers and airmen of the RAFSAA arrived at St Helena on the *RMS* from Ascension Island early in April and on 14th April raised a bronze cannon, which had probably been on board the Dutch East Indiaman *Witte Leeuw* (the White Lion) sunk in James Bay after a brief naval action in 1613. The cannon had been completely preserved in the sand on the seabed in which it had been buried for over 380 years. Flotation bags, and then the crane on the wharf, had salvaged the cannon from the depths of James Bay, and put it ashore almost at my feet. Whereupon and under the provisions of an ancient Ordinance, I claimed the cannon for the Crown. It now has pride of place in the Jamestown museum.

The airmen were to return to their military life via Ascension, and by pure coincidence we travelled with them on the *RMS* en route for discussions with Foreign Office departmental officials on Ascension Island. During the voyage I explained to them the difficulties that I had encountered in finding a way to land on Gough Island that we had sighted during our visit to Tristan da Cunha in the previous January. *"We must make a plan"* was the response of Sqn Ldr Paul Marshall. And, over the next few months we did. The outcome of the planning is described in the following chapter.

*　　　　　　*　　　　　　*

Although Chief Justice Geoffrey Martin had continued with his regular visits as and when needed, he had not always been able to get away from his judicial responsibilities in Leicester. But fortunately an apparently chance visit while on a cruise on the *St Helena* led to another English judge, Bill Hannah, declaring himself able to visit and act in Geoff Martin's stead, which he did on a couple of occasions. In the meantime, however, Geoff Martin had been working quietly away in the background with the aim of fulfilling our wish to see a Court of Appeal sit on St Helena. It was, therefore, a disappointment that he could not have been on the Island in the spring of 1998 when the first three Judges of Appeal had arrived to be sworn in and hold the very first Session of the St Helena Court of Appeal on 29th May.

*   *   *

The negative vein in which the MLCs had acted early in 1998 continued for the rest of the year, demonstrating a gut adverse reaction to reforms in the public sector and refusing to accept that things were actually getting better. Unemployment, quite naturally, a major cause of concern, had dropped from 20% to 15% over the course of 1996/97; the Development Agency had created or sustained over 100 jobs; and inflation was less than 1%. The Census, the results of which were published in September 1998, also clearly illustrated the general increase in the quality of life on the Island. Even so, the MLCs not in Executive Council openly referred to themselves as 'the Opposition', and most of their colleagues in Executive Council failed to put any distance between themselves and those MLCs for fear of being identified with the Castle or the Governor – where, as they glibly told the world the decisions were made. It was not them it was the Administration! Hence, possibly, their determination not to be seen to be acquiescing in the fiscal regime that necessarily flowed from the Aid Agreement and their decision to block the passage of the appropriation legislation again the following year.

Underlying the opposition to the policies that had been introduced as a result of HMG's responsibility for the good governance of St Helena lay the fundamental discontent with the arrangements for governing the colony that had had been set out in the 1988 Constitution. This legislation took account of the desire for more powers expressed by St Helena's politicians of the day, but seemed to me to have been framed from afar, with insufficient consideration for the context within which it had to work. While giving more power to MLCs it did little to increase their sense of responsibility, either to their fellow Legislative Council members or to the Officer Administering the Government of St Helena. At the same time it rather diminished the Governor's ability to govern effectively in the situation where the Island was a long-term recipient of Budgetary Aid.

It would be a simplification of the result to suggest that the transfer of powers effected by the 1988 Constitution was a step too far given the political immaturity of the democratic process in St Helena. Nevertheless, one eminent lawyer, with wide experience of the Overseas Territories and other small island democracies, described the exiting Constitution to me as "*an interesting experiment in colonial constitution drafting*" of a kind that he had not previously encountered; or could see working in St Helena's state of political immaturity. To which I could only reply: "*Quite so!*" The inability of Government to bring simple matters of policy to fruition, or legislation through the Legislative Council, because of the lack of collective responsibility had been illustrated by our inability to effect simple but obvious privatisations and by the failure of the Government's appropriation legislation.

Nevertheless, ever since the introduction of the 1988 Constitution, MLCs had voiced their discontent with the arrangements in it to anyone whom they could persuade to listen. A fine example was the Motion debated in the Legislative Council on 19th March 1997 that "*This House requests Her Majesty's Government to review our Constitution to reduce the power of the Governor to enable Elected Members to have more say in running this Island.*" In effect the FCO replied to the effect – make specific proposals and we will consider them.

Yet, when asked what the Constitution did actually provide; how it could best work; or how specifically it could be improved, they displayed a considerable view of confusion and disagreement. The fact that it did not provide for several of the political hobby-horses mounted by various of the MLCs, or that it didn't include provisions for other views voiced during the consultation exercise before the Order was drafted, was offered as proof that it was flawed. By omitting the reasonable suggestions of Saint Helenians, it seemed to be argued that, it could not therefore be satisfactory or work to St Helena's benefit. MLCs, for example, would argue that St Helena should move to a ministerial system of government and then that all the elected representatives should be involved in making all the decisions, effectively removing any distinction between Executive and Legislative Councils. Even those MLCs who formed the Government as Unofficial members of ExCo frequently acted as though they formed the

Opposition, treating the *Ex-officios* as if they alone were the Government.

I had hoped that the Commonwealth Parliamentary Association advisory visit in 1997 might have provided the advice MLCs evidently needed on the respective rôles of the members of Councils and the Governor; on Committee rules and procedures; and formulating proposals for the constitutional advancement of St Helena. Unfortunately it was nine months before a copy of what the authors had translated into 'The St Helena Constitutional Review' had been received on the Island. Most noticeable was that the views expressed in the report were heavily coloured by the authors' respective experiences in Norfolk Island and one of the Channel Islands, with their vastly different economic and constitutional development and maturity of population, which meant that the recommendations didn't link into the context of St Helena. Indeed much of the report played back suggestions for constitutional changes made to them by MLCs, but without studying the impact that these would have, particularly given St Helena's chronic dependence on funding from HMG. The report, thus, generated expectations that would have been impossible to meet. Scope for progress did exist were MLCS to accept that it was as important to identify what could not be done as it was to recognise what might be done. Nevertheless, as so often the case in St Helena, the politicians could not agree on how the report should be used, and it was, effectively, shelved.

So, by October 1998 and with continuing rumbles from MLCs about the powers of the Governor and the 'defective Constitution', I realised that it was up to me to do something so that suggestions for amendments to the constitutional arrangements could be put to London. I therefore constituted the 'Governor's Commission on the Constitution', chaired by a respected and well educated Saint Helenian, Corinda Essex, which produced its report in April 1999. This I forwarded to the FCO, putting the ball firmly back in their court.

*   *   *

What we had earlier called the Diplomatic Wing, i.e. the main body of the FCO, started to show a greater degree of interest in what was happening in St Helena following the appointment of John White as Head of, what in a re-organised post-May 1997 election FCO, had become Overseas Territories Department, reflecting the New Labour belief, that this was a less condescending reference to the UK dependencies. We had met briefly in Ascension Island in April and again in London in July, when Sandi and I were on leave. The FCO were working on a White Paper outlining a new relationship with the fourteen remaining Dependencies and it was pretty well guaranteed to include a commitment to bring forward legislation to restore full British citizenship. But I had to keep that to myself until the White Paper, *Partnership for Progress and Prosperity: Britain and the Overseas Territories* was published (in mid-March 1999). Even so, and as I told the writer Richard Madden, which he quoted in his article *St Helena: A Green and Pleasant Alcatraz* published in March 1999, the granting of full British citizenship might not be the panacea for the island's ills that many hoped for. I went on, *"I and my predecessors have been pressing hard for full citizenship rights for a long time, but it's debatable whether or not it will help solve the social problems facing the island. If a lot of young people leave for the UK it remains to be seen whether they will want to return. The really big question is whether or not it will salve the emotional wound"* [of, what seemed to many, to be the confiscation of their British nationality and freedom of access to the mother country under the 1981 Act of Parliament].

In the meantime life continued on St Helena with its round of official engagements and skirmishing with MLCs, leavened with the odd ship's visit, occasional cricket match for the Governor's XI, and preparations for the second Governor's Cup Race. During our leave break in May 1997 I had been invited by the journalist Brendan Boyle to be his guest at a luncheon at his livery company in the City – the Worshipful Company of Leathersellers. The Leathersellers Company's origins dated from the Middle Ages and the company was granted its first Royal Charter by King Henry IV in 1444. A century later the Leathersellers Company purchased the former Priory of St Helen's in the City of London and subsequently have owned that land: their current Livery Hall is in St Helen's Place, London EC3. This is the same St Helen, or Helena, upon whose day in 1502 it was believed that St Helena Island was first sighted: hence the association, and the invitation.

Like all the ancient livery companies the Leathersellers have ample funds for their activities and have established various funds for charitable purposes. I took advantage of being sat next to the Master to suggest that the Leathersellers might consider funding the purchase of two dinghies to allow a sail-training project to be set up for young people on St Helena. The idea had the Master's immediate support. With £5,000 from the Leathersellers and Nina MacLennan's £1,000, supplemented by a further sum from the Governor's Discretionary Fund, we were able to purchase two Saldanha dinghies and equipment in South Africa to start the scheme which built upon the enthusiasm that I had seen among the young people that had participated in the informal racing after the 1996 Governor's Cup Race. After the establishment, and success, of my sail-training project I proposed that a sailing club might be set up and said that the remaining project funds that I held could then be transferred to it. The St Helena Yacht Club was formed on 10th November 1998. Sandi and I were founding-members, and upon our departure were invited to be the SHYC's first honorary life members.

As well as lunching with the Leathersellers, I had been busy encouraging participants from the British yachting fraternity to enter the 1998 Race. This was successful in attracting a yacht and crew from the Army Sailing Association; a yacht sponsored by the international security organisation Group Four; and an entry sponsored by Curnow Shipping Ltd. These latter two yachts then used some of the first of the sailing project trainees as crew members.

We left St Helena on the *RMS* for Cape Town and the Race on 28th November, which allowed us to attend the RCYC's Blue Peter Supper for the Governor's Cup Race (a feature lifted from the proceedings attending the Cape to Rio Race); picnic again at Boschendal; and meet our last guest from our life at home, David Rowden, owner and skipper of my summer cruising boat. David joined us on the *RMS* and stayed at Plantation House until leaving for home in time for Christmas in England, via Ascension and the RAF Airbridge, on 19th December. Out in Table Bay on the *St Helena* we had to await the sailing of the yachts taking part in the 1998-99

'Around Alone' single-handed race circumnavigating the world. Once they were off, Sandi was able to sound the ship's siren to start the 1998 edition of the Governor's Cup Race.

During that call at Cape Town we were also to meet up again with South African friends; enjoy some good meals out; and see the musical sensation, the Soweto String Quartet perform in the open air amphitheatre at the Cape Town Waterfront, a leisure development of the former Victoria & Alfred Docks. The Waterfront was customarily our first destination on arrival at Cape Town – Quay Four our favourite venue at which to enjoy a Castle beer and a plate of delicious calamari and some chips!

*　　　　　*　　　　　*

Although 1998 had started inauspiciously in St Helena, I reported to London at the end of the year that at the same time in 1997 I had looked forward to the following year with a degree of optimism. Yet, and while there were hiccups along the way, we had demonstrated conclusively that the Country Policy Plan worked; and that tight financial control and good management were producing the results to enable SHG to live up to its part in the bargain struck in the 1996 Aid Planning Agreement. Our discussions with our DfID visitors in January had gone well, with the visitors welcoming the greater clarity and transparency of the Government's accounts. Furthermore we had been able to agree our joint objectives for the year.

This was nearly all lost by the belief that MLCs had that, after their sponsored visit to the UK, they could deal directly with the Secretary of State over my head. They were once again resistant to their own policies of structural adjustment, but the stiff reply to their petition from London had eventually led to an improvement in their behaviour. Thus, despite the recalcitrance of some of the politicians there had been some positive achievements. However, constitutional reform was creeping up the agenda, partly directly due to having their attempted interventions with the Foreign Secretary thwarted. Optimistically, I judged the outlook for 1999 to be "*steady as she goes*" and thus, perhaps, that my optimism had not been misplaced.

154

CHAPTER TWELVE

Adventure in the Roaring Forties

Gough Island, in common with the other islands of the
South Atlantic, is a volcanic outcrop. It was
discovered in 1505, during the voyage of the *Santo
Espirito*, and was marked on Portuguese charts thereafter as
Gonçalo Álvares Island. However, as the determination of
longitude was such an inexact science until the late
eighteenth century – two St Helena Islands appeared on
some charts at one time - the island's position was subject to
some conjecture, so enabling the British naval captain,
Charles Gough, to claim its (re-)discovery in 1732.

Gough Island is in the Roaring Forties and, although
forming part of the Tristan da Cunha Colony from the time of
the claim on behalf of the British Crown on 14th August 1816
it had no permanent population. It has been a UNESCO
World Heritage site since 1995. Being over 200 miles south of
Tristan da Cunha, it is only infrequently visited by its
Administrator and is rarely seen by its Governor. However
and as mentioned earlier, following our annual visit to
Tristan da Cunha in January 1997, when the *St Helena* had
made its first voyage south of the Fortieth parallel to
circumnavigate Gough Island en route for Cape Town I was
determined to find a way to achieve a landing on this furthest
flung part of my parish.

Although technically uninhabited, the South African
Government had maintained a weather station on the island
for over forty years. So, quite apart from the opportunity to
observe the teeming wildlife, there was the matter of 'showing
the flag' at this South African establishment on British soil,
and meeting the personnel there.

The seas in the latitude of Gough Island are always tricky
and the weather station no longer possessed its own boat
following a near fatal fishing expedition by some of its
members a few years previously. The weather station team
normally arrived on the island, and was supplied annually,
by helicopter from the South African Government survey ship
the *SA Aghulas*. Governors were unable to whistle up

helicopters, so the first requirement for a landing was to find an independent means of getting ashore from the *RMS*. This seemed to boil down to two boats with strong engines and intrepid crews. One boat would have done the job, but given the dangerous seas a back-up was vital in case of difficulties. No doubt volunteers for the rôle of boatmen could have been found readily enough among the complement of the *RMS*, but the provision of a boat or boats did not immediately suggest itself.

What had seemed to be an almost insurmountable problem, however, was solved by the RAF Sub-Aqua Association team, which had recovered the cannon of the *Witte Leeuw* in 1998. A visit to Tristan da Cunha to undertake some 'necessary' underwater survey could provide an opportunity, on the return voyage to Cape Town, for a call at Gough Island to land me from one of the team's rigid inflatable boats (RIBs). Only shortly before Christmas 1998 did the Service authorities finally sanction '*Exercise Roaring Endeavour*'. '*Roaring*', as its leader Sqn Ldr Paul Marshal explained, as it was to be conducted in the Roaring Forties, and '*Endeavour*', because the objective was to get the Governor ashore at Gough – some endeavour!

After our official visit there, and the successful underwater survey of Calshot Harbour and its approaches, the '*Roaring Endeavour*' party, plus the Administrator and his wife travelling on leave, embarked the *RMS* in a confused swell at the Edinburgh anchorage on Sunday 24th January, before setting course off Stoltenhoff Island for the 210 mile run to Gough Island.

The weather forecast for 25th January was not propitious. The task of required the *RMS* to anchor, so that the team's two RIBs could be launched by crane over the ship's side. Both operations required relatively calm seas, as would the recovery of the boats. Sunrise was at 05:40, but long before that it was obvious from the violent motion of the ship that the wind had intensified during the night. Indeed, the early morning light revealed swells of 10 - 12 feet and a lot of white water. By six o'clock the *St Helena* was two miles off North Point and turning into wind (Force 6, gusting Force 8) to pass down the west coast of Gough Island. The ship took heavy spray across the fore deck and hatches, occasionally obscuring the view from the bridge where I sheltered from the wind and rain fearing that the weather had defeated the planned landing. However, the weather began to improve, the rain cleared and visibility increased until, passing South Point in a moderating swell, the first contact was made with the weather station where the meteorologists confirmed that there was a strong wind blowing.

On reaching the bay off the weather station the swell conditions and strong south-south-westerly wind made it impossible to anchor there. So, Captain Smith, after surveying other possibilities on the leeward side of the island decided on Quest Bay as the safest and most sheltered anchorage that morning. Coincidentally, this was offshore an area of the island known as the Glen, where an earlier weather station had been located. Thus, shortly before eight o'clock the anchor went down and the RMS St Helena was making her first call at Gough Island, 40° 20' S, 10° 00' W. The anchorage had the advantage of being completely sheltered yet only some 2 to 3 miles down the coast from the site of the weather station.

The sun was shining brightly, reflecting strongly off the sea, which was strangely calm in the shelter of the bay, as the two RIBs were swung out and lowered into the sea at the ship's side. The boats departed in a welter of spray and were soon lost to the sight of those on board in the choppy waters around the point as we left Quest Bay and headed up the coast towards the inlet below the weather station.

We made radio contact with the weather station as we made our approach in the RIBs. We spotted the station crew far above shortly before the boats slipped out of their sight below the overhanging cliff. The only way ashore here (apart from using a helicopter) is in a cradle with a base some 3 feet square with rope supports with cross splicing, rather like the first rungs on the rigging of a sailing ship, onto which to hold. The cradle was lowered by a crane, the operator of which cannot see over the cliff top about 120 feet above the surface of the sea. Using the VHF radio link it was possible to 'talk' the cradle down to enable me, accompanied by Sqn Ldr Marshall and RMS cadet Andrew Greentree, to make the first upward trip. The progress was rather slow and the cradle spun slowly round as it lifted us ever higher. Jokes about plummeting down into the sea below became unamusing as the cradle approached the level of the cliff top when it came to a halt. The brake on the crane had jammed! There we literally hung around, gently spinning and swinging, for almost 15 minutes while first a hammer and then buckets of water were induced to free the brake.

Having finally succeeded in freeing the brake, the cradle swung to earth on Gough Island. Shortly before 9am on 25th January 1999 I became the first Governor believed to have set foot on that most southerly part of the island territories comprising St Helena and Its Dependencies. Following quickly behind was the first Saint Helenian (Andrew Greentree) to visit Gough Island, and probably the first officer of the Royal Air Force, Paul Marshall. "*Roaring Endeavour*": Mission accomplished. There was, however and as I was later to be reminded, nothing explicit in the plans that had been laid for the exercise about getting me off again!

As we had hung, gyrating gently in the breeze 120 feet above the sea, we had been within sight but not conversational distance of the weather station crew for fully fifteen minutes. By the time that we were finally swung ashore, we were greeted like long lost friends by the leader of the 'Gough 44' team, Anke Kotze, and her five companions - three meteorologists, a radio technician and a diesel mechanic, who made up this forty-fourth team to man the Gough Island weather station for the South African Antarctic Programme. Having landed there in September and not seeing any visitors since, they were anxious to talk and show the visitors their home and talk, and talk! Once the Administrator (Brian Baldwin), his wife and Andy Melling, another of the RAF team, had joined us via a well-behaved crane journey, we repaired to the Station, where we were shown around; photographs duly taken; and finally congregated in the mess room for the rather more serious part of the expedition.

I presented a new Union Flag to Ms Kotze, on behalf of the station crew, as a friendly but formal reminder that the weather station was in fact on British soil. I also presented the 'Gough 44 Mess' with a plaque of the St Helena Coat of Arms and an artist's rendition of the Arms for Tristan da Cunha (which had not then been formally granted) as a reminder of this unique and historic visit of the Governor to that part of the Territory.

I had been in correspondence with Professor Nigel Wace of Melbourne University about Gough Island during the previous year. Professor Wace had been a member of the 1955-56 Gough Island Scientific Survey that had surveyed and mapped Gough Island. *Inter alia* he had suggested that we could rectify what in retrospect the Survey team considered to be an omission on their part some forty years earlier. I agreed with his recommendation that it would be appropriate to name a feature of the island after its original discoverer. He suggested that we might rename Expedition Peak. So, I read the Declaration that had been prepared in advance at the Castle in Jamestown to rename the former Expedition Peak, Gonçalvo Alvarez Peak (the Expedition's spelling followed that of other references) after the sea captain who had originally discovered the island, thus commemorating half a millennium of European imperial history.

Gough Island is the most spectacular of all the islands in the South-east Atlantic and which comprise St Helena and Its Dependencies. It is remote and somewhat lonely place some 1,700 miles west of the Cape of Good Hope. Ringed with cliffs, with rugged and yet beautiful mountain scenery, it is has been described as one of the least disrupted ecosystems of its kind and one of the best shelters for nesting seabirds in the Atlantic. It is home to two indigenous land bird species, spectacular penguin and seal colonies, and what ornithologists claim to be the world's finest population of seabirds. Gough Island has been identified by BirdLife International as an 'Important Bird Area', (IBA). It is fitting that it should be a World Heritage Site. The passengers on board the waiting ship all believed themselves lucky to have had the unexpected opportunity to gaze upon its beauty – as, of course, did those of us who went ashore.

The journal of the Royal Air Forces Association, *Air Mail*, covered the landing in its July/September 1999 edition under the headline "*Historical event in South Atlantic Ocean*" and concluded by quoting me as reflecting on departing Gough Island that "*I feel particularly privileged that not only have I, as an individual been able to gaze upon its beauty, but as its Governor, have actually managed to stand upon its shores.*"

The landing was duly reported to Buckingham Palace. Her Majesty graciously replied by telegram which read:-

"I received with pleasure your message of 25th January. It was good news that you are the first Governor to land on all four of the major islands of the Tristan da Cunha Group. Many congratulations.
Elizabeth R."

The official Hydrographer at Taunton also acknowledged that, with respect to future chart editions, the former Expedition Peak on Gough Island would henceforth be known as Gonçalvo Alvarez Peak.

However and before we had re-embarked on the *RMS*, the party relocated down the coast to the beach at the foot of The Glen where I was able to photograph 'our ship' gently swinging at anchor at 40° 20'S – 10° 00'W, framed by Archway Rock at the head of The Glen. The photograph mirrors one taken of *HMY Britannia* from Gough by The Duke of Edinburgh during his visit to the Southern Ocean in 1956. The photograph appeared in his book *Birds from Britannia*, which was published in 1962. Curnow Shipping Ltd later used the photograph that I had taken for their company calendar for 2000.

There is, however, an interesting postscript to this adventure. In acknowledging receipt of confirmation that the task of renaming Expedition Peak in honour of the discoverer of Gough Island had duly been completed, Professor Wace wrote that he believed that this was not the first time a Governor had landed on the island. His information indicated that Governor Thomas Oates had landed on Gough Island in the 1970s. It took some considerable time and research to discover the facts.

At the time of the 1999 landing the Tristanians had believed that the *'Roaring Endeavour'* attempt would, if successful, be the first time that a Governor had set foot on Gough Island. On return to St Helena in February 1999, after the successful landing, contemporary received opinion was also that it was indeed a 'first'. Nevertheless, it was clear that the identity of the first Governor of the Dependency to set foot on this furthest part of the Territory had to be established beyond doubt.

The Administrator of Tristan da Cunha, by then Bill Dickson, came up with the anecdotal evidence that there had been no gubernatorial landing on Gough Island before 1999. Later he confirmed that there was no record in the Tristan da Cunha Government files to indicate otherwise, and - following a visit there himself - that there was no entry in the Gough Weather Station Visitors Book in 1973 or 1974 to confirm Thomas Oates' presence on the island. The Government of St Helena Archivist also joined in the search – there should have been, at least, a report of the landing in the Castle Archive. But, after extensive research, she too came up with no record – as too did a search of the local newspaper archives for the period of Governor Oates' term.

Our attention then turned to the Foreign & Commonwealth Office records. Reference was found there of Sir Thomas Oates preparing to go to Tristan da Cunha during both 1973 and 1974. But, he was apparently unsuccessful on both occasions. Finally a file note to the effect that he was to take passage aboard a Royal Fleet Auxiliary vessel from Cape Town in November 1974 was found; and then, a cryptic signal from the *RFA Reliant* that bad weather had precluded the Governor going ashore at Tristan da Cunha on 13th November. But, nothing more could be found in the FCO archive to establish whether or not the Governor had landed on Gough Island.

Nonetheless, there was the clue that Governor Oates had been aboard the *Reliant* at the material time. A search of the Royal Fleet Auxiliary records in the Ministry of Defence archives unearthed the log of the *RFA Reliant*. The log entries showed that Sir Thomas Oates had embarked *Reliant* at Duncan Dock, Cape Town on 7th November 1974 and that *Reliant* had sailed that evening.

At 0800hrs on 12th November the log records *Reliant* "...*stopped and drifting off Gough Island*" and at 1313hrs "*Closing Gough for passengers*" who, at 1442hrs, were embarked. There is no log entry to indicate that the Governor either went ashore or was one of the passengers embarked on the *RFA*'s 23ft cutter that had been deployed for this exercise. This is in marked contrast to the log entry on 14th November when, after *Reliant* had been lying off Tristan da Cunha since 1500hrs on 13th November, it refers to making a lee off Edinburgh's harbour for an approaching boat, which came alongside at 0710hrs and *"0720hrs. Governor in boat."* and again *"0720hrs. Governor away."* The log shows that *Reliant* sailed from Tristan with H.E. and others embarked from the island shortly after 1800hrs on 17th November 1974; and that Governor Oates disembarked at the St Helena anchorage at noon on 21st November.

All this would seem to be pretty conclusive proof that Sir Thomas Oates did not in fact land at Gough Island in the 1970s, although he certainly sighted the island in 1974 – his only visit to the southern extremity of his parish - and that 'Governor Smallman' was the first Governor to land on the island during the voyage of the *RMS St Helena* in January 1999.

*   *   *

Also onboard the *RMS* during that voyage to Tristan da Cunha and Gough were a Swiss couple, Birgit and Adrian Bührer, owners of the Chateau Capion in the South of France. The couple had purchased the Saxenburg wine estate at Kuilsriver near Stellenbosch in 1989, renovated the homestead built in 1701 by Joachim Sax, and employed the renowned winemaker Nico van der Merwe as the estate's wine grower and cellar master. Saxenburg had since become a prize-winning estate producing top quality red and white wines – particularly Shiraz, Cabernet Sauvignon and Sauvignon Blanc.

During the return voyage to Cape Town Birgit and Adrian had been sat with us at the captain's table, where we had enjoyed their company. They owned horses and both rode. Shortly before we arrived at Cape Town they invited Martin Smith, Sandi and me to visit the estate on 31st January and take the opportunity for a ride. Sandi very sensibly declined the ride – there had to be someone able to drive back to Cape Town if either Martin or I fell!

Adrian arrived alongside the *St Helena* in a white cabriolet Rolls Royce to convey Capt Smith in sedate grandeur, while we followed in a small hire car. At Saxenburg we changed into some clothes more suitable for riding. Our horses were frisky, having had no exercise during the absence of their customary riders over the previous two weeks, but provided a superb way to see the estate. It extended to nearly 500 acres, of which a little over 220 (90 hectares) were planted to vineyards. Sandi remained at the homestead while Martin Smith and I made our tour on horseback with Adrian; and then Birgit and she joined us in the courtyard as, still in the saddle, we were offered a glass of sparkling white wine from a silver tray. A delicious lunch followed before we had to make a hasty return to Duncan Dock to enable Capt Smith to take command of the *RMS* for the voyage to St Helena.

CHAPTER THIRTEEN

Drawing to a Close

Once more it was Eric George who became the cause of political conflict; and once more the lack of any in-built Government majority in its 'Cabinet' – ExCo - and the political immaturity of the Island's elected representatives that brought the St Helena Government to crisis point.

In the light of the problems experienced with the Budget for 1998/1999, officials had been at great pains to ensure that the elected members were onboard and understood each step along the way towards the preparation of the 1999 Budget. As a consequence there was little detailed debate in the Executive Council when the Appropriation Bill was discussed on 16th February 1999. The detail had been thrashed out in the Finance and Development Group – which itself comprised a majority of MLCs - and, in various forms, by ExCo itself, over the previous weeks and months. It was, thus agreed unanimously at the ExCo meeting on 2nd March that the Bill should be printed, published and presented to Legislative Council as Government business. However, at the end of that meeting Eric George announced that he had *"made a mistake over the Appropriation Bill"*. He would not support it and withdrew his support from the Budget. He was not moved by later reminders, in private discussion, of his collective responsibility for Executive Council decisions - the Government of which he formed part – neither did he see this as a resigning matter! However, his apparent *volte face* was not altogether surprising, given his previous lack of enthusiasm for Government policy and his failure to vote with Government on the Budget in 1998. With Executive Council member Bill Drabble absent abroad, Councillor George implacably opposed to his own Government and most Members of the Legislative Council having already announced that they would vote against the Government's Budget, regardless of its provisions, the result of the vote on the Appropriation Bill after the Financial Secretary's Budget Speech on 16th March was, perhaps, a foregone conclusion. The Appropriation Bill duly fell when it was introduced at the start of the Legislative Council Budget Session on 19th March.

Negotiations with individual members of the Legislative Council over the next few days failed to produce anything resembling a majority for the Government's Appropriation Bill. As I explained earlier, under the terms of the St Helena Constitution, the Governor is not obliged either to consult, or accept the advice of, Executive Council in the exercise of his Reserved Powers. However, it was agreed that both within, and in the wider world outside, St Helena, it was important to show that the use of the Governor's Reserve Powers was a course recommended by the Government of St Helena (i.e. Executive Council); and that the Government respected its obligations under the Aid Planning Agreement and the need to provide for the services and policies agreed as a result. In the knowledge that funding for all Government activities would cease on 1st April, Executive Council agreed unanimously that use of the Governor's Reserved Power over finance was required urgently. On the evening of 30th March Radio St Helena broadcasted my message to the Island explaining what was to be done and why. The Appropriation Ordinance, 1999 was enacted - under the powers reserved in Section 34 of the St Helena Constitution Order, 1988 - the next morning.

To lose appropriation legislation once - as had been the case in 1998 was unfortunate, if unique in the island's history - but to be defeated twice in successive years might seem to indicate gross carelessness! However, the nub of the problem lay in the total unwillingness of Councillors to act upon what they had agreed with HMG. There was also an element of what MLCs believed to be the inadequate response of the British Government to meet the island's needs over the years. Although on the one hand Government, in the shape of an Executive Council in which elected members formed a majority, had set out a policy to reform the public sector, the dinosaurs amongst them failed in public to support the policies they had agreed upon within the confines of the Executive Council, and called into question the Aid Planning Agreement to which they had subscribed. No amount of explanation seemed to bring them to the point of enlightenment.

*   *   *

I was struck down by dengue fever on 4th March. The Island's Chief Medical Officer, who was on duty as the general practitioner at the hospital declared that there was no dengue on St Helena and that notwithstanding my temperature of 104°, should Sandi want him to see me I had to be taken to the hospital in Jamestown. We did go, but to no avail. I was hallucinating – and remember very little about the couple of days as my temperature soared. Sandi was naturally very worried about the high temperature, and the Plantation staff were very sympathetic.

Finally one of the staff said to Sandi that, "*You should try vinegar socks, Madam*" and explained that wrapping a patient's feet in socks soaked in vinegar would bring down the temperature. (It is quite possible that this folk remedy has been immortalised in the nursery rhyme, *Jack and Jill* - remember when Jack fell down and cracked his skull it was wrapped "*in vinegar and brown paper.*"). Shirley Yon (no relation to Ethel) arrived in my bedroom, Sandi later related to me, with a bowl of vinegar on a silver tray together with two of the best linen table napkins. She could not be persuaded to find something, perhaps, a little more suited to dowsing in vinegar and wrapping round my feet! Once dunked in the vinegar, the napkins were then tied around my feet. The next morning my temperature had gone! However, I did take it easy for a while after that experience.

The White Paper, on the United Kingdom's relationship with its Overseas Territories, Cmnd No. 4264, was published on 16th March 1999. It duly included a Chapter on citizenship, which specifically mentioned the sense of injustice felt by Saints on account of the promise in the King Charles II Charter, and undertook that "*...British citizenship – and so the right of abode – should be offered to those British Dependent Territories citizens who do not already enjoy it and who want to take it up*" (Gibraltarians and Falkland Islanders already had that status). This I had expected, but I hadn't expected to have a phone call from London and an interview on John Humphreys' BBC Radio Four morning news programme, *Today*.

I had, nonetheless, gained quite a lot of experience in speaking on the radio. Radio St Helena had a very special place in Island life on St Helena. It operated on a shoestring budget, having only a handful of permanent employees; and relied very heavily on both material provided by, or re-broadcast from the BBC, and amateur contributors for much of its programming – as with the *From my Collection* series of music programmes that I have earlier mentioned. As Governor I was also given access to air time to enable me explain what Government doing; and I had a prime time spot on Christmas Day for a message to the Island immediately after the Station broadcast the Queen's Christmas message. In 1988 I co-presented a monthly programme of West Indian music, which I understood gained quite a following!

*   *   *

The Governor's Commission on the Constitution concluded their enquiries and studies in April. As I had reported to the FCO over the years, members of the Legislative Council had on the one hand consistently articulated a call for constitutional reform but, on the other hand, been unspecific and sought to put the onus for deciding what changes might be practicable on to HMG. Having been closely involved in the issue during my term, and observing the Commission's consultation exercise and the confusion of the 'Unofficial' Members of Government, I had a degree of sympathy with their view that they required guidance from London. Indeed, having conducted the consultation, in which all MLCs had been closely involved, they particularly, and the Islanders in general, needed a lead from HMG, indicating what, if any, of the Commission's recommendations might form the basis for further discussion. They all needed to be told what could not be done as much as what changes might be made.

Thus, on 28th April I wrote a comprehensive treatise covering the pros and cons for constitutional change so far as St Helena was concerned. My Despatch was simply headed '*A Case for Constitutional Change?*' I led with a quote from Lewis Carol' - "*If you don't know where you are going, any road will get you there*" as spoken by the Cheshire Cat in

Alice in Wonderland, the latter being particularly appropriate as I saw it. I made the suggestion that the Legal Advisers Department might review my Despatch and the Commission's recommendations and subsequently enter into a dialogue with the St Helena Government's principal legal adviser, the Attorney General, to determine the viability, or otherwise, of the recommendations and any other proposals for constitutional change which might form the basis for amendments acceptable to HMG in the constitutional arrangements for St Helena. After further consultation and debate here, I suggested that the outcome may well be that what emerged could form the drafting instructions for a revised Order-in-Council.

It is doubtful whether much if any serious thought can have been applied to either the Report of the Governor's Commission on the Constitution or my lengthy Despatch No. 2 of 28th April 1998 examining the case for constitutional change before I left the Island. I have no first hand knowledge of the process that followed other than to comment that it was not until 2009 that an Order-in-Council – The St Helena, Ascension and Tristan da Cunha Constitution Order, 2009 was promulgated. Obviously several of my successors must have been involved; and a case made for an umbrella constitutional instrument to cover each of the three Territories.

*   *   *

I was sufficiently recovered from my brush with dengue fever by 30th April to join in a match on Francis Plain. This time it was one with a difference. A young man employed by Solomon & Co had told me at an earlier social occasion that the Island's football team had been challenged to a game by the crew of the *RMS*. I foolishly said that I would be available to play if numbers were a problem as it was to be played on a working afternoon. I soon realised how ridiculous that was – I might have been fit, but surely not that fit? I made my excuses – I had no boots – but that wasn't a problem they could be found. Socks? The same. Shirt? Buy a yellow T-shirt at Yon's in the High Street. I had no excuses left. I was in the starting line up! But there was a mitigating offer – I could play for the first ten minutes or so, and a substitute would be on-hand to relieve me. However, I forgot the substitute until about fifteen minutes from the end and wondered why a young man wearing a yellow shirt was jogging up and down the touchline. The penny dropped and I quickly left the field. After the game, as we gathered around the couple of cases of beer that I had brought along for the teams, one of the young players said that he knew that I played and enjoyed cricket, but that he didn't know that I played football. I said that I didn't really play football any more and that indeed my last game had been in June 1997 (in Singapore). *"Wow, I wasn't even born then"* was the reply! Nevertheless, that game gave me great 'street cred', among the younger generation, at least for a few days.

*   *   *

Looking wider, it was true to say the even in a digital age, the Island's remoteness militated against exponential growth. Intellectual accomplishment had been hindered by a lack of ready interchange with the outside world and by an ungrammatical English usage, itself the result of inadequate resources and an historic lack of emphasis put upon an academic education. There was also a willingness to tolerate lower standards in education than the Island demanded to achieve a well-qualified and articulate work force capable of competing internationally. Learning was considered, by a wannabe-macho youth culture, as being for girls, with the consequence that for the most part women filled the majority of senior positions in public service and the boys become the Island's manual workers. A lucky few got cadetships on the *RMS* or, latterly, to join the Armed Forces (but so too did the girls). Others went off to labour on Ascension or the Falkland Islands.

The Island's same conservative tendency has meant that politicians were unresponsive to suggestions that St Helena actually needed to encourage immigration. There was no new immigration during the nineteenth century, and prospective settlers during the twentieth century had been viewed as threats to local employment opportunities. But, in a first, small step, towards recognising that a managed immigration can have positive economic and social benefits ExCo did approve a statement of Immigration Policy, but it had not started to fulfil its objectives of filling labour market shortages, improving public finances and contributing to the development of new industries and jobs; but the structures were in place by early 1999 to use inward migration as a means to achieve a degree of economic growth whenever the opportunities arose.

As the pages above have demonstrated, more than half of the island's GDP was generated through the British Government's grant-in-aid of administration and by remittances from overseas workers. However, this is something of a double-edged sword. There was genuine concern that were there to be any substantial economic development of Ascension Island, attracting further Saint Helenian migration to better paid jobs, that St Helena and its fragile economy would be adversely affected. The objective of financial independence, embraced in Jamestown as well as in London, while utterly laudable, was still so far from achievement that it remained difficult to see quite how it might be fulfilled.

So, by 1999 the ground for progress had, nevertheless, been prepared, but it was for St Helena and Saint Helenians to take advantage of the opportunities that the twenty-first century might offer. If St Helena's politicians continued to seek to avoid taking responsibility publicly for difficult decisions, in the fear of being blamed for those which their constituents found unpopular, and as a result to represent themselves as separate from the Government of which they were in fact part, there would, I thought, be very little political progress. After all, unwillingness to take the blame is an attitude not altogether far removed from the general character of a significant part of the Island's very conservative population. Together they exhibited a velleity in the pursuit of progress that made West Indian lassitude look positively dynamic! However, there was still hope. They did not actually represent the up-and-coming generation with their 'get-up-and-go' attitude who had gone - but will hopefully return in the future to help build that *"...prosperous, peaceful and democratic society for all."*

For all this, there comes a time in the governance of that remote colony when one realises it is time to go. A latter day Hudson Janisch, a Canadian descendent of his namesake, visited the Island in November 1998 and presented me with a copy of the letters of his illustrious predecessor, father of Hudson Ralph Janisch, Governor of St Helena from 1872 - 1890. In that slim volume I found that Georg Wilhelm Janisch, when writing to his cousin Joachim in Hamburg on 12th May 1843, declared that:-

> "...the dreadful contrast between tropical heat and icy storms makes all those who are driven here by fate become prematurely old and pass away..."

While not passing early away, I recognised that four years on that inhospitable rock was enough and that these words would aptly find a place as the heading of my farewell Despatch from St Helena. The next milestone in the island's cycle of development was a second three year Aid Planning Agreement for the period 2000/2001 – 2002/2003. This was due to be negotiated in December 1999, and it seemed only right and proper that the Governor who would have to live with the results of that Agreement should be able to lead the St Helena Government team in those negotiations.

CHAPTER FOURTEEN

Farewell to St Helena

As I reflected on the successes and travails of our four years in St Helena I had once more put pen to paper and composed a final Despatch to the Secretary of State for Foreign & Commonwealth Affairs in London.

I had had no illusions about the island of St Helena before our arrival in September 1995, although on reflection I fear that my first impressions, as essayed to the Foreign Secretary of the day, were the view of an outsider and coloured with the experiences of other times and places. Saints had, at least during our time on the Island, referred to three day and seven day visitors. The first category covered those who stepped ashore for the time that the *RMS St Helena* was in port. The seven day visitor was one who came to the Island and stayed for the additional days when the *RMS* was away on its trip to and from Ascension Island. They might find out a little more about St Helena, but when the *RMS* departed for Cape Town or specially when the ship was away on its call in the UK, the atmosphere in Jamestown changed: it was very different. Very few casual visitors saw or experienced that Island. And, hence the more idyllic references to Saints and their Island that were made in books about St Helena, which depended to a great extent on the author's impressions of so short a visit.

An old chum, whom we had first met on St Helena in 1995, and who has visited the Island on many occasions, wrote to us from Jamestown on 13th January 2018 saying *inter alia*:-

> *"As to St Helena (here from 10th to 17th Jan) I now find that it's not the same island that I knew when you and Sandi were there, or even five years ago. Everything more expensive than ever . . . On the RMS' arrival here – the same old story – no eggs, no fish, no butter, etc.. The new "4 star" Mantiss Hotel with about 40 rooms is truly splendid – but at £210 per night it's not surprising that guests average 4 to*

6 nightly. It's on the site of 1, 2, & 3 Main Street, opposite the entrance to the Castle Gardens. . . . .

"This will be my very last visit to St Helena as the 'magic' of the place has now definitely gone for me, and the ship [the RMS St Helena] *will now also cease operating. One must move on."*

First impressions can be valuable, but cannot stand in place of the truth of experience. My belief that I expressed that attitudes were slowly being transformed was certainly very wide of the mark in the case of the politicians – the Members of the Legislative Council – they certainly had no *"will to experiment with change"* as I had optimistically stated in my first Despatch from the Castle. Nevertheless, those attitudes were, in varying degrees, shared by sufficient a number in the public service to enable what can only really be described as 'an experiment in public sector reform' to gain traction. It was a stiff and steep path for a very fragile economy to tread, but it was beginning, I believe genuinely, to gain a wider acceptance by the time I wrote my *'Farewell to St Helena'* in May 1995.

I used the quotation from Georg Wilhelm Janisch mentioned in the previous chapter as a heading for my despatch. Although not passing prematurely away, as the former Secretary to Major General Hudson Lowe, and father of the only Governor (Hudson Janisch) to be born and die on the Island, put it in his remarkably touching letter to his cousin in Hamburg, I did, nonetheless, recognise that there came a time in the governance of this remote island Colony when it was, indeed, time to go.

Economically our 'experiment' in structural adjustment had some success, but it had little acceptance politically. Indeed, the Island's politicians seemed unable to think outside of the box into which they regularly retreated when any new idea was floated. They seemed to believe the fact that it had 'never been done like that' meant that it was impossible or even wrong to try. They completely failed to be able to grasp whether it might actually be for the greater good or in the Island's best interests. Nevertheless, I hope the reader will bear with me as the successful bits have found the most coverage within these pages.

Our Administration had had its successes during what the Chief Secretary described as 'the Smallman Years' in his valediction on our departure. Of the four major issues I identified on my arrival in 1995 - national status, access, public sector reform, and the need to stimulate the creation of a private sector and to reduce the financial dependence on the United Kingdom, progress had been made on all.

A commitment had been made to restore full British citizenship. But this, we had always recognised, could be a double-edged sword. The reinstatement of a full British citizenship opened the prospect of employment in the United Kingdom where, in a competitive labour market full of immigrants from the eastern fringes of the European Union, young Saints without good academic qualifications could well find themselves unable to take other than the more menial of the job prospects on offer. Nevertheless, another exodus from the working population - which now in the second decade of the twenty-first century seems to have happened – would compound the natural decline in numbers remaining on the island, with the danger that it could eventually become something of a 'theme-park' attraction which would be even more economically unsustainable. There was a body of conservative opinion on the Island which believed that, as in earlier years when access to the United Kingdom job market was unhindered, the numbers seeking employment in Britain would be manageably small and act to relieve unemployment on St Helena rather than be the cause of skill shortages. Nevertheless, history has shown that of those going abroad to seek employment few ever returned to use their skills or capital to local advantage; and 1990s experience demonstrated that a skills shortage already existed in St Helena, as the better qualified, notably teachers, nurses and policemen took up offshore employment in the Falkland Islands or on Ascension.

Building on the 'Vision for St Helena', a pattern of freeing up resources and creating greater efficiencies within Government emerged to help in growing a private sector. Public sector reform meant moving from an economy in which Government dominated to one where more was done by privately operated enterprise. In a small and fragile island economy like St Helena this can be immensely disruptive. Faced with entrenched opposition the choice was to try to press ahead and not come to a shuddering halt, as the politicians tried continually to engineer. We had sufficient a degree of success to demonstrate that keeping the hands of bureaucrats and politicians off the management of enterprise did actually work. The allied requirement to grow a private sector – to attract foreign investment - proved, Argos Helena apart, much more difficult

There is no doubt that the four years in what *The Daily Telegraph* called the 'diplomatic equivalent' of "...*a weekend in Swanage...*" were difficult, but as the Foreign Secretary put it when writing to thank me for "...*the splendid job you did as Governor of St Helena...*" it appears that I also "...*ruled with great aplomb...*" Well, it could only happen in St Helena!

We finally took our leave of St Helena on 7th May 1999. My adc and Comptroller of the Household, Patrick Young, folded the Governor's Ensign, which only very shortly before had been flying from the flag-pole above Plantation House, and handed it to me ceremoniously. Sandi and I then boarded the official Jaguar, with it own smaller ensign mounted on the wing, for our last journey down to Jamestown.

The House staff, with whom we had had a group photograph taken minutes previously, lined up to bid us farewell: almost a mirror image of the welcome that we had received from them in 1995. They had served us well and we had established an easy rapport. Suddenly it seemed, we were at the Castle for a final leave-taking of the staff there. My final official act was to present the St Helena Certificate and Badge of Honour (a cupro-nickel medal with a yellow ribbon) to the Deputy Secretary, Ethel Yon, and Chief Personnel Officer, Ivy Ellick, for their loyal and valuable service and particularly their outstanding support to me on 19th April 1996.

Then, together with Ethel Yon, Sandi and I walked the last few yards, through the Town Gate and past the Cenotaph, where the previous year a personal initiative had led to the mounting of a bronze plaque bearing the names of all St Helena's servicemen who had died in action in the two World Wars. The knots of Saints gathered there to bid farewell to their own relations hardly acknowledged us as we passed. We bade a final muted farewell to Ethel and walked down the quay to the Steps. Within moments we were in the launch ferrying us out to where 'our yacht' awaited us. We boarded the *Royal Mail Ship St Helena* for the two-week voyage to Cardiff.

During our four years in the South Atlantic we totalled some 54,500 miles aboard the *RMS* travelling to and from St Helena and its Dependencies. We were now no longer part of the Government or government of those islands and were sailing into retirement from diplomatic life.

After the fifteen-day voyage from Jamestown the *RMS St Helena* docked at Cardiff on Saturday 22nd May 1999. Officers of HM Customs came aboard and, in addition to clearing the ship's papers, kindly dealt with our declaration in our cabin while the bulk of the passengers disembarked. The little red Rover 100 car that had acted as our runabout on the island was carefully extracted from its place in the hold and gently placed on the quayside adjacent to the companionway. We packed the car with our portable possessions and by 3:30 that afternoon we were back in Northamptonshire – home and on retirement leave. I formally retired from HM Diplomatic Service on 18th June, packing away the sword and feathers and tropical uniform that had been my official props during the four years tenure of the appointment as Governor and Commander-in-Chief, St Helena and Dependencies.

POSTSCRIPT

St Helena is an island moulded by the elements, and by its inhabitants who, in their turn, were fashioned by the influence of the East India Company. The nineteenth century was an age of British expansion, fuelled by the industrial revolution of the late eighteenth century - an age of mechanisation, of urbanisation and wealth creation, and an age of railways and steamships. It was a second age of discovery and colonisation, but St Helena profited from none of this. With no new immigration following the Company's final departure in 1836, St Helena's character was cast, and progress destined to pass the island by.

Julia Blackburn, writing her account of a journey to discover *'The Emperor's Last Island'* in the early 1990s, wistfully summed it up by saying:-

> *"if only it could break from the habit of its own history. Instead the island has grown accustomed to serving as a prison; the rules and regulations that were needed to turn it into a factory under the control of the East India Company metamorphosed...dressed in modern clothes, but still controlling every aspect of people's lives."*

The dependence (on the Company) and defiance of its writ (witnessed by the several mutinies) had, however, taken root deep within the Saint Helenian psyche long before the Company left, and colour the attitude to the mother country and to authority locally, even today.

The veneer of 'Britishness' is often quite thin. It is certainly thinner than that in Gibraltar or the Falkland Islands. Years of subsidy, most recently under colonial development and welfare auspices (CD&W funds) and then overseas development aid, have led, if anything, to a greater degree of reliance on expatriate assistance. Partly, this must be said, due entirely to the lack of opportunities that the island offers to native born Saints. Nevertheless, it is an unfortunate, but inescapable fact, that a culture of dependence has produced a somewhat feckless characteristic. Such people, when placed in positions of political power or authority are content to exercise themselves to the minimum, while making every possible use of their positions to improve their own standing. A sense of public spiritedness, as more widely recognised, simply does not generally exist. A change in this attitude, the result of a 'slave mentality' and the authoritarianism of the East India Company's rule, is a Herculean task.

However, salvation is to be found in the generation that has been away (either in the United Kingdom, or on the *RMS*, and to a lesser extent on Ascension Island) who are beginning to emerge as personalities in their own right. There is an efficient public service, which compares very favourably to those in the West Indian dependencies, and St Helena's senior public servants are second to none. However, to make progress, to get on a par with the developed dependencies, will need an honesty of purpose and belief in moral values not yet entirely evident in the majority of political figures. But it is clearly possible, as the countless Saints who quietly get on with their own lives, holding those values dear while keeping out of politics, amply bear witness. The other necessary ingredients, of course, are responsible government and a sympathetic ear in the corridors of power in London that recognises that St Helena is, indeed, different.

The island had its 'Vision' to aspire to, but its achievement will be no easy task even if still remembered. Emigration and demographic trends, which point both to a falling birth rate and to an increasing longevity, are building up problems for the future. An ageing population, in which many earners are working overseas and thus contributing little to the public purse, will impact on the public services required to meet this challenge as much as the resources needed to provide those services. De-population is no longer the realistic alternative that it might have been during the first fifty years of life as a Crown Colony in the nineteenth century. To paraphrase former US Secretary of State, Dean Acheson, St Helena has lost a rôle and needs to find its destiny.

Part of this destiny is believed to lie in providing an attractive destination for small-scale tourism. The East India Company and Napoleonic connections are obvious and marketable aspects, but so too is the island's attraction for eco-tourism. Although the early years of the islanders' relationship with St Helena's natural history are a sorry tale of despoliation, punctuated by apparently vain efforts of environmental conservation, the tide has definitely been turned. Environmental conservation now plays a central part in the Government's agricultural and forestry strategy.

Many endemic flora have been lost, and others are on the verge of extinction due to the depredations of man and his animals; and at least six endemic land birds are known to have become extinct since 1502. Nevertheless, there are still forty-five endemic species of plants, over 300 endemic invertebrates, ten shore fishes and one endemic bird, the plover-like wirebird, to be found in and around the forty-seven square miles of this remote island

St Helena, thus, has many endemic and unusual indigenous plants and shrubs. Redwoods and the St Helena ebony were much used for tanning, which together with the local demand for building timber and firewood led to the extinction of the redwood in the wild and the near extinction of the ebony. In fact in 1980 it was believed that the ebony had been extinct for something like one hundred years. However, it was re-discovered by George Benjamin near Castle Rock and its identity confirmed by Dr Quentin Cronk. Cuttings were carefully nurtured at the Island's Scotland nurseries and it now thrives once more. A hybrid species, the result of close planting to the redwood has been named *Trachetiopsis Benjaminii* after its 'creator'. Another endemic thought to have been extinct for over a century was the St Helena boxwood, popular in its time as kindling. Islander Stedson Stroud discovered a specimen in 1998 in the scree in the shadow of Lot's Wife, and I visited the site with him shortly afterwards to wonder at its survival.

Gumwoods covered about a third of St Helena's land area before human habitation and the release of alien domestic animals into the wild. The largest collection of remaining gumwoods is to be found at Peak Dale, although there is a small number of naturally occurring trees still surviving in Deep Valley. Conservation efforts to regenerate the gumwood forests began in the late 1980s; and, in preparation for the biggest re-forestation project yet attempted on the island, plans were put in hand in 1998 for the re-establishment of a native gumwood forest. Situated at Horse Point, an area that has suffered from acute soil erosion following de-forestation, and to be known as the Millennium Forest. The land was prepared to enable the first four thousand saplings to be planted in 2000 in celebration of the millennium.

The Peaks are home to other endemic trees and shrubs. Clearance of flax and other imported plant species (notably buddleia, bilberry, and whiteweed) to enable re-plantings have been a feature of the conservation and regeneration of the native flora of the central mountain range of the island in recent years. These have led to the strengthening and extension of thickets of tree ferns and cabbage trees with the aim that these may clothe the slopes once more, and increase the rainfall over the northern slopes. A Gubernatorial Declaration announced the Peaks as St Helena's first National Park - The Diana's Peak National Park - in March 1996. The Park covers an area of almost 160 acres across the three main peaks of the central ridge where the last vestiges of the tree fern thickets exist.

Coffee, although neither endemic nor indigenous, has been grown on St Helena since the 1730s. Although winning a commendation at the Great Exhibition in London in 1851, it was not cultivated on a scale large enough to become an export commodity to rival Jamaica or Kenya. Nevertheless, the root-stock remained and following on from the East India Company coffee continued to be grown under Government auspices, notably in Sandy Bay Valley. The 1990s saw a sudden growth in the industry as the excellent quality of the product was demonstrated and the realisation that there were a number of areas in which it might flourish.

Although private enterprise had led to the export and sale of St Helena coffee locally, on the *RMS* and through a specialist outlet in Harrogate, it was not until a young Englishman of Saint Helenian ancestry who returned to the island and negotiated a lease on the 'Coffee Grounds' with the St Helena Government that the full potential was realised. Allied with a resuscitated East India Company, re-established as a London registered public limited company, this high quality coffee has been sold as a gourmet beverage, especially in the discerning Japanese market. Other growers, encouraged by the Government, have planted at a number of promising sites around the island and are starting to produce more strains of St Helena coffee. Production was a little over 3 tons in 2000, but could grow tenfold in the next few years.

It will require more similarly innovative thinking to find niches in the global market with which to secure a viable future for St Helena in the twenty-first century, but there are still major problems of local inertia to overcome in introducing and sustaining new industries. In Governor Gallwey's words *"...the islanders'...utter helplessness to do much for themselves without material assistance from outside"* is much to blame. The lace industry, for example, has been allowed to die on more than one occasion, despite its employment and foreign exchange earning potentials. It was first rescued by funding from the British Government and the expertise of an English lace-maker in 1907, but had almost died out by the mid 1940s, when further expatriate teaching experience resuscitated the industry. In 1999 there remained a mere handful of excellent but elderly lace-makers turning out the fine traditional St Helena lace. But, with a younger generation apathetic to learning its intricacies it seems to face virtual extinction again in the twenty-first century.

No-one is blind to the need to create employment and activities that will generate new money. Steps have been taken to attract inward investment and promote tourism. The response has understandably been somewhat mixed to date, given the lack of comparative advantage that St Helena offers. However, the island's remoteness, a disadvantage to most conventional economic development, does provide an advantage in promoting the island as a special tourism destination, once the air connection becomes well known. No bucket and spade holiday venue, but one rich in historic and ecological interest. Nevertheless, the fact still remains that St Helena needs to find solutions pretty quickly and before the current deflationary cycle accelerates towards an economic implosion.

*   *   *

The airport saga continued to run and run well into the twenty-first century. Despite Government's other access priorities an active pressure group for air access remained. Its activities were largely responsible for ensuring that by

1998 the United Kingdom Department for International Development, with the approval of the Government of St Helena, agreed to commission a further and comprehensive phased feasibility study into the whole question of air access to St Helena.

The final phase of this process led, in June 2000, to the production of a report examining the comparative costs of both air and sea access. This study suggested that while the cost of a new passenger ship was likely to be in the region of £26 million, the provision of a modest airport and allied services would be in excess of £38 million. These estimates grossly underestimated the cost of providing an airport, which in the event amounted to ten times that sum. The calculation also omitted the extra costs of providing a dedicated cargo-carrying capacity in a *St Helena* replacement: somewhat disingenuously it was suggested that the carriage of freight to and from St Helena was a common factor in both cases examined. Arrangements for the island's freight would be left to another commercial carrier. This would, of course, be at additional cost to the island. In 2001/2002 the operating subsidy paid from British Government aid funds to maintain the Royal Mail Ship passenger and cargo service to St Helena amounted to some £1½ million.

In July 2001, using the conclusions essayed in the access study, agreement was reached between the St Helena Government and the Department for International Development over a way forward which could lead to the development of an air-strip and access by fixed wing aircraft. The Department for International Development suggested that the British Government might make available funding up to the equivalent cost of a new ship build; and opportunities for private sector financing were to be pursued by the St Helena Government.

An intensive public consultation exercise, setting out some of the pros and cons of the provision of an airport as opposed to a replacement for the *St Helena*, culminated in a *referendum* in 2002. As has so often been the case in St Helena, the result was tinged by the unwillingness of many to make a decision for which they might later be held responsible (or be blamed!).

As in 1997, the result of the *referendum* was that there was still a majority of those registered to vote who did not express any support for the proposal. Nevertheless, the proportion of those voting in favour of an airport over a replacement for the *RMS St Helena* had risen to 27% in St Helena. This was a clearer proportion in favour of the proposal, but still less than half of those entitled to vote exercised their democratic right to express an opinion at the ballot box. Adding those working offshore and also entitled to vote in the *referendum* on this occasion, the proportion in favour of an airport rose to 35%. But this still left some two thirds of Saints either opposed, or at best apparently indifferent, to the loss of the dedicated sea link. Anecdotal evidence indicated strong support for an airport among the young and those working offshore, but an almost equally strong resistance to the idea from the older generations who were, nevertheless, unwilling to stand up for their convictions and vote.

Given such an inconclusive result, there were then few material developments. The final economic, environmental and social costs were calculated to be high, whatever final conclusion was reached; and the equation was then complicated by the existence of the *RMS St Helena*. Had Aid agencies insisted on an assumed rate of return on capital investment in an airfield in the same way as, for instance, as had been the case when considering a much needed breakwater development, then it was difficult to see how it might realistically be financed from Aid funding, whether from the United Kingdom, the European Union or the United Nations Development Programme, in each of which broadly similar rules apply. Commercial financing customarily sought even higher returns.

Furthermore, even were a decision taken for such a development to be undertaken, there remained a concern whether St Helena could provide either the organisation or adequate funding to cope with the day-to-day maintenance, and problems likely to arise in due course, in keeping an airport runway and safety equipment (radar, ILS etc) functioning to the appropriate international standards. It was seen as both ironic and costly if, in a few years time and with no shipping service to fall back on, the St Helena Government might have been pushed into seeking an expensive rescue operation after vast and then scarce aid funds had been poured into what many already considered to be a white elephant.

And finally, there was the question of which airline had the equipment and willingness to operate an air service over the sort of flight sectors that the island would require; and would Governments (United Kingdom or St Helena) be prepared to subsidise such operations, in the same way that the shipping subsidy operated were the service to be shown to be uneconomic? Big questions: a solution to which necessarily had to be found before the expiry of the projected life expectancy of the *RMS St Helena* in 2015.

Rumour had it that Lord Ashcroft, a 'non-dom' tax exile with dual British and Belizean citizenship, a private jet and an historic connection to St Helena was behind the resuscitation of the 'airport project'. He had visited in 1948 when his father had stopped off en route to his own Colonial posting in Africa, and, although only two years old the present Lord Ashcroft was said to remember the occasion clearly. The rumour said that at some time in the early 2000s he had flown over the Island en route from southern Africa and finding that his aircraft could not land at St Helena he took the matter up with the Government – he had been a former deputy Chairman of the Conservative Party. Nevertheless, after a long period of rumour and consultation, in March 2005 the British Government announced plans to construct an airport on St Helena funded by the Department for International Development, which it was expected would be completed by 2010. Whether this was after pressure from St Helena, by concerns over tensions in the South Atlantic, or other pressures it is impossible to discern. Whatever led to the decision, it was then and is now a 'special case' in that it cannot hope to achieve the normally expected rate of return on capital, used as a measure of the value of Aid, on the vast amount of funding needed. By late September 2006 all the companies that had entered the competition to build and run an airport on St Helena had withdrawn.

Apparently DfID restarted the procurement process to identify a suitable design, build and operate contractor in October that year. Four bidders had been identified for the project by March 2007 and visited the island for six months from June 2007 before submitting their final proposals. By

January 2008 DfID was down to a shortlist of two bidders. There were delays within the British government as the Prime Minister (Gordon Brown) apparently insisted on personally reviewing the paperwork allowing an approved bidder. Nevertheless the outcome was that the Italian company Impreglio was appointed in 2008. Then, in November of that year the project was suspended, as the Secretary of State at DfID announced a pause due to the financial pressures brought on by the financial crisis of 2007-2010.

No contract had been signed by January 2009, but after pressure from St Helena the British Government finally announced agreement in July that year to assist in the payment for an airport. Contracts for the construction were signed with a South African company, Basil Read (Pty) Ltd, in November and construction started in May the following year.

The final runway at St Helena airport is shorter than first planned – meaning large jets are not able to land but saving the habitat of a rare flightless bird. The St Helena plover, known locally as the wirebird, is unique to the island. It nests on the ground, catches tiny insects by scurrying after them, and lives in open clearings rather than trees. Experts feared the design for the airport would destroy huge areas of land where the wirebird and the invertebrates it eats live, threatening it with extinction. A redesign of the airport in 2011 reduced the runway by 200 metres to 1,950 metres, saving much of the bird's territory and meaning that less engineering works were required in creating the level area for the runway. But the redesign meant that smaller jets carrying up to 125 passengers would be able to use the runway, rather than the hoped-for larger jets carrying more passengers.

St Helena Airport should have started operating in May 2016, but test flights a month before revealed problems with wind shear. Charles Darwin had noted the problem of wind shear on St Helena on his voyage on the *Beagle* in 1836; and an RAF officer visiting during my time said that nothing would induce him to land at the proposed site. The first and only largish passenger jet, a Comair Boeing 737-800, landed on 18th April 2016 on an implementation flight to test the route, ground operations and handling ahead of the commencement of scheduled services. The landing was not straightforward, with the aircraft only successfully landing on its third attempt due to the crew experiencing severe windshear. The Comair pilot reported that the aircraft had encountered significant turbulence and that the instruments had triggered a windshear caution. The company put commercial operations to St Helena on indefinite hold. On 26th April 2016, the St. Helena Government announced a further indefinite delay to the opening. The plan had been that the airport would be opened on 21st May – St Helena Day – and HRH Prince Edward was due to arrive and perform the official opening. However, this was also abandoned in the wake of the alarming flight reports from the first two jet pilots to land at the new airport. The airport started small operations in June 2016, but could not open to commercial flights. MPs challenged DfID about why it had commissioned an airport paid for by the British taxpayer, without properly appreciating the danger of the windshear effect. Officials told the MPs that it had commissioned a feasibility study from engineering consultancy Atkins for the airport build and acted upon its recommendations, as well as taking advice from the Met Office and aviation regulators. No heads rolled, though!

The late postponement caused extra local costs, and the need to attract and contract an airline with aircraft suitable to operate under the conditions. It also meant extending the use of the *RMS St Helena*, which originally was due to be decommissioned in 2015. On 9th June 2017 a South African company, Air Link, won the bid to operate scheduled flights to St Helena using an Embraer E 190 aircraft from Johannesburg and Cape Town via Windhoek, with a monthly link to Ascension. Due to the limitations placed on operations by the windshear problem, the aircraft will operate utilising only 76 of the 99 seats from Windhoek to St Helena. However and possibly with a sigh of relief, the airport was finally opened to commercial traffic on 14th October 2017.

Matthew Engel's article *Last Boat to St Helena* in the *Oldie* magazine in April 2016 also serves a reminder that, *"The arguments about the airport persist."* The late Rodney Young captain of the *RMS* on Engel's trip and a Saint himself was reported in the article as saying *"I genuinely believe that tourists will come. Saints will find it much easier to travel. What we have now is not the way forward."* The Chief Purser, John Hamilton, with over 20 years experience of the service, disagreed. He accepted that it will be much easier to deal with medical emergencies but said that freight arrangements will be much worse. His view, no doubt held by many Saints themselves was that, *"For the price of the airport you could build a brand-new ship, 50 metres longer and run it for 20 years. Cape Town in three-and-a-half days, not five."* And, it has to be said that the 'holy grail' of the airport construction saga - a self sufficient Island built upon the proceeds of tourism - is as much a *chimera* today as at any time.

*   *   *

Looking back now, it is quite a surprise to me just how much the Royal Navy and the RAF have been elements in the story that has unwound in the preceding chapters; and that is without my own brief attempts at the outset to be part of both. Perhaps it is simply a coincidence that one could point to my old school, St Clement Danes, as being the connecting factor? The emblem of the church (and badge of the school) is an anchor, which in itself is a very naval device and forms the central motif of the RN cap badge. While in 1958, shortly after I had left the school, the rebuilding of the church in London's Strand was completed after the damage from incendiary bombs had destroyed the interior during the Blitz in May 1941. At the time Cecil King, Chairman of *The Daily Mirror*, had recorded in his diary, published in 1970 as *"With Malice Towards None: A War Diary"*, that *"St Clement Danes had been gutted, and only the spire was alight half way up the top and sending out showers and sparks - an odd and rather beautiful spectacle"*. The walls, tower, and steeple of the church emerged intact however, but the church remained a fire-blackened bomb site in the middle of the Strand until 1956 when an appeal was launched to raise over £¼million to fund its rebuilding. The church had been taken over by the Air Council in 1953 and on 19th October 1958 the church was re-consecrated as the Central Church of the Royal Air Force.

My life would obviously have been far different had I followed either of the military paths that I had sought to tread early on. But, I had much to be grateful for in a career that finally ended, by coincidence, on son Neil's birthday in 1999. I was able to retire on my 'notional sixtieth' - a throwback to service in unhealthy climes when time served in those countries known as Scheduled Posts counted as time and a half for pensionable purposes. Although the arrangement was withdrawn in the 1970s I had by then earned time enough to retire early on full pension shortly after my fifty-ninth birthday.

I joined HM Diplomatic Service when I was seeking a way out of the hole that I had dug for myself during my early years, and looking for a real career. Nevertheless, the moment was finally right. Whether it was 'written in my stars', or the moment was finally right, who can say? I had certainly never been consciously aware that there might be an option of a foreign service life, but I was ready, just as one of those periodic fundamental changes in the way Government conducted its business, and which brought together Colonial, Commonwealth, Trade and Foreign Services, happened.

Subsequently, during my years in the Service, I rubbed shoulders with princes, prime ministers and peons; travelled through the Khyber Pass; seen the Taj Mahal; explored the edges of the South Arabian Desert, and the Shan Hills of Burma; learnt to ride a horse well and win rosettes; sailed in the South China Sea; travelled thousands of miles in the South Atlantic Ocean where I became the first Governor ever to have set foot on the Islands of Nightingale, Inaccessible and Gough in the Tristan da Cunha Group; played competitive sports in half-a-dozen countries far from home; learnt to play the guitar and clarinet, and languages that I had never imagined I would ever hear, let alone comprehend. For the most part I had enjoyed those experiences, and been proud to have represented my country overseas. To have been entrusted with the governance of a Dependent Territory was the high point in a career full of fascinating challenges and opportunities.

Another former Governor writing in the mid 1990s of *The loneliness of the long distance Governor* remarked that being the Governor of a small group of islands, though often rewarding, was far from a sinecure for elderly diplomats preparing for retirement. Although I declined, then as now, to describe myself as elderly I could, nonetheless, fully endorse the remark. Having had no part in their choice of their new head of state, local politicians and the public at large have no built-in goodwill as for one elected to the post. A Governor has to have the patience of Job and be able to develop the skills of a Machiavelli in trying to solve apparently intractable problems when to give way can be a sign of weakness: compromise is not always the right answer! One lives on one's wits, drawing on a lifetime of diplomatic experiences, as often there is no one set answer to the problems that a Governor can face. He needs the support of his colleagues in London just as much as those around him *en poste*, and it was an insight to observe from far distant Saint Helenian shores how little our advice was heeded once we had left the fold in London, and just how much our erstwhile colleagues there turned to reinvent the wheel at frequent intervals.

I had reached a point where I could look back on the plethora of debilitating reports, 'initiatives' and 'scrutinies' that had both coloured and changed the environment in which I had served. It was not the same Service that I had joined: efficient, effective and self-confident: an elite, chosen, not privileged – especially when taking into account the difficult and dangerous places in which one could be directed to serve. But, change is surely inevitable? Good management, according to one school of thought, means, as the former chairman of ICI and business guru Sir John Harvey-Jones was wont to say *"The achievement of maximum change in an organisation"*. But that need not, indeed surely should not, result in 'the baby being thrown out with the bath water'. I, for one, regretted the demise of the simple practice of scholarship and courtesy; the use of grammatical written English and correct forms of address; and receiving replies to correspondence. Before even the twenty-first century embedding of New Labour 'values' and its concomitant 'political correctness', I believed that we were already in danger, through endless navel gazing, of spending so much time in administering ourselves and our objectives that the pursuit of the Service's core functions were in danger of being lost in the chimera of a spurious modernisation.

I had an enjoyable and, I hope, productive career, much of it spent in interesting places in interesting times. Sandi and I were able to spend almost all of our married life together, unlike contemporaries in the armed services and others for whom overseas travel is part and parcel of their calling. Our three children had a broad experience of life in the third world that has helped prepare them for much of what life might later have in store for them. My Valedictory Despatch of 6th May 1999 to Robin Cook, the Secretary of State for Foreign and Commonwealth Affairs, gave me a platform to pay tribute to Sandi of whom I wrote *"I would not be here today without the love and encouragement of my wife, Sandi, who has been both friend and wisest counsel and to whom I pay tribute and offer thanks for the many hundreds of hours she has contributed in the cause of GB Ltd and, more recently, SHG & Co, to enable me to carry out my job adequately over the past many years."*

The recognition of one's services takes many forms. It was a custom, as Alan Lennox-Boyd (Secretary of State for the Colonies, 1954-59) emphasised when arguing for its retention in the mid-1970s, for a Colonial Governor to be granted a knighthood on assuming office. It recognised his elevated position in the Territory that he was to lead. But, I think rightly, the custom fell into disuse when the direction of colonial affairs became subsumed in those of foreigners and members of the Commonwealth. Nevertheless, a system of honours, indeed a special order of chivalry, the Most Distinguished Order of Saint Michael and Saint George, exists for award to men and women who render *"extraordinary or important non-military service in a foreign country"* and *"important or loyal service in relation to foreign and Commonwealth affairs"*. Thus it is that the most senior and distinguished members of Her Majesty's Diplomatic Service might receive a knighthood (KCMG) today, and those in the next echelon can be invited to become Companions of the Order (CMG).

Ralph Selby, HM Ambassador at Oslo (1972-75), had written in his valedictory despatch of 12th March 1975:-

> *"It is true.........that honours used in the old days, to offer some compensation for all this;* [the disadvantages of living abroad in not always

congenial conditions] *and it is in my view, absurd to argue, as some do, that honours are fundamentally an irrelevance and that it is sufficient honour itself to represent Her Majesty abroad. Of course it is while it lasts......... It is still essentially honours, which give to the public an indication of the esteem in which jobs are and ought to be held. I am not however at all sure that this argues for more honours for the Diplomatic Service..."*

Thus, there existed within the Service even at the time I retired, an informal rule of thumb that ascending the Ambassadorial heights at, say Ankara (and not being responsible for souring international relations there) might result in a KCMG or were it to be Paris a GCMG (especially at the end of one's career), and that making a good job of being HM Consul-General at Toronto would probably earn a CMG.

In February 1990, after three years heading the secretariat dealing with Royal Matters at the FCO and after he learnt of my future career move, Sir William Heseltine, The Queen's Private Secretary, wrote to me and said that *"The Queen . . .knows well how much her office has depended on your assistance"*. His letter went on to say," *. . .we have all come to depend on you so heavily and to appreciate the help and advice you have given so readily"* and *"We shall miss you enormously from* [Buckingham Palace telephone] *extension 3629"*. I was, and I remain, very proud that Her Majesty felt that my service to Her and the Royal Family should be recognised by my appointment (being 'granted the dignity') as a Lieutenant of Her Royal Victorian Order (LVO). When I retired in 1999, I considered that was that.

However, one of the first questions I was asked by colleagues when I became a Foreign Office Historical Records Adviser in the year after my retirement was - why had I turned down a CMG? There was an air of incredulity when I said that I hadn't. My predecessor at St Helena had been awarded a CMG and his predecessor a CBE. I must have turned down something, surely? But I had not. Is recognition in the so-called honours system simply a matter of being in the right place at the right time, of having friends in the right places, or doing what 'London' wanted? Should not one's official life be more a matter of doing what one knows to be right – and doing it well regardless of what others think? I believe that experience over a long and varied diplomatic career gave me the answer to that one! In any case and most unfortunately for the concept of honours as rewards for outstanding service to the nation, the whole system fell into disrepute during the years that New Labour was in power (1997-2010). It has neither changed nor improved over subsequent years. Indeed, it can be argued that it has become more degraded with political failure being marked by a knighthood. So, perhaps to have been commended on my retirement from Her Majesty's Diplomatic Service by the FCO's senior administrator, the Chief Clerk, for my *"...performance and the committed way in which you have carried out your duties"* and that Sandi and I would be *"much missed in the Service"* was recognition enough. For having *"ruled with great aplomb"*, as Robin Cook put it to me in his letter of 29th April 1999 on my retirement and thanking me for my *"service...loyalty and commitment"*, and specifically for the *"...splendid job you did as Governor of St Helena"*, added a ministerial seal of approval, to the official recognition, that I found of far more reward.

When my appointment was announced the *Peterborough* column in *The Daily Telegraph* commented along the lines that among the riches of the Posts available to a senior officer of Her Majesty's Diplomatic Service an appointment as Governor of St Helena was considered by some to be akin to opening the winning envelope in the then popular TV show *Blind Date* only to find that the prize was a weekend in Swanage! There is no doubt in my mind that the four years in the 'diplomatic equivalent' of *"...a weekend in Swanage..."* were difficult. But of the four major issues that I had identified on my arrival in 1995 - national status; access; public sector reform; and the need to stimulate the creation of a private sector and to reduce the financial dependence on the United Kingdom - progress was made on all.

Four years on that lonely rock were indeed a difficult time. But, a working life time of diplomatic experience, I like to think, enable me to produce positive results for the people of St Helena; and that I did do some good! That this was not far from the truth was brought home to me very shortly before departing when a Saint with years in England confided *"Leave them wanting more . . ."*

In the period before my departure from St Helena we set up a committee to plan the celebration of the Quincentenary of the Island's discovery; and after I left, realising that there was no contemporary publication on the history of St Helena I made my own contribution to 1502-2002 by recording that history in my book *'Quincentenary'*, published in 2002. Her Majesty The Queen sent her own message of congratulation:-

On the occasion 500th *anniversary of the discovery of St. Helena I have much pleasure in sending my warmest congratulations to the people of the island on this special day. I know that many Saints have travelled overseas to seek employment on the Falkland Islands, Ascension Island, the UK, South Africa and elsewhere, but their love for their homeland remains undiminished. They truly look forward to the first sight of the island on the horizon, as it appears rising from the ocean.*

St. Helena was discovered in 1502, but it was not until 1658 that the British East India Company colonised and fortified the island. St. Helena has had many distinguished visitors throughout its history. Napoleon Bonaparte was exiled to St. Helena in 1815 and remained there until his death in 1821. Other visitors, who have been as famous in their own fields, have included Edmund Halley in 1677, Captain Cook in 1775 and Charles Darwin in 1836.

The loyalty and affection of the Saints for the Crown is well known and greatly valued. I remember with much pleasure my own visit to St. Helena in 1947 with The King, The Queen and my sister, Margaret. I have an abiding memory of the arum lilies, understandably the island's national flower, growing in the wild as we drove to Bamboo Hedge and back to Plantation House. There we met Jonathan, still the oldest living inhabitant of St. Helena, and many Saints. The warmth and informality of our welcome remain with me to this day. My family has continued to enjoy strong links with the island and its people. Princess Margaret launched the first RMS St. Helena, the island's only regular cargo/passenger shipping link to the outside world in 1978 and the Duke of York enjoyed his own visit to St. Helena in 1984. I know that he is delighted to join you in your celebrations in London today to mark the Quincentenary and the launch of the St. Helena National Trust. The Princess Royal is very much looking forward to her own visit to St. Helena later this year.

My thoughts are with the people of St. Helena, wherever you are in the world, on this special day, and I send you every good wish for a peaceful and prosperous future.

Elizabeth R
21st May 2002

The *RMS St Helena*, the service life of which had been extended once again, paid a first and final call to London in June 2016. London was the ship's port of registry, but she had never called there. So, as a finale to the ship's life as the St Helena Lifeline there were two days of celebratory functions on board as she lay alongside *HMS Belfast* in the Pool of London. A fine celebration of a fine vessel's life; and an opportunity to catch up with many of those aboard who had eased our passage to and from St Helena. These included Matt Young, my former Financial Secretary, who had gone on to serve for many years with distinction as a member of the St Helena Line board; Capt Rodney Young, who had been the First Officer during our 54,500 miles of travel in 'our yacht'; Capt Andrew Greentree – 'Gough' Greentree – who as a cadet, had accompanied me ashore at Gough Island in 1999; Chief Purser John Hamilton, with whom we had also travelled on some of many occasions we had been aboard the *RMS*; and many other familiar crew members, together with travel industry representatives.

If from what appears in the foregoing chapters suggests that St Helena was a somewhat Ruritanian society it is because it was true. The lacuna in taking responsibility for one's actions and hiding behind the veneer of respectability and status, particularly so far as the politicians were concerned could perhaps be due to the inherited dependency culture since the establishment of the Honourable East India Company on the Island. Its politicians of the 1990s were, however, a caricature of democracy at work: members of the Government who took no responsibility for unpopular decisions that they themselves had made, blaming the Governor, or anyone other than themselves, coming together as 'the opposition' to justify their position to their electorate. No wonder that there was no political party system – it wasn't needed – all could appear to be the Opposition! It might seem easy at first glance to conclude that being the Governor of such an unimportant Ruritania, a speck of rock in the South Atlantic with relatively few inhabitants, would be a sinecure. As my predecessors, and no doubt successors, could show, that was far from the truth. Politicians and officials in London demanded the same from the likes of St Helena as they did for more mature colonial administrations like Bermuda. It was a hard ask, and how ever much one tried to explain the basic facts to one's erstwhile Foreign Office colleagues, they simply saw the suntanned Englishmen of St Helena myth and assumed that London knew best . . .

St Helena's story is remarkable in the absence of any mention of an historic female figure paying an overt rôle in the Island's development. This is even more remarkable given the senior positions in public service occupied by Saint Helenian women. In 2002 there were the Deputy Secretary, Ethel Yon, who frequently acted for the Chief Secretary and who on occasions had also been the Governor's Deputy; Corinda Essex, with a doctorate in educational studies and then Chief Development Officer; Lynn Thomas, Managing Director of the St Helena Development Agency; Ivy Ellick. Former Chief Personnel Officer and later Chief Administrative Health Officer; and Barbara George, Chief Personnel Officer, to name but a few. Uncounted among these, of course, is the wife of the Governor – as St Helena, along with the other United Kingdom Overseas Territories, awaited its first lady Governor – until the appointment of Lisa Phillips in April 2016.

Formerly the First Lady, would be the wife of a colonial service officer, and more recently the spouse of a diplomat, adept at moving home from post to post at regular intervals, inured to frequent and long separation from children and other family, skilled in administration and expert at making her husband think that his job is by far the most important. Ms Philips' arrival will herald many changes!

Throughout the four years of my own appointment, as Governor Sandi, as my wife, was the First Lady. We undertook an extensive programme of engagements, both separately and together, ceremonial and official. Plantation House, like most other Residencies, is a representational tool rather than simply a home. We maintained a constant and busy cycle of entertainment at Plantation House from 'Cocktails and Carols' for 300 hundred guests before Christmas to the annual reception in June for over 500 in honour of the Official Birthday of Her Majesty the Queen. The First Lady ran that business, entertaining and accommodating large numbers of guests in the interests of the St Helena Government each year. Although there was a staff with which to achieve these tasks, diplomatic wives received no salary or allowance from either the British or St Helena Governments to manage the eleven permanent staff at Plantation House or the arrangements to cater for some two thousand cocktail party guests, several hundred lunch and dinner guests and scores of other callers on official business in the course of a year. In addition, the First Lady was her husband's partner and expected at a variety of official engagements – on his arm, so to speak – and then expected to head various charitable and other island organisations as 'Mrs Governor'. She thus had a busy, and not necessarily rewarding, programme - on parade - because of what her husband chose to do as a job. What now then?

I certainly could not have made a success of any of those jobs to which I had been posted and especially not that as Governor of St Helena & Its Dependencies during four quite difficult years without her unstinting support. Yet, at the end of the day and save *en passant*, she received neither thanks nor the praise that she deserved from any official direction, and it is without question that she was successful in her own right.

Appendix I

The Governors of St Helena

The island of St Helena became a possession of the English East India Company in 1659 and a Crown Colony in 1834. Today, as a United Kingdom Overseas Territory, St Helena has a Governor appointed by Her Majesty The Queen, upon the recommendation of the Secretary of State for Foreign & Commonwealth Affairs and with the approval of the Prime Minister. Prior to the island's Crown Colony status the East India Company appointed its own Governors to administer St Helena under the terms of Royal Charters obtained by the Company for that purpose. The Company's first Governors were:

John Dutton	1659-1661
Robert Stringer	1661-1670
Richard Coney	1671-1672
Anthony Beale	1672-1673

Governor Beale fled St Helena on 1st January 1673 following the Dutch invasion the previous day. Capt Richard Munden, commanding the escort flotilla sent to await the returning East Indies fleet, retook the island on 4th May 1673 and assumed charge. Once order was restored and the returning East India Company ships assembled in James Bay he departed. He left Capt Richard Keigwin of the man-of-war *Assistance* to take charge of the island until the East India Company was able to appoint a new Governor, who arrived the following year. The Company's succeeding Governors were:

Capt Richard Field	1674-1678	Capt Robert Jenkins	1740-1742
Major John Blackmore	1678-1690	Major Thomas Lambert	1742
Capt Joshua Johnson	1690-1693	Col David Dunbar	1744-1747
Capt Richard Kelinge	1693-1697	Charles Hutchinson	1747-1764
Capt Stephen Poirier	1697-1707	John Skottowe	1764-1782
Capt John Roberts	1708-1711	Daniel Corneille	1782-1787
Capt Benjamin Boucher	1711-1714	Col Robert Brooke	1787-1801
Capt Isaac Pyke	1714-1719	Col Robert Patton	1802-1807
Edward Johnson	1719-1723	Maj-Gen Alexander Beatson	1808-1813
Capt John Smith	1723-1727	Col Mark Wilks	1813-1816
Edward Byfield	1727-1731	Lt-Gen Sir Hudson Lowe	1816-1821
Capt Isaac Pyke	1731-1738	Brig-Gen Alexander Walker	1823-1828
John Goodwin	1738-1740	Brig-Gen Charles Dallas	1828-1836

With the passage of the Government of India Act, 1834 the East India Company's jurisdiction over St Helena was transferred to the British Government. After this enactment the island's Governors were commissioned by the Monarch to exercise the executive authority of the Crown in St Helena. As such, and the direct representatives of King William IV, His Heirs and Successors, Governors became 'His Excellency' (there had not, until 2016, been a lady Governor) rather than the 'Honourable', as they were when the Company's representative. St Helena's Governors are commissioned additionally as Commander-in-Chief and, since the inclusion of Ascension and Tristan da Cunha as Dependencies of St Helena, as Governor of those two Territories as well. The Governors appointed under the Crown are as follows:

Maj-Gen George Middlemore	1836-1842	Sir George Joy	1947-1954
Col Hamelin Trelawney	1842-1846	Sir Thomas Harford	1954-1958
Maj-Gen Sir Patrick Ross	1846-1851	Sir Robert Alford	1958-1962
Col Sir Thomas Gore Browne	1851-1856	Sir John Field	1962-1968
Sir Edward H Drummond Hay	1856-1863	Sir Dermod Murphy	1968-1971
Admiral Sir Charles Elliot	1863-1870	Sir Thomas Oates	1971-1976
Vice-Admiral C.G.E. Patey	1870-1873	Geoffrey Guy	1976-1981
Hudson Ralph Janisch	1873-1890	John Massingham	1981-1984
W. Grey Wilson	1890-1897	Francis 'Dick' Baker	1984-1988
Robert Armitage Sterndale	1897-1903	Robert Stimson	1988-1995
Lt Col Sir Henry Galway*	1903-1912	Alan Hoole	1991-1988
Maj Sir Harry Cordeaux	1912-1920	David L Smallman	1995-1999
Col Robert Peel	1920-1925	David Hollamby	1999-2004
Sir Charles Harper	1925-1932	Michael Clancy	2004-2007
Sir Spencer Davis	1932-1938	Andrew Gurr	2007-2011
Sir Guy Pilling	1938-1941	Mark Capes	2011-2016
Maj William Bain Gray	1941-1947	Lisa Phillips	2016-

The Governor's commission from The Queen states that his appointment is effective from the day of his arrival on the island. However, before he can take up his duties it is necessary to swear the oath of loyalty to The Queen. The formal inauguration of the Governor and Commander-in-Chief of St Helena is customarily conducted in public on the steps of the Supreme Court in Jamestown. The Chief Secretary reads the Royal Commission appointing the Governor and then presents the Sheriff, who administers the Affirmation of Office. The Sheriff reads an illuminated Address of Welcome, which is then presented to the Governor. The Governor has the opportunity then to make a formal reply before inspecting the Guard of Honour and taking the salute as the uniformed contingents march off. After the ceremonial is complete the Governor and his wife proceed to the Council Chamber in the Castle, where the *aide de camp* presents the members of the Legislative Council, Senior Government Officials and members of the public.

* With effect from the 1912 edition of The Colonial Office List Lieut.-Colonel Sir Henry Gallwey's entry is shewn spelt Galway. Who was Who shows that he 'assumed the present surname in place of Gallwey, 1911'. The parchment list of Governors' names displayed at Plantation House shows the Governor's name spelt Galway. References to him in the text of this publication are spelt Gallwey, as they are contemporaneous with the Governor's usage at the time.

Appendix II

The Governor's Inauguration Speech, 8ᵗʰ September 1995

"Madam Sheriff, thank you for your warm words of welcome. My wife and I have had some months in which to anticipate with pleasure our new life here in St Helena. We extend our greetings to all the people of St Helena, and of Its Dependencies.

I am greatly honoured to have been appointed by Her Majesty as the twenty-ninth Governor under the Crown. I realise, however, that even so I am but the last in a long and distinguished line of Governors stretching back to 1659.

The World has seen many changes since then. One has only to look at neighbouring southern Africa to be aware of momentous change. Further afield, the command economies of Eastern Europe have been abandoned for free open markets. Even the countries of the former Soviet Union have recognised that the State cannot effectively own and control the commanding heights of the economy. From massive India to tiny Trinidad, the industrialising nations of the world are competing fiercely for foreign investment with which to build their economic development. These, and other Governments, have realised that their rôle is not to manage business or to control enterprise, but to act as facilitators, creating an economic environment to enable dynamic growth to flourish.

The management of change is a core component of current business school curricula. It is a subject familiar to the Government of St Helena. A fine tradition of representative democracy has been established in this country and your Councillors are implementing policies to effect changes which will stimulate the development to which you, Madam Sheriff, referred. The Ordinances setting up the St Helena Development Agency, and that providing for a commercial bank, are good examples.

I look forward to working closely with the elected representatives of the people of St Helena to ensure that the momentum is maintained. Our aim must be to create the conditions in which St Helena can meet the challenges and the opportunities that the twenty-first century will surely present.

I cannot canvass your votes. But, I do seek your support.

Long live The Queen.

Long live St Helena."

Appendix III

Ascension Island

In common with the other South Atlantic islands, which together form St Helena and Its Dependencies, Ascension Island was discovered during the great age of Portuguese maritime exploration in the sixteenth century. It was the Portuguese navigator, Alfonso de Albuquerque, who first sighted the island on Ascension Day in 1501 and who named the island Ilha da Ascensão in consequence.

Also in common with those other islands of the South Atlantic, Ascension Island is volcanic. Of more recent origin than St Helena, the island's 34 square miles are dominated by the oldest and highest evidence of volcanic activity, Green Mountain, the summit of which towers some 2,817 feet into the skies above a landscape almost devoid of vegetation. This and the other major peaks, White Hill and Weather Post, are well eroded now and are in the south-east quadrant of the island. The remainder of the island is largely covered by lava flows and low volcanic cones, the last of which was active within the last six to seven hundred years, which explains the disparaging descriptions of 'Hell with the fire put out' and 'Slag-heap on sea'.

Ascension is located 7° south of the Equator at 14° 25' W, and has a very dry equatorial climate. Being barren and inhospitable it had no indigenous population and was never settled by any of the other seafarers who came to its shores in the succeeding centuries. Mandelslo, who wrote a glowing account of St Helena, said of Ascension that "...*it affords no water, nay it hath not so much as any verdure*"; and Peter Mundy, visiting in 1634, also noted the lack of water and recorded that "...*no ship would willingly put in there, except* [it] *put by St Helena, which if they overshoots... is hard or noe fetching it again, by reason of wynde or current settinge to the NW*". Nevertheless, as a breeding ground for seabirds and turtles, sailors seeking eggs and fresh meat to supplement their shipboard diet frequently visited it.

In 1816 Admiral Cockburn, in command at St Helena, ordered the island's occupation to prevent it falling into the hands of French forces sympathetic to Napoleon. It was annexed to the British Crown and commissioned as a 'stone frigate', *HMS Ascension*, under the command of Post Captain Cuppage, and attached to the Royal Navy's Cape of Good Hope Squadron. In 1821, following the death of Napoleon and the removal of the prime reason for its occupation, rather than abandon the island the British Government decided that the garrison should be retained. The naval personnel were withdrawn and replaced by Royal Marines. Later it became an additional victualing base for the West Africa Squadron patrolling the Atlantic for slave ships, and a convalescence centre for sick and wounded seamen

What is now Georgetown began to grow in the mid nineteenth century with the establishment of a military headquarters, barracks and hospital. Barracks were also built on Green Mountain in 1833 and the farm facilities on the mountain, where vegetables had been grown from 1817, were improved. The Residency of the island's Administrator today, set in a commanding position on the mountain overlooking Georgetown and the anchorage, was initially built in the 1860s as a sanatorium for the garrison.

In 1844 the command of *Ascension* passed back to a naval officer, although the garrison was still a Royal Marine detachment. Life was bleak and apparently pointless: no one wished to wrest the island away from Britain. However, the beginnings of its present day point emerged in 1899 when the Eastern Telegraph Company extended the cable from St Helena to Ascension, and then onward, via the Cape Verde Islands to England. Ascension too became a cable regeneration station, and an important link in the telegraphic network extending out from Britain to South Africa and beyond. In 1915 a naval wireless station was built on the island, but in 1922 the Royal Navy finally withdrew. The local manager of the Eastern Telegraph Company was appointed as resident magistrate, and responsible to the Governor of St Helena for the island's administration. Cable & Wireless absorbed the Eastern Telegraph Company in 1934 and by the outbreak of the war in 1939 there were still less than one hundred and fifty inhabitants, of which about one hundred were Saints.

The Second World War was to change Ascension beyond recognition. A small Royal Artillery detachment strengthened the island's defences in 1941, with the mounting of two large calibre naval guns, taken from *HMS Hood* and which still stand on Cross Hill above Georgetown. But the big, and enduring change, was to be provided by the Americans. As part of the Lend-Lease Agreement the Americans established a base on Ascension, 'Wideawake', which became one in the logistical chain of Atlantic airfields through which they ferried fighter and bomber aircraft from the United States to Europe. By 1943 Ascension housed about 4,000 American airmen and soldiers, manning anti-submarine patrol aircraft and the defences for the airfield and island. With the ending of hostilities the base was run down and by 1947 the island, with its airfield, had emptied of US servicemen and the population dropped to a mere 170 persons.

However, the Americans were soon to return, as the airfield facilities were to prove useful as a down-range centre for the missile testing carried out from Cape Canaveral in Florida. In 1956 the British and United States Governments signed an agreement on the *"Extension of the Bahamas Long Range Proving Ground by the Establishment of additional Sites in Ascension Island"* (The 'Bahamas Agreement') confirming these facilities and others in the Bahamas and Antigua. Ascension became a staging point for the support to the Eastern Test Range in 1957 and later a valuable logistics centre for the Apollo moon-landing programme and other American space projects. Wideawake Airfield was developed in 1965 to provide alternative landing facilities for the space shuttles and back up for the re-entry of space vehicles. Its use is still controlled by the United States Department of Defense. In 1999 (last figures available) the US Base employed 121 American military and civilian personnel and 165 Saint Helenians.

In 1964, following the British Government's decision to build the BBC Overseas Service relay station, and facilities for the Composite Signals Organisation (CSO) on Ascension Island, it was agreed that it was no longer appropriate for Cable & Wireless to run Ascension. As a result, an Administrator was appointed by the Colonial Office to be responsible to the Governor of St Helena for the administration of the island. His main rôle was to be a co-ordinator between the various agencies of the British Government, including the Ministry of Public Buildings &

Works, which was to assume responsibility for the construction and maintenance of the Government and quasi Government installations to be established there. All this, it was agreed, should be done at no additional cost to the Government of St Helena: the running costs were to be met by the British organisations using Ascension. These bodies were later to become known as 'the Users'.

The review conducted by the Colonial Office in 1966 (Future Policy in the Smaller Colonial Territories) concluded that *"As Ascension has no permanent inhabitants no question of political development arises...It seems likely that we shall want to retain Ascension* [for Bahamas Agreement, BBC and Cable & Wireless reasons] *for the foreseeable future, and to insulate it from any political development in St Helena."* Thus, in conveying the information to the Governor about the new constitutional proposals on 2nd September 1966 the Colonial Secretary wrote: *"...In future, however, the members of the Executive Council will be drawn from persons elected to the* Legislature (sic) *to represent constituencies in St Helena only. In view of this, and having regard to the fact that both Ascension Island and Tristan da Cunha have Administrators with their own consultative bodies, I have concluded that it would be more appropriate for the functions of the Executive Council, like those of the present Advisory Council and the proposed Legislative Council, to extend to St Helena itself, the legislative and executive authority for the dependencies resting with the Governor."*

The British Government of the day had excluded any thought of a federal arrangement for the governance of the two territories. It had become the received wisdom that in colonial administration that binding together separate social and economic units, especially if they were widely separated, was a pretty hopeless exercise. It becomes more difficult as political developments are polarised in the different parts and it becomes virtually impossible when economic developments create disequilibrium between the different parts. The Colonial Office experience of the late 1960s was that the precedents for contrived federations were not encouraging. St Helena and Ascension Island were to follow the separate paths of development most appropriate to them.

In 1984 the Users set up a co-operative arrangement to deliver common services for all but the military organisations operating on the island and known as Ascension Island Services (AIS). This organisation took on public works; provided health and education services; managed the island's civil estate and accommodation; ran pierhead and stevedoring operations; and undertook the financial and management back-up to these services on a non-profit making basis, taking an employee capitation fee from the Users to finance the operation. The system worked adequately, if somewhat unaccountably, until the late 1990s. Then the number of employees (upon which the financial contribution was assessed) began to fall at the same time as costs rose sharply and the Users reacted against what they considered to be the inadequate contribution towards the running costs by the British Ministry of Defence on behalf of the military component at RAF Ascension.

The population of Ascension had expanded rapidly after the Argentine invasion of the Falkland Islands in 1982 when the United States Government gave permission for the British Forces to use Wideawake Airfield as a staging post and support for the Task Force and as a logistical base for men and materiel in transit to the Falklands. The Royal Air Force later established itself permanently at RAF Ascension where it provides support for a regular 'Airbridge' connecting Stanley to Brize Norton in Oxfordshire. Many Saint Helenians were employed by HM Forces and the supporting civilian organisations at that time and, despite military cut-backs, there is still a substantial establishment working for the RAF and its contractors on Ascension Island.

In its 1999 review of the Overseas Territories, 'Partnership for Progress and Prosperity' (Cmnd 4264), the British Government promised that *"Studies will be conducted to establish how the governance of the Island should be organised for the future."* Ministers had concluded that there was a democratic deficit and that government should become more inclusive and more accountable. The first step, after a wide exercise of public consultation, on St Helena as well as Ascension, and further detailed examination of the administrative and economic situation, was the establishment from 1st April 2001 of an expansion of the Administrator's governmental responsibilities to include the government-type functions of AIS (e.g. education, health); an Ascension Island Services to run other essential functions such as the pierhead; and a new – Ascension Island Commercial Services (incorporated in London) – with the BBC, Cable & Wireless, and the British Government as equal partners to manage the commercial functions, such as the Guest House and the Shop - the longer term objective being to spin off these activities into private ownership in the shortest possible time-frame.

It is for debate whether a complete hiving off to private enterprise (which would reflect the degree of commitment by the private sector in maintaining the 'enterprise zone' nature of Ascension) should not have been the most obvious route to follow, avoiding public cost and liabilities difficult to slough off at a later date. Ascension is not a conventional settlement and it would be unlikely to be viable as such were it to be treated as any other colonial territory. An interim period was required while change was introduced slowly to enable the inhabitants to gain rights and more say in how the island is governed.

There is no indigenous population, and all civilians on the island are there on an employment contract and leave at the end of their contracted tour. The total population, including military personnel from both the United States and the United Kingdom, amounts to less than one thousand. In 1999 it amounted to 958, including 113 children under working age, and has reduced by 12% over the past ten years.

Ascension's utility as a communications facility is likely to be limited by technological advances in the future. Indeed, it is probably true to say that were the BBC and Cable & Wireless not already established on the island, neither would find the need to locate their communications hubs there today. In the longer term, therefore, it is perfectly possible to envisage their eventual closure on Ascension. The island is remote, has a harsh climate and terrain and possesses no conventional civil administration. It does, however, provide an interesting venue for eco-tourists and can offer diving and sports fishing to those sufficiently hardy and adventurous to travel by military aircraft. The barriers to normal economic activities are high, but not completely insurmountable, especially were the United States Government to re-negotiate the Bahamas Agreement to allow flights by long-range commercial aircraft to use Wideawake Airfield.

Such development would not automatically create the political institutions that the British Government might wish to see in place to address the democratic deficit. There has been little initiative for changes of this nature from the Saint Helenian community, which makes up about 75% of the population on Ascension. Indeed, many are happy to be free of the politics altogether. Neither was there any evidence that might suggest that any significant number would wish to acquire rights of residence and stay on Ascension at the end of their contracts or on retirement. Saint Helenian employment on Ascension has often been predicated on saving for a home of one's own on St Helena and a nest egg for retirement. Although there are some among the longer-term residents who would naturally welcome more account being taken of their views, it is a quantum leap to infer that this suggests that any significant number wish to see a conventional democratic system established on Ascension Island: anecdotal evidence actually suggests the opposite.

However, after a considerable amount of work on the modalities, the first step in the British Government's plan to reduce the democratic deficit - putting the island's finances into a recognisable colonial-style fiscal regime – was taken on 1st April 2002. An island-wide consultation followed - to establish what sort of representative system the residents would most prefer. An electoral roll was then drawn up, and Ascension's voters asked to show their preference for one of two forms of Council (an 'island only' council, or one linked to the Government process in St Helena). Although only 337 persons voted on 22nd and 23rd August, the overwhelming majority, unsurprisingly, voted for the first option – i.e. one with no linkage to the St Helena Legislative Council. The first General Election for seats on the Ascension Island Council was held on 1st November. Seven Ascension residents were elected to the Council who, together with the Administrator, Attorney General and Ascension's Director of Financial Services, were to be responsible for the running of the affairs of the Ascension Island Government as a British Overseas Territory.

The first meeting of the Island Council took place shortly after the election – on 7th November - when the following message of congratulation from the Foreign & Commonwealth Office Minister responsible for the British

Overseas Territories, Baroness Amos, was read by the Administrator to the Councillors assembled at the Obsidian Hotel:-.

> *"I wanted to send my congratulations to you following your election as Councillors to the first Island Council on Ascension Island. I am pleased that island residents have been actively involved in the moves to democratic representation, which led to the vote on 1st November. This is an historic step for the island. You will play an important rôle in shaping the future of Ascension Island. I hope that Councillors will work in close partnership with the Governor and the Administrator for the benefit of the island."*

But, this exercise in imposing a paternalistic democracy upon an unwitting but compliant territory was a unique experiment, which subsequent events seem to have unravelled.

On 12th December 2002 the tanker, *Maersk Gannet*, set sail from the Georgetown anchorage for Nigeria where the vessel was to be sold: the 32,500 ton tanker had replaced the *Maersk Ascension* in 1999. To provide readily available fuels for the military on the island, the Maersk Company had had a vessel permanently moored off Ascension as a floating storage tank since 1983, when *Maersk Ascension* was positioned there, primarily to supply the airfield and HM Ships. The view from the pierhead will not be the same again!

In the heyday of New Labour Foreign Secretary Robin Cook's 'ethical foreign policy', and as mentioned above, a new deal for the Ascension's mainly Saint Helenian residents was promised. Plans were drawn up for democratic institutions, a legal right of abode and the right to own property with the stated aim of ensuring that Ascension could be a viable community. But the promise that the residents of Ascension could forge a permanent presence on the island has been discarded. With no right of abode, anyone who retires or reaches 18 without a job, or whose contract ends, has to leave. Businesses set up during Robin Cook's 'Ascension Spring' have lost their value because they cannot be sold and have no secure land tenure. Some would have it that

Whitehall was forced into the about-face on right of abode by American security fears about potentially troublesome Saint Helenian/Ascension Islander neighbours; and that HMG in the UK wanted to avoid contingent liabilities such as providing pensions, unemployment benefits and beefed up security. When constituted the first Island Council planned to develop eco-tourism. The only downside to brave plans to develop Ascension Island for residents seeming to be the introduction of taxes: but, whereas, the planned developments have all been abandoned, the taxes have not.

The Island has been losing professional Saint Helenian jobs, such as teaching at the island's only school, to ex-patriate Britons on short-term contracts; but the biggest cause of Ascension's depopulation has been the privatisation of most Government and military services on the island. The British contractor Interserve is now the island's biggest employer. Jobs are being shed and workers moved onto short-term contracts. The result is that the population is shrinking. The loss of families means that three-quarters of the population is now male.

Together with the Tristan da Cunha colony, Ascension Island had been bracketed constitutionally with St Helena as one of Its Dependencies, and so described. This had allowed for each island to follow its own path, but for the one Governor to be responsible for the governance of them. However, following the introduction of the St Helena, Ascension and Tristan da Cunha Order, 2009 (which replaced the 1988 Constitution Order and confirmed the allegiance of the three to The British Crown) what some consider to be a more balanced relationship was outlined. While establishing that the three Territories now formed a single territorial grouping, the Order also placed some limits on the Governor's powers which have been suggested offer more of a union between the Governor and the two Administrators.

However, the remaining Saint Helenian population – all ex-patriates, for as Ministers have consistently said, *"there is no indigenous population, or 'islanders"* and everyone on Ascension is an expat, present solely by virtue of an employment contract – believe that they have been hoodwinked. The most suspicious among them believing that the British Government is deliberately planning to abandon

Ascension, evacuate the resident Saints, and leave it to the Americans with a view to it becoming the Diego Garcia of the Atlantic . . .

In the meantime Ascension may be enjoyed for its beaches and its wild life, particularly its seabirds and, in season, the truly wonderful sight of the greenback turtles coming ashore to lay their eggs before they swim back to the coast of Brazil.

Appendix IV

Tristan da Cunha

The United Kingdom Overseas Territory of Tristan da Cunha comprises the islands of the Tristan da Cunha group: the three significant islands being Tristan da Cunha itself, and Nightingale and Inaccessible Islands; together with Gough Island, a little over 200 miles to the South-east. All are volcanic, but only Tristan da Cunha has a permanent population.

Tristão da Cunha discovered the islands of the immediate Tristan da Cunha Group in 1506, but little is recorded of the occasion other than the naming of the principal island after da Cunha, the master of the *Santiago*. The *Globe*, in 1610, was the first vessel from the British Isles to sight Tristan da Cunha; but the first recorded landing was not made until 1643, when a party from the Dutch ship *Heemestede* landed on 7th February that year. In 1655 the Governor of the Dutch Colony at the Cape sent a party to survey the islands; and in 1696 the Dutch East India Company carried out a further survey. In 1790 a party of sealers from America spent seven months on the island; and three years later a French expedition visited Tristan da Cunha. On 27th December 1810 three Americans settled on the island and sought British protection, but by 1812 the settlement had been reduced to a single person; and was uninhabited in 1816.

Information about the history of Nightingale Island is scarce, and there seems to be no record of whether or not the island was sighted during the first voyage of discovery in 1506. However, since it is visible from Tristan da Cunha it is assumed that it was sighted, although there is no indication whether it was separately named at that stage. In 1760, Captain Nightingale, a British naval officer, is assumed to have landed, or at least have sighted the island, as from that time it has borne his name on the charts. Inaccessible Island was so named on account of the steep cliffs and difficulty in landing there.

Gough Island, a little over 200 miles from the main archipelago, has no permanent population and it is out of range of the *Wave Dancer*, the Island's Fisheries Patrol vessel. Gough Island was only infrequently visited by its Administrator, courtesy of a passage on the *SA Aghulas*, and only very rarely seen by its Governor. However, following the circumnavigation of Gough Island in January 1997, I was determined to find a way to achieve a landing on Gough. As recorded in Chapter Eleven, I set the ball rolling to achieve this aim with the assistance of a team of RAF Sub-Aqua Association divers and, as Chapter Twelve records, landed there with members of the RAF-SAA on 25th January 1999.

In common with the other islands of the South Atlantic, Gough Island is a volcanic outcrop. It was discovered in 1505, during the voyage of the *Santo Espirito*, captained by Gonçalo Álvares (some references show the Captain's name as Gonçalvo Alvarez). The island was marked on Portuguese charts thereafter as Gonçalo Álvares Island. However, as the determination of longitude was such an inexact science until the late eighteenth century the island's position was subject to some conjecture, so enabling the British naval captain, Charles Gough, to claim its discovery in 1732.

In 1811 Captain Peter Heywood sailed from Tristan da Cunha to Gough Island to seek out a party of American sealers who had been left on the island during the previous year by the US ship *Baltic*. The following account by Captain Heywood of his visit on 8th January 1811 makes fascinating reading, and is an interesting counterpoint to the description in Chapter Twelve of that other visit in 1999.

"At day light, the wind, having hauled to the south, the weather cleared up, and Gough's Island was in sight about six leagues from us, the base and extreme points of it only to be seen, the higher parts being obscured by clouds. Made sail and approaching observed the rock off the North East point making as is described exactly like a church with a spire. The contour of this whole island is steep, rising up almost perpendicularly from the sea in high cliffs, down the fissures of which fall several beautiful cascades. About eight o'clock observing a hut in a small cove sheltered by some of the high peaked rocks whose base is completely perforated, and supposing it might be the habitation of the

*American seamen whom the master of the Baltic
had left here last year, I hove to and sent the
lieutenant away in the Cutter, with orders to land if
he should find it safely practicable, to try to get
some tidings of them and to offer them any
assistance they might need. He landed just to the
eastward of the large rock, but finding no person in
or near the hut returned about noon, and just at the
same time a boat was observed pulling up from the
south east part of the island round the Church
Rock, which I bore for and picked up. In it were the
people left by the master of the Baltic, and not a
little overjoyed when I told them that they might
expect to see their ship daily to take them off the
island. Not that they were in want of food, for they
informed me that they caught a great variety of
excellent birds up in the hills by lighting a fire there
in the night time, at which they flew in such
numbers that they knocked them down with sticks.
They had also some of the provisions left them
when they landed, and could always catch more
fish than they could eat, in a quarter of an hour.
But they had not been so successful as they hoped
when they first landed...for in all this time they had
only been able to cure eleven hundred sealskins so
that, as they were all on shares, they would
scarcely clear as much for their labour as would
find them "new gang rigging", and truly they
needed some, for they were all in a most ragged
plight, full of grease and filth and clothed chiefly in
seal skins"*

The islands were included in the claim made in 1816 by the
British Government for Tristan da Cunha at the time of
Napoleon's imprisonment on St Helena. Lord Charles
Somerset, the younger son of the Duke of Beaufort, then
Governor of the Cape of Good Hope, was instructed to occupy
Tristan da Cunha and hold it as a precaution in case of its
use as a base to mount a rescue bid for Napoleon on St
Helena. A naval party took possession of Tristan da Cunha
and the neighbouring islands of Nightingale and Inaccessible

on 14th August 1816, and in the following November a garrison of troops was established under the command of Capt Josias Cloete who, although a Dutchman, went on to become a General in the British Army. The perception of a threat to intervene in Napoleon's imprisonment on St Helena diminished with time and the garrison was withdrawn in late 1817.

However, one of the soldiers, Corporal William Glass, opted to make his family's future there rather than return to the Cape with his wife, Maria Leenders, and their children. William and Maria Glass's descendants remain there to this day. In the late 1990s a twentieth century James Glass was the Chief Islander. Shipwrecked sailors, settlers of European extraction and five women, including the two adolescent daughters of one of those, sent at the islanders' request by the Governor of St Helena, joined those who remained over the years. By 1888 there were 97 inhabitants. It became a Dependency of St Helena, whose Governor also became Governor of the Tristan da Cunha Colony, in 1938. With a population of a little less than 300 today, Tristan da Cunha claims to be the remotest populated island in the World: it is also one of the most stunningly beautiful and unspoilt.

Following the Island's acquisition of its first fisheries patrol vessel in 1996, I became the first Governor to set foot on Nightingale Island, a wildlife haven on the nearest of the island group to Tristan da Cunha (1997), and Inaccessible Island (1998).

*   *   *

The *RMS St Helena* maintained the only regular passenger service to Tristan da Cunha and in the 1990s had a three-day call at the Island but, even in the southern summer when she normally called, the weather could not always be relied upon to allow passengers ashore on each of the days. On these occasions the ship might slip away to anchor in the shelter of either Nightingale or Inaccessible Island both some 30 miles from the anchorage at the settlement on Tristan da Cunha. These two uninhabited islands are home to hundreds of thousands of sea birds, penguins and seals. In January and February the seashore is lined with scores of moulting rockhopper penguins.

Seals bask in the sheltered bays and their pups, like tiny puppy-dogs, roll around in the rock pools unfazed by human intrusions. Here large areas of the sea itself appear in the bright sunshine to be paved with shiny cobbles, only to be revealed on closer inspection as hundreds of thousands of resting shearwaters. They, like the skuas, petrels and stately albatross all breed on these islands and provide a day long and absorbing flying display for us rather more earthbound mortals.

The yellow nosed albatross breeds on Tristan da Cunha's Base, the land at the foot of the mountain atop the 2,000 ft cliffs, which towers over the settlement known formally as Edinburgh-of-the-Seven-Seas, named for the eponymous Duke and son of Queen Victoria who, as a naval officer, visited in 1867. The Village, as it is more commonly called, is situated on the only habitable area of land at the north-western corner of the island and which appears to have been formed by a large landslip from the cliffs above. No more than a half mile wide for most of its extent and some three or four miles in length this area of land forms the settlement and its main agricultural resource for crops and grazing. For the visitor it provides a fascinating glimpse of a world far removed from the industrialised and consumer oriented 21st century of shopping malls and motor-car dominated existence in which most of us are accustomed to live.

Nevertheless, some forty years ago a generation of Tristanians chose their way of life over what the outside world had to offer. During 1961 the island experienced a series of minor earth tremors. Starting in August, these tremors and resulting rock falls became more frequent and by early October a fissure had opened up to the east of Edinburgh. The fissure began to show signs of volcanic activity and the islanders removed themselves and a minimum of possessions to the arable area two miles west of the village, known as the Potato Patches, where most households had a small tool-shed in which they could take shelter. By 10th October lava was beginning to flow from the fissure and the Administrator, Peter Wheeler, ordered an evacuation to Nightingale Island in the island's longboats. As good fortune would have it the *Tjisdane* a Royal Interocean Line passenger vessel had been scheduled to call at Tristan da Cunha on 11th October. As luck also had it, 380 of the liner's 400 berths were empty, so enabling the whole Tristanian population to be embarked and carried safely to Cape Town. The islanders were then transferred to the *Stirling Castle*, which was conveniently at Cape Town and had sufficient capacity to take all 290 of the evacuees to Southampton.

On arrival in the United Kingdom they were temporarily accommodated in disused army barracks near Reigate before a more permanent home was found for them at the former RAF camp at Calshot overlooking Southampton Water. Many of the islanders found employment in the area and the Colonial Office appeared to believe that one minor remnant of Empire had been satisfactorily tidied away. That was not, however, as the islanders saw it.

Nevertheless, at first the volcano remained active and eventually a major lava flow engulfed the fish processing factory and the two landing beaches. Clearly the islanders could not return while the volcano posed a threat, but they clung strongly to the belief that one day they would be able to return. Although not tasked to determine whether the island was safe for the Tristanian population to return, a scientific expedition to examine the volcano, mounted under the sponsorship of the Royal Society, spent three months on the island in early 1962. Their safe return and positive reports led to increasing pressure for an organised repatriation of the islanders, but the British Government prevaricated until an unofficial Resettlement Survey Party was mounted with voluntary funding. The Colonial Office was impelled to add a representative to the group.

The party landed on Tristan da Cunha on 8th September 1962. Amazingly the lava flow had missed the village and only one house been damaged by fire. By November the favourable reports coming from the Party on the island and the pressure thus put on the British Government led the Colonial Office to concede that arrangements would be made for those wishing to return to do so. A ballot held on 3rd December led to all but five Tristanians opting to return. The first group of fifty-one returned on 9th April 1963. The remaining evacuees had to wait a further six months before they were able to make the journey back to Tristan da Cunha, where they made their landfall on 11th November, more than two years after hurriedly leaving their island home. The core of the volcanic flow remains hot to this day and a wisp of steam can be seen rising from the lava field when it rains.

It rains frequently on Tristan da Cunha and the island experiences many gales during the winter months, but both struck with devastating effect on 21st May 2001. Hurricane force winds, gusting up to 120 miles an hour, hit the Village damaging many buildings and destroying its communications with the outside world. No one was injured, but most homes were damaged. The hospital and the fish-processing factory were severely damaged and the island's community centre destroyed. The British Government made a grant of £75,000 for immediate relief including medical supplies and communications equipment, while the islanders' natural resourcefulness ensured that homes were quickly made weather-proof and much of the damage quickly repaired. However, much seed and livestock were lost in the storm and a full recovery to self-sufficiency took a little longer.

The volcanic eruption in 1961 and the publicity surrounding the islanders' resettlement, and the hurricane of 2001, certainly increased public awareness of Tristan da Cunha. It is no longer a philatelist's speciality interest. Nevertheless, Tristanians have always been careful in protecting their environment and never sought to attract mass tourism. Nonetheless, it is a popular call for ocean going cruise ships and until January 2018 was an annual cruise destination for the *RMS St Helena*.

A small harbour, built after the volcanic eruption of 1961 had obliterated the traditional landing, now nestles beneath the cliffs below the village and is the visitor's point of entry after disembarking the *St Helena* in the anchorage by launch. Most of the visitors make straight for the Handicraft Shop where hand knitted woollens and other local handicrafts are popular purchases. But a pullover or sweater from Tristan da Cunha is really different, not simply for its design but because, as with all the other knitted items available here, the wool from island sheep has been processed completely by hand on the island. Most of the island ladies card and spin their own wool after the shearing in the Spring and, although knitting is very much a cottage industry, selling the finished goods to visitors is a useful additional income for them as well as providing a sought after souvenir for the tourist. These and other traditional skills are still alive and well on Tristan da Cunha.

The fishing concession; the need to provide island services; and increasing tourism have broken down the early subsistence economy of the island and introduced a wage-based economy, imported foodstuffs and other goods; and recently satellite telephone has added to the accessibility to the outside world. Nevertheless, the traditions of a self sufficient community die hard and, as there are no contractors, builders or plumbers in business, families help one another with the essentials of house maintenance and building a home for young marrieds; and each family has its own sheep, a cow, and plot to grow vegetables at the Potato Patches west of the village. And yet progress to some is measured by the fact that today the island's senior citizens can travel the two miles to work at the 'Patches' by a Government owned mini-bus rather than walk, as formerly.

Nonetheless, the day can start for many of the islanders by a walk to the pasture to milk the family cow before going off to work in the Administration or the island's single store, to teach, or perhaps to spend time with family and elders and work on the next piece of knitting. The weather dominates life on Tristan da Cunha and it can change very quickly. Every islander is an amateur weather forecaster, able to judge whether the apparently balmy breeze and sunshine will enable them to sail to Nightingale for the weekend, or turn into a raging gale. In the season, if the weather looks at all promising, community leaders will decide that it is a 'fishing day' and tools are downed at the Public Works Department and elsewhere while the men take their boats out to lay pots for crayfish and to put out a line for some fish for the table. For those of us softened by the conveniences of our consumer society life seems hard on Tristan da Cunha, but it has produced a close-knit community of amazingly resilient and hard-working people.

Appendix VI

The Chief Secretary's Valediction for Governor Smallman

"The leaving of every Governor is marked in three main ways. Two of these are tangible and durable. First the Governor's portrait has been added to those of previous Governors in the Council Chamber. Secondly in the Library at Plantation House there is a board recording the names of all twenty-eight previous Governors from the establishment of the [Crown] Colony in 1834. Governor Smallman's name will be added as the 29th Governor of St Helena. The third way of marking the departure is the event this evening. It is clearly more ephemeral but none the less important for that. Over the years we have enjoyed the hospitality of the Governor and Mrs Smallman at Receptions and other events. This evening we turn the tables and Members of the Legislative Council, public servants and others have an opportunity to host a Reception for the Governor and Mrs Smallman. Sir, it is a pleasure to be able to join with others in hosting this Reception for you.

It is traditional for the Chief Secretary to make a short speech on this occasion. It is nevertheless an honour, which I approach with some trepidation. The difficulty, which I face, is how to encapsulate the contribution of a period approaching four years in a speech of several minutes. This is all the more difficult because I have not been here for the whole of that period. But I have my sources! I have consulted the embassy – also known as Dot's Café – and have found out what 'the street' is saying.

In future when we reflect on the Smallman Years we may see them in two lights – as the years of change and the years of raising St Helena's profile.

Let us look at the years of change. From the Governor's arrival in 1995 planned development was top of the agenda with the Strategic Review, the first ever Country Policy Plan and the Three Year Aid Agreement. Since 1995 St Helena has gone through great changes. The most recent and certainly the most welcome is the promise to restore British Citizenship and the Right of Abode to Saint Helenians. Governor Smallman has fought consistently and persistently within the appropriate channels for this welcome change. I have no doubt that the Governor's efforts added significantly to the efforts of all involved in the citizenship issue.

The Governor, of course, has special responsibilities for the Public Service and the major change here is in terms of public sector reform. The Governor has overseen significant developments so that we have a leaner, more efficient and better trained public service with improved pay and conditions. There have been some problems, of course, especially in nursing and teaching, but the Governor responded without delay with a task force, the recommendations of which have been implemented. Business cases have been conducted and several services to the public have been improved and/or privatised.

Turning to another area of change, the Governor has been a tireless supporter of private sector development. This has ranged from strategic support in Government to the support of individual businesses and managers. It is not an exaggeration to say that the Governor has visited all the businesses on the island. This has given him a vital insight into the ambitions of, and challenges facing, business. He has used this insight to help inform the development of policies. Businesses on the island have also been involved in consultations on matters like shipping and have been given a voice though the Development Forum which the Governor set up last year.

The Governor has also had to cope with significant political change. The elections in 1997 required considerable work and the Governor played a key rôle in encouraging the briefing of the many new Members in the Legislative and Executive Councils. Seminars were held and visits were organised. The programme of visits for Councillors continues and has been widely welcomed.

Change has also been reflected in the large legislative programme, which the Governor has encouraged the Executive Council to consider as Government business. We have seen legislation covering significant tax reforms, a media board, legal aid assistance, updated and improved immigration procedures and a better pension deal for public servants, to name but a few. Of course, some of these have a long gestation period and involve different players. They happened because Governor Smallman encouraged a consultative approach on issues like fiscal reform, and recognised the potential of the public service to implement change.

Some advances occurred only because Governor Smallman applied his strong determination, and this resulted in successes as diverse as Diana's Peak National Park and the appointment of a Public Solicitor.

My second theme is raising St Helena's profile. Governor Smallman has made sure that many more people knew where to find St Helena on the map. Which reminds me of a clerihew:

> *The Art of Biography*
> *Is different from Geography*
> *Geography is about Maps*
> *But Biography is about Chaps*

So, in this potted biography of Governor Smallman, let us look at maps.

The Governor's Cup Yacht race has helped put St Helena on the map. Like many new ventures, I think it is fair to say it was initially greeted with some scepticism. However, some 40,000 people accessing the Internet to enquire abut the race, and thousands more being reached through radio and yachting magazines demonstrated that the race caught the imagination. Last year we saw the participation of a St Helenian crew. Much valuable publicity has been generated for the island.

Governor Smallman has also supported the development of the new Tourist Office and assisted the Tourism Director to build up links in South Africa.

He has been an enthusiastic supporter of Radio St Helena Day, which is another event, which strengthened our links with the rest of the world.

The Governor has not flinched from difficult issues. Hence, RMS scheduling has been reviewed with the aim of improving access to the island – not just for tourists but also for off-shore workers.

I have focussed on two main areas of change and St Helena's profile. There are many other achievements, which I could have mentioned. I have not touched upon the Governor's involvement with St Helena's Dependencies; on being the first Governor to land on Gough and Nightingale; on involvement with charities; promoting cricket; on the fair wind given to the sailing club; on the Commission on the Constitution; and on the Governor's part in the publication of Lady Field's 'History of Plantation House'. I can only plead too much to mention – too little time.

The motto of the eco-tourist is:
Take only photographs; leave only footprints.

Our farewell message to you chimes with that:
Take only fond memories: leave only the footprints of your endeavours."

The Castle,
Jamestown, St Helena
30th April 1999

Bibliography

The Foreign Office	Anthony Seldon 2000
The Diplomatic List 1999	HMSO 1999
With Respect, Ambassador	Simon Jenkins & Anne Sloman 1985
Inside the Foreign Office	John Dickie 1992
The Honourable Company: A History of the English East India Company	John Keay 1991
The East India Company	Antony Wild 1999
Quincentenary; a Story of St Helena, 1502-2002	David L Smallman 2003
One of The Queen's Men	David L Smallman 2012
St Helena	J C Mellis 1875
St Helena Records	Hudson Ralph Janisch 1885
Georg Wilhelm Janisch - Three Letters from St Helena	Hudson Janisch 1998
Despatches from St Helena	Government Printing Office, St Helena 1999
St Helena Lifeline	Ronnie Eriksen 1994
The History of Plantation House	Margaret Field 1998
Outposts: Journeys to the Surviving Relics of the British Empire	Simon Winchester 1985
The Last Pink Bits	Harry Ritchie 1997
Tristan da Cunha	Allan Crawford 1962
Birds from Britannia	HRH The Duke of Edinburgh 1962
Parting Shots	Matthew Parris and Andrew Bryson 2010
The Emperor's Last Island	Julia Blackburn 1992
Last Boat to St Helena	Matthew Engel 2016

Lightning Source UK Ltd.
Milton Keynes UK
UKHW01f1938300718
326523UK00001B/184/P